The Buddhist Campus Chaplaincy Sourcebook

Edited by Ji Hyang Padma & Jonathan Makransky

with contributions from
Harrison Blum
Julian Bowers-Brown
Eli Ryn Brown
Lama Döndrup Drölma
Zoketsu Norman Fischer
Victor Gabriel
Rev. Jitsujo T. Gauthier
Trudy Goodman
Roshi Joan Halifax
Rev. Victor Kazanjian, Jr.
Jonathan Makransky
Rev. Ivan (Kusa) Mayerhofer
Nathan Jishin Michon
Ernest C.H. Ng
Rebecca D. Nie
Ji Hyang Padma
Henry C.H. Shiu
Ven. Priya Rakkhit Sraman
Jessica Thomas
Mark Unno
Matthew Weiner

The Buddhist Campus Chaplaincy Sourcebook
Edited by Ji Hyang Padma & Jonathan Makransky

Text © by Ji Hyang Padma, Jonathan Makransky and the respective contributors, 2025
All rights reserved

Book design: Karma Yönten Gyatso
Cover illustration: Lotus, by Woman from Baku, Shutterstock

Published by
The Sumeru Press Inc.
PO Box 75, Manotick Main Post Office
Manotick, ON K4M 1A2

ISBN 978-1-998248-07-0 Paperback

LIBRARY AND ARCHIVES CANADA CATALOGUING IN PUBLICATION

Title: The Buddhist campus chaplaincy sourcebook / edited by Ji Hyang Padma & Jonathan Makransky ; with contributions from Harrison Blum, Julian Bowers-Brown, Eli Ryn Brown, Lama Döndrup Drölma, Zoketsu Norman Fischer, Victor Gabriel, Rev. Jitsujo T. Gauthier, Trudy Goodman, Roshi Joan Halifax, Rev. Victor Kazanjian, Jr., Jonathan Makransky, Rev. Ivan (Kusa) Mayerhofer, Nathan Jishin Michon, Ernest C.H. Ng, Rebecca D. Nie, Ji Hyang Padma, Henry C.H. Shiu, Ven. Priya Rakkhit Sraman, Jessica Thomas, Mark Unno, Matthew Weiner.
Names: Padma, Ji Hyang, editor | Makransky, Jonathan, editor.
Description: Includes bibliographical references.
Identifiers: Canadiana 20240475631 | ISBN 9781998248070 (softcover)
Subjects: LCSH: College chaplains. | LCSH: College students—Pastoral counseling of. | LCSH: Pastoral counseling (Buddhism)
Classification: LCC BQ5305.C4 B83 2024 | DDC 294.3/61—dc23

 For more information about The Sumeru Press
visit us at *sumeru-books.com*

*To the lineages of teachers who have transmitted the lamp –
may we reflect their compassion and mercy.*

*To the students, who are the future Sangha –
may we together become Buddha.*

A brief note about typography

In keeping with the voice of each contributor, Pali and/or Sanskrit have been used for Buddhist terms, along with diacriticals and transliteration methodologies from the authors themselves.

Contents

Introduction 7

PART I: PRACTICES OF PRESENCE
Introduction to Part I 15
1. Compassion is Not a Luxury, *Joan Halifax* 17
2. Ministry of Presence: Wandering and Street Retreats, *Jitsujo T. Gauthier* 27
3. Stand Like a Tree, Relax Like a Flower, *Julian Bowers-Brown* 33
4. Buddhist Meal Prayer: Offering to the Three Jewels, *Lama Döndrup Drölma* 35
5. One Heart Grace, *Zoketsu Norman Z Fischer* 37
6. Metta for the Body, *Trudy Goodman* 39
7. Stone Fruit: An Invocation, *Eli Brown* 41

PART II: SPIRITUAL CARE MODELS
Introduction to Part II 45
8. Nurturing a Culture of Spiritual Friendship and Intentional Community, *Ven. Priya Rakkhit Sraman* 47
9. Traditional Buddhist Healing as Spiritual Care Model, *Ji Hyang Padma* 55
10. Chaplain Formation for Buddhist College Chaplaincy, *Ernest C.H. Ng* 67
11. What is Self-Care for Buddhist College and University Chaplains? *Jonathan Makransky* . . . 85
12. Towards a Multi-faith Community at Wellesley College, *Rev. Victor Kazanjian* 95
13. Buddhist Ceremonies for Higher Education and Related Considerations, *Rebecca Nie* . . . 107

PART III: UNIVERSITY SYSTEMS
Introduction to Part III 125
14. How to Survive Your Promising Life: A Baccalaureate Address, *Zoketsu Norman Fischer* . 127
15. Hidden Chaplains: A project for Buddhist seeing and reflection, *Matthew Weiner* 133
16. Canadian University Chaplaincy: A closer look at the distinctive role of Buddhist chaplains, *Henry C.H. Shiu* 141
17. "Buddhism is a Whole Life Practice!" Building relationships with Asian and Asian heritage Buddhist communities to work against Neo-Orientalist tendencies in Buddhist Chaplaincy, *Rev. Ivan (Kusa) Mayerhofer* 151
18. Managing and Transforming Conflict, *Nathan Jishin Michon* 161

PART IV: UPAYA
Introduction to Part IV 173
19. Queer Buddhist Prayers, *Victor Gabriel* 175
20. Sangha Synergies: Dance and prayer as Dharma modalities, *Harrison Blum* 179
21. Buddhism and the Calling of No-Calling, *Mark Unno* 191
22. A Contemplative Approach to Family Systems, *Jessica Thomas* 211

Epilogue 219
Contributor Biographies 223
Acknowledgments 227

Introduction

The field of Buddhist college chaplaincy has come into fruition over the last thirty years. In 1995, when I began this work, there were just three other Buddhist college chaplains, and the field of interfaith chaplaincy was also nascent. However, as the Pluralism Project has well demonstrated, America's religious landscape has changed. The number of college-aged Buddhist practitioners has been steadily growing. According to the Pew Forum's Religious Landscape Study (Pew Forum, 2017), Buddhism in America grew 170% between 1990 and 2001, and is currently the third largest religion in America behind Christianity and Judaism with Islam as a close fourth. A PRRI study completed in 2020 (PRRI Census of American Religion) found that the median age of Buddhist American adults is 36, significantly lower than the median for all Americans (47) and among the youngest of all religious groups. The Pew study (2014) found that one third of Buddhists were between the ages of eighteen and twenty-nine, a 55% increase since the study was last completed in 2007. A PRRI study completed in 2020 found that more than one third of American Buddhists have at least a four-year college degree. From this data, we can discern that there are an increasing number of young Buddhists within our college communities.

It is evident from this cursory glance at the research that there is more need for Buddhist spiritual care and community-building among young adults than we chaplains are currently able to provide. Advocacy is needed, to tackle issues of funding and other structural obstacles. And yet, the university setting is a fertile ground for practice endeavors. The need that students have for Buddhist teaching and spiritual care is real – particularly in this turbulent time.

Student mental health has been adversely affected by the pandemic, increased racial and cultural stratification, and other vectors of change. As a society, we face rapidly increasing mental illness rates that experts describe as a mental health crisis on college campuses, nationally and globally. On college campuses there has been a reported 135% increase in depression and 110% increase in anxiety from 2013–2021. Covid has contributed to further isolation and disconnection, which are precursors to mental health problems. Ninety-six percent of US adults report that the pandemic has impacted their overall stress. Forty percent of US adults report struggling with mental health (Maio et al., 2022).

Anxiety and depression, specifically, are significant concerns. When left untreated, these concerns can lead to a variety of health-compromising attitudes and behaviors, including impaired relational skills, alienation, addiction, and suicidal thoughts and behaviors – which disrupt students' lives and the lives of our communities (Kass, 2017). Buddhist chaplains can promote positive health outcomes through one-on-one counseling as well as through mindfulness programs, which can increase resilience and enhance learning. The intervention that a Buddhist chaplain makes is exponentially increased by the resource of peer sangha, within which the student experiences a spirit of unity and interconnection, within which other divides propagated by a modern culture of stratification diminish. As anthropologist Victor Turner noted, the peer sangha provides *communitas*, a sense of oneness of spirit, love and acceptance of the other (2017). This experience of belonging can provide resiliency in times of crisis and catalyze greater intimacy in other interpersonal relationships. (Griffith, 2012).

In particular, the sense of communitas and resiliency that mindful communities provide is an antidote to the stratification and bias which have been re-surfacing in universities as it re-surges within the global commons. Societal injustice and inequity perpetuate patterns of cross-group tension and disconnection, which adversely impact students' lives. These patterns of social inequality and systemic racism are very significant concerns within university life (Jordan, Hartling &Walker, 1999; Kass, 2017). Campus-based mindfulness interventions can promote intersectional awareness and compassion and ground students in the body, which diminishes reactivity, strengthening the capacity for critical self-reflection (Magee, 2019).

Need for a Buddhist Practical Theology

Bhiksuni Lozang Trintae (2014) and Rev. Monica Sanford (2016, 2021) have argued effectively for an academic discipline of Buddhist *practical theology*. The term *practical theology*, pioneered within Christian theology, refers to the testing of theology praxis through cycles of critical reflection and action. We can see the historical records of commentary upon texts such as the *Prajna Paramita*, the Lojong slogans developed by Atisha, or the *Blue Cliff Record* as an "indigenous practical theology" (Trintae, 10). Within my Zen tradition, the capacity to provide an incisive and appropriate response to these pointing-out instructions is the measure of a seasoned teacher. On one level, this process exists in a dynamic, empirical way within the lineages of Buddhism. And yet, as scholar John Makransky has noted, there is a need for Buddhist scholar-practitioners to contribute to new understandings of Buddhist teaching and practice through "critical-constructive reflection" (2023): this can described as Buddhist theology (although this term may be considered an oxymoron, there are advantages to using the term theology in its broader sense, to mean a discipline of conceptual reflection upon the sacred from within that wisdom tradition). The field of Buddhist practical theology, then, includes adaptation of traditional teaching to the contemporary settings through contemplative research, the interdisciplinary work of Buddhist psychology and certainly, specific teaching strategies and praxis related to college chaplaincy.

The Practical Theology of Buddhist Chaplains

Buddhist college chaplains play an important role in the spiritual life of emergent adults. They are often students' first encounter with the Dharma. They provide spiritual teaching and meditation practice on campus, and by so doing, create a sangha, spiritual community, which then becomes an important resource for students who are seeking a sense of belonging. For a certain number of these students, the Buddhist chaplain may be the first friend that they make in the university. In order for the chaplain to do this work, the Dharma must be strategically adapted to the community and setting.

For instance, chaplains provide many kinds of spiritual counseling. They facilitate discernment about career and vocational choice. They play an essential role in providing pastoral (spiritual) counseling as a confidential and preferred resource. A pastoral counseling session ranges from an introduction to the path of meditation or actual *dokusan* (Zen koan interviews), to actively helping a student work with anxiety or depression, to providing good counsel with regard to relationships, to crisis counseling. Pastoral counseling often includes referrals to mental health resources, sexual health resources, and other networks of support services. While the Buddhist chaplain is not expected to provide long-term counseling, this spiritual accompaniment often plays a pivotal role in the lives of the students they serve – and it is quite different from temple life. Buddhist chaplaincy interventions are not exactly like the work of other student life professionals, in that they are rooted in Buddhist ontology and axiology, and contemplative praxis. The development of such a body of work by a chaplain requires cycles of critical reflection and action, through which traditional teaching on right speech, *kalyanamitta*, and other Dharma teaching and teacher formation is integrated with relevant training in pastoral care or other social sciences – this is Buddhist practical theology. In recognition of the pressing, ongoing need for these adaptations within the context of higher education, and to advance the professionalization of our field through engagement in peer-to-peer cycles of teaching and learning, we have compiled this first Buddhist college chaplaincy sourcebook.

In this volume, we have organized the varieties of Buddhist chaplains' practical theology into four themes: *Practices of Presence, Spiritual Care Models, University Systems,* and *Upaya.*

As Jonathan Makransky has noted, "At the core of the Buddhist college chaplain's work are practices of presence, skillful means through which we can embody on deeper and deeper levels the qualities of boundless wisdom and compassion that are inherent within the nature of mind, Buddhanature." We begin with the G.R.A.C.E. model pioneered by Joan Halifax Roshi, a model for opening to grounded, conscious attunement that amplifies our capacity to respond with compassion. Therein follow several different practices of presence that are adapted to contemporary life.

Spiritual Care Models are the theme of the second section. Most of us embarked upon this work at a time when there were very few Buddhist theologians – and yet, it is so helpful to have an appropriate framework, to clarify our intention and understanding and do this work. One of the core paradigms brought forth by the historical Buddha is the *Kalyanamitta* (noble friend) model, described here by Venerable Priya. I have contributed a reflection on the Medicine Buddha and the *Trikaya* (three bodies of Buddha), an ancient healing paradigm embedded within our Buddhist tradition that can help us to differentiate between different strategies of care.

In the third section, we bring awareness to the circles of interdependence which are the context of this work, the college and university systems. Zoketsu Norman Fischer offers a powerful Baccalaureate address, in which he critiques the impossible expectations embedded within the traditions and privileges of higher education, in a way that invites the listener to reconsider what, in the final analysis, matters most. We then examine the campus-wide multi-faith spiritual care model, developed by Rev. Victor Kazanjian in response to the rich diversity of religious traditions and spiritual beliefs which are now present within the cultural landscape of our campuses. This pluralistic model made it possible for Buddhist chaplains, together with chaplains of other faiths, to work together to support the spiritual life of the campus as a whole. This work was considered essential to fulfill Wellesley College's educational mission, a multi-cultural learning community in which spiritual and cultural differences are recognized and celebrated.

Thus, spiritual care provided by a Buddhist chaplain extends beyond the particularity of this tradition: the Buddhist chaplain serves as a community organizer of sorts, strengthening the fabric of community among faculty, fellow chaplains, university core staff and students, through which students can be held in the wholeness of their educational journey. One particularly powerful example which appears in this volume is "Hidden Chaplains", a program at Princeton University. Hidden Chaplains is a skillful means of recognizing and uplifting the moments of transformative connection which are taking place throughout the campus – quite often through the kindness of the dining hall worker, secretary, or facilities staff who smile at the student, ask them about their day, know their name, engage in small talk for a moment. The nomination process is itself an opportunity for critical reflection: students "nominate" a hidden chaplain by reflecting on their interaction and its' meaning. Nominees are then honored at a dinner. Hidden Chaplains is not explicitly Buddhist, and yet the initiative serves as a means for engaging the wider community with Buddhist sensibility in terms of practical application, and relationships to Buddhism in both doctrinal and lived terms.

Henry C.H. Shiu expands this volume's vision of Buddhist chaplaincy through a survey of Canadian Buddhist college and university chaplaincy. While the diversity of the traditions represented within Canadian university chaplaincy demonstrates the nation's commitment to inclusivity and religious pluralism, funding levels do not support many full-time positions. There is an ongoing need for chaplains to promote their work, and advocate for their organizations.

Some of the particular strengths of the Buddhist chaplain's position are based on the chaplain's embeddedness within the higher education structure. Spiritual advisors are generally considered to be trustworthy mediators in times of conflict who can ease the growing edges of community. Nathan Michon's contribution to this volume reflects on processes for conflict transformation and reconciliation that are deeply rooted in Buddhist principles.

In the fourth section, Upaya, we inquire into expedient means that support the extension of the Dharma universally, to every human being and place within the campus community that might benefit.

Buddhist theologian Victor Gabriel illuminates the need to illuminate the path of intimacy, particularly among the LGBTQ+ community. Recognizing the lack of guidance and Buddhist resources addressing sexuality and queerness when he was a student, Gabriel offers a queer Buddhist theology, *gathas* and visualizations.

Harrison Blum, Director of Religious and Spiritual Life at Amherst, draws upon his training in dance to develop *Dharma Jam*, a path of mindfulness expressed through movement, supporting a surrender to *what is*. There is a sequence, through which rhythms shift and change, so that students are taken through an evolutionary journey. Blum has found it especially powerful to incorporate an element of prayer, through which *metta* (lovingkindness) is amplified in the community's shared experience.

Buddhist chaplains are trusted as confidential and privileged resources who can provide healing support in cases of trauma, especially related to Title IX (prohibiting sex discrimination in education). Due to this, they may be entrusted to hold space for students who suffer spiritual trauma from other religion or dharma centers so that these students may reestablish spiritual groundedness. Chaplains often serve as an important source of attachment security, and thus it is common that students may bring family matters which adversely impact their academic and spiritual life into the spiritual counseling session. Jessica Thomas offers a contemplative family systems approach, with practices that can be used to help students gain clarity and find resources within their family system.

Buddhist chaplains, through the spiritual education that they provide, invite students to integrate the values and ethics inherent in Dharma practice with their path of service in the world, through the life choices of family and career. Within the contexts of community teaching and individual counseling, Buddhist chaplains are called to support students' discernment related to career and vocational choices: Mark Unno's contribution grounds such reflection skillfully in Buddhist text and case studies. This integrative spiritual education can also prepare students to provide mindful and non-violent leadership in the world at large.

Through these skillful ways of adapting the teaching of the Dharma to the context of university life, Buddhist chaplains guide students to rediscover their wholeness through clarity of the mind and the heart's own wisdom. These pathways then support the achievement of such values as integrity, compassion and inclusivity that are central to a university's mission, and we empower students to become compassionate actors in this increasingly connected world.

REFERENCES

2020 PRRI Census of American religion. PRRI. (2024, February 23). https://www.prri.org/research/2020-census-of-american-religion/

Griffith, J.L., & Griffith, M.E. (2012). *Encountering the sacred in psychotherapy: How to talk with people about their spiritual lives*. Guilford Publications.

Jordan, J.V., Hartling, L.M., & Walker, M. (2004). *The complexity of connection: Writings from the Stone Center's Jean Baker Miller Training Institute*. The Guilford Press.

Kass, J.D. (2017). *A person-centered approach to psychospiritual maturation: Mentoring psychological resilience and inclusive community in higher education*. Springer International Publishing.

Lozang Trinlae, B. (2014). Prospects for a Buddhist Practical Theology. *International journal of practical theology*, 18(1), 7-22.

Magee, R.V., & Kabat-Zinn, J. (2021). *The inner work of racial justice: Healing ourselves and transforming our communities through mindfulness*. Tarcher Perigree.

Maio, H.A., (2022, April 21). *Mental health of college students is getting worse*. Boston University. https://www.bu.edu/articles/2022/mental-health-of-college-students-is-getting-worse/

Makransky, John. (2023, June 21). *Buddhist Constructive Reflection Past and Present: Recurrent Reinterpretation in Meeting New Cultural Needs and Challenges* [Keynote]. European Academy of Religion Conference, St. Andrews University, St. Andrews, Scotland.

Pew Forum. (2017, April 5). Pew Research Center. *The Changing Global Religious Landscape*. https://www.pewresearch.org/religion/2017/04/05/the-changing-global-religious-landscape/

Sanford, M. (2016). Practical Buddhist Theology: Methods for Putting Wisdom into Practice. In *A Thousand Hands: A Guidebook to Caring for Your Buddhist Community* (pp. 3-15). essay, Sumeru.

Turner, V. W. (2017). Liminality and communitas. In *Ritual* (pp. 169-187). Routledge.

Part I
Practices of Presence

Part I: Practices of Presence
Introduction

At the core of the Buddhist college chaplain's work are practices of presence, skillful means through which we can embody, on deeper and deeper levels, the qualities of boundless wisdom and compassion that are inherent within the nature of mind, Buddhanature. Grounding within these practices allows chaplains to show up for students in moments of joy, sorrow, and the day-to-day life experiences in between, to be fully present to them in a mode of wise and skillful care. Each contributor to the first section of this volume illuminates practices of presence in ways that are both specific to their contexts and broadly relevant to Buddhist spiritual care providers in higher education settings.

Roshi Joan Halifax opens this section with a crucial reminder that "compassion is not a luxury," and that compassion can be viewed as an emergent and contingent process of attuning to our capacity for care. She provides a review of contemporary psychological and neuroscientific research on the beneficial effects of compassion-based meditation in improving chaplain and client outcomes. In doing so, she demonstrates the ways in which compassion can transform what she calls "edge states," qualities that are integral to a life of wisdom and care but that can manifest dark sides if internal and interpersonal resources break down (due to burnout, for instance). One skillful method of embodying compassion in this way is Upaya Zen Center's GRACE, a contemplative framework for cultivating care in relationship with others. In closing, Roshi reminds us that "compassion is the path that the great healers and teachers of the past have walked. And it is a path of sanity that chaplains can discover, step by step."

Rev. Jitsujo T. Gauthier writes of the practice of wandering and street retreats as a means through which to cultivate a ministry of presence through which compassion can manifest effectively. For university students, street retreats present a possibility of radical learning outside the classroom, in which they are prompted to go beyond their comfort zones in order to cut through the illusion of separation between beings. This necessitates a ministry of presence, particularly with unhoused communities, that allows for healthy boundaries while simultaneously fully witnessing and being with the suffering encountered on the street. In this context, "fearless compassion means stepping outside our comfort zones, loosening our identity, and seeing the societal norms that perpetuate barriers that separate individuals and communities." Students thus become familiar with Buddhist frameworks of engaged compassion such as the Brahmaviharas, the Three Tenets, and others, in a lived way.

Julian Bowers-Brown provides us with a practice of centering and grounding that allows us to be compassionately present to ourselves in an embodied sense so that we can be fully present with others in chaplaincy work. We all have the capacity to "stand like a tree" and "relax as a flower."

We conclude the section with four invocations of our radical interconnection with all sentient beings. Lama Döndrup Drölma provides us with an adaptation of the traditional Tibetan meal offering to the Three Jewels, and Zoketsu Norman Fischer offers a different meal grace emphasizing gratitude for all beings connected to the food: both prayers can be adapted easily for programs at which food and drink are consumed (nearly every program, in many university settings!) Trudy Goodman offers a Metta for the Body – as she notes, this turning toward our bodies with love satisfies an eternal hunger. Eli Ryn Brown offers a prayer of "intergenerational embrace," connecting us with our ancestors, teachers and lineage elders with all of their loving revolutionary resistance; the accompanying still-life photograph is an offering in itself.

1
Compassion Is Not a Luxury
Roshi Joan Halifax, PhD

Compassion is not a luxury; it is a necessity for the human being to survive. *His Holiness the Dalai Lama*

The intent of this chapter is to outline briefly some of the challenges chaplains face, and why and how cultivating compassion for others is a source of psychological and social wellbeing. It also explores some of the neuroscientific underpinnings of compassion, and the value of compassion in supporting chaplain resilience. Finally, the chapter briefly outlines a model of compassion and a compassion intervention that can be used while immediately interacting with others.

Giving care to people who are suffering has many challenges, including the shadow side of "edge states" that affect chaplain well-being. These include pathological altruism, empathic distress, moral suffering, disrespect of others and self, and burnout. These five core challenges can be compounded by the possible denial of suffering; the angst around pain, suffering, and death; the inability to discuss the reality of unpredictability and pain; the inability to communicate about stresses in caregiving; workaholism, self-neglect, and perfectionism; engaging in negative cognitive appraisal; moral conflicts and distress; and futility with client demands, institutional demands, and interventions not benefiting clients.

The question then arises: how do we address chaplain suffering, and what are some relevant spiritual and contemplative perspectives and practices that might give relief to caregivers, and foster greater resilience and compassion in chaplains and caregivers?

In the work that the Upaya Zen Center has done over several decades in training chaplains, we have, among other things, explored seven core contemplative strategies that support chaplains in developing resilience and cultivating compassionate and mindful caregiving. These include: focused attention; insight practices; practices that assist caregivers in presencing pain and suffering; practices that develop prosocial mental states (kindness, compassion, sympathetic joy, equanimity, altruism, empathy); GRACE (cultivating compassion while interacting with others), imaginal processes that track the psychophysiological aspects of dying; and open presence.

In the extensive neuroscience research on meditation being done around the world at this time, contemplative practices have demonstrated the following benefits:

- The cultivation of attentional balance: the capacity to have a sustaining, vivid, stable, effortless, and nonjudgmental attention (the base of presence).
- The cultivation of emotional balance: cultivating prosocial mental states, including altruism, empathy, compassion, kindness, joy, equanimity.
- The establishment of cognitive control: the ability to guide thought and behavior in accord with one's intention and override habitual responses; as well, to downregulate, and the cultivation of mental flexibility, insight, meta-cognition, and the capacity to reappraise.
- The enhancement of health and resilience: stress reduction, relaxation, and enhanced

immune response, and decreased inflammation.

Compassion and Mindfulness

In exploring compassion meditation, an important feature of compassion practice is mindful attention of the present moment. The meditation teacher Jon Kabat-Zinn (2005) has defined mindfulness as "…moment-to-moment, non-judgmental awareness, cultivated by paying attention in a specific way, that is, in the present moment, and as non-reactively, as non-judgmentally, and as openheartedly as possible" (pp. 143-161).

Mindfulness is associated with self-reported positive affect, less anxiety and depression; greater relationship satisfaction and less relationship stress (Barnes et al, 2007); and profiles of brain activity associated with greater emotion regulation during affect labeling (Brown and Ryan, 2003). These qualities form a base where compassion can unfold.

Mindfulness is a process that also makes the regulation of emotion possible. It can create a stable mental state where insight arises that makes the distinction between self and other more obvious, without which we could experience empathic over-arousal, and move into personal distress (Baer, 2006). Over-arousal, leading to personal distress, inhibits healthy compassion. Thus, mindfulness is an essential component of compassion (Brown and Ryan, 2003).

Mindful and compassionate caregiving entails listening with full attention; emotional awareness and self-regulation while caregiving; prosociality and positive regard for self and other; the ability to prioritize and be attuned to one's surroundings; and bringing compassion and nonjudgmental acceptance to interactions (Decety, 2007).

To support these qualities, chaplains need to value well-being, insight, compassion, integrity, respect, and self-respect. They also need to recognize challenges and stresses associated with caregiving. A commitment to physical, emotional, mental, spiritual, and relational balance is essential. Chaplains also need to engage in strategies supporting compassionate action toward the person, community, colleagues, and self.

Research on Compassion

Compassion is one of those experiences that deeply affects those who give it, those who receive it, and those who observe it. In terms of physical health, research indicates that the social connections associated with compassion appear to reduce inflammation, support immune function, speed recovery from illness, and lead to increased longevity. An example of this is the study conducted by Dr. Sara Konrath (2014), where volunteers lived longer than non-volunteering peers if the reasons for volunteering were altruistic rather than self-serving.

In another study, nonverbal communication of compassion calmed patients' autonomic nervous systems and regulated breathing and heart rate variation. Research also suggests that receiving compassion reduces post-surgical pain and decreases surgical recovery time, improves trauma outcomes, prolongs the survival of terminally ill patients, improves glucose control, reduces mortality at better rates than smoking cessation, and boosts immune function. By creating all these health benefits, compassionate interactions with patients might reduce systemic health care costs and the costs of stress on chaplains (Epstein, 1999).

What happens to long-term meditation practitioners when they are exposed to pain and suffering? Neuroscientists Richard Davidson, Antoine Lutz, and colleagues at the University of Wisconsin (2007) discovered that open awareness meditation appears to reduce negative anticipation to pain. In the same study, these long-term practitioners also experienced pain less adversely and recovered more rapidly from being unpleasantly stimulated. In another study,

Dr. Davidson and his colleagues learned that expert practitioners, while generating compassion, responded more strongly to emotion-laden human vocalizations than novice meditators did. They also saw that the expert practitioners' capacity for cognitive and affective empathy was greater than novice practitioners. These are important discoveries on how contemplative practices might enhance resilience in relation to being subjected to unpleasant stimuli, as well as supporting caregivers to be more attuned to the suffering of others.

In a study led by neuroscientist Dr. Helen Weng, also in the laboratory of Dr. Davidson, young adults trained to increase their experience of compassion behaved more altruistically when playing an economic game in the experiment. When they evoked feelings of compassion while viewing images of people who were suffering, they also showed increased activity in brain areas associated with empathy and understanding of others, as well as in emotion regulation and positive emotions.

Years ago, Dr. Gary Pasternak, the medical director of Mission Hospice in San Mateo, California and a long-term meditator, sent me an email I've never forgotten. He wrote,

> I'm up late admitting patients to the inpatient hospice unit. Just when I think I'm too old for these late nights without sleep, a person in all their rawness, vulnerability and pain lays before me and as my hands explore the deep wounds in her chest and my ears open to her words, my heart cracks open once again…. And this night a sweet 36-year-old woman with her wildly catastrophic breast cancer speaks of her acceptance and her hope for her children, and she speaks with such authenticity and authority. And her acceptance comes to me as the deepest humility a person can experience and then again, once again, I remember why I stay up these late nights and put myself in the company of the dying.

Dr. Pasternak's words reflect respect, humility, and courage. He was able, in a world of distractions, time pressure, and sleep deprivation, to slow down and open to life and death. In the midst of his patient's pain and his own, he remembered who he really was. This is compassion – the ability to turn toward the truth of suffering with the wish to relieve that suffering. And then awakening with humility to the precious gift of serving others selflessly.

Experiencing compassion also seems to diminish depression and anxiety because it opens our horizon beyond the narrowness of the small self. Dr. Emma Seppälä (2013) wrote, "Research shows that depression and anxiety are linked to a state of self-focus, a preoccupation with 'me, myself, and I.' When you do something for someone else, however, that state of self-focus shifts to a state of other-focus."

Another powerful aspect of compassion is related to moral character. Albert Schweitzer understood this when he wrote: "I can do no other than be reverent before everything that is called life. I can do no other than to have compassion for all that is called life. That is the beginning and the foundation of all ethics" (1979). He affirmed Arthur Schopenhauer's perspective that "compassion is the basis of morality" (1998). Research has found that being compassionate upholds our moral principles and gives meaning to our lives. According to the psychology researchers Daryl Cameron and Keith Payne (2012), when we restrain compassion, we will feel that our moral identity is compromised.

Psychologist and specialist in ethical leadership Jonathan Haidt (2014) has conducted studies on morality, culture, and emotion that suggest that when we see someone help another, it creates a state of "moral elevation" that inspires us to do the same. University of California – San Diego professor James Fowler, who studies contagion mechanisms, also confirms that helping is contagious.

Challenges to Compassion

In terms of healthy compassion, I want to briefly address recent work I have been doing around what I call Edge States. Understanding Edge States can enhance resilience and give us insight into the obstacles that inhibit compassion.

What are Edge States? Over the years, I became aware of five internal and interpersonal qualities that are keys to a compassionate and courageous life, a life that is grounded in wise hope, and without which we cannot serve, nor can we survive. Yet if these internal and interpersonal resources deteriorate, they can manifest as toxic landscapes that cause harm. I call these bivalent qualities *Edge States*.

The Edge States are altruism, empathy, integrity, respect, and engagement, assets that exemplify caring, connection, virtue, and strength. Yet we can also lose our firm footing on the high edge of any of these qualities and slide into a mire of suffering where we find ourselves caught in the toxic and chaotic aspects of the harmful edge of an Edge State.

For example, *altruism* can turn into *pathological altruism*. Selfless actions in service to others are essential to the well-being of society and the natural world. Altruism is a psycho-social imperative and arises naturally, like the right hand taking care of the left hand, should the left hand be injured. But sometimes, our seemingly altruistic acts harm us, harm those whom we are trying to serve, or harm the institutions in which we serve. This is when altruism gets compromised; when small hope for an outcome, or hope for recognition, or fear of failure drive us toward helping others at a cost to all. This is what social psychologists call pathological altruism (Klimecki & Singer, 2012).

A second Edge State is *empathy*, which can slide into *empathic distress*. When we expand our subjectivity to include the suffering of another person physically, emotionally, or cognitively, empathy can bring us closer to another's experience. This can inspire us to serve and can enhance our understanding of others. But if we take on too much of the suffering of another, and identify too intensely with the suffering, we may find ourselves unable to serve (Batson, Fultz, & Schoenrade, 1987). Our practice allows us to see that impermanence will prevail. It also helps us to understand that we cannot ever really know the experience of another. Thus, our practice and insight can engender humility and ground our experience of empathy to keep it healthy and balanced.

A third Edge State is *integrity* which points to having strong moral principles. But when we engage in or witness acts that violate our sense of integrity, justice, or beneficence, *moral suffering* can be the outcome. Moral suffering includes moral distress, moral injury, moral outrage, and moral apathy. We have to be aware that we can violate our integrity when we are at the effect of our expectations or the expectations of others. On the other hand, integrity is founded on the recognition of the basic goodness in others and ourselves.

The fourth Edge State is *respect*, a way we uphold beings and things in high regard. Respect can disappear into the swamp of *disrespect*, when we go against the grain of compassion-based values and principles of civility, and when we end up disparaging others or ourselves. Disrespect is an attitude that reflects cynicism and futility. Our practice provides the space in which we can see the goodness as well as the suffering of others, and where we hold all in equal regard.

The fifth Edge State is *engagement* in our work which gives a sense of purpose and meaning to our lives, particularly if our work serves others. But overwork, a toxic work-place, and an experience of a lack of efficacy can lead to *burnout*, which can cause physical and psychological collapse. Our expectations and the expectations of others often lead to burnout. Futility is also a cause of burnout. Our practice and insight can prevent burnout, and fuel and inspire healthy engagement.

Like a doctor who diagnoses an illness before recommending a treatment, I felt compelled to explore the healthy and destructive sides of altruism, empathy, integrity, respect, and engagement. Along the way, I was surprised to learn that even in their degraded forms, Edge States can teach and strengthen one, just as bone and muscle are strengthened when exposed to stress, or if broken or torn, can heal in the right circumstances and become stronger for having been injured.

In other words, losing our footing and sliding down the slope of harm need not be a terminal catastrophe. Being caught in the grip of unrealistic hope or abject futility need not be the worst thing in the world. There is humility, perspective, and wisdom that can be gained from our greatest difficulties.

In her book *The Sovereignty of Good*, Iris Murdoch defines humility as a "selfless respect for reality." She writes that "our picture of ourselves has become too grand." This I discovered from sitting at the bedside of dying people and being with caregivers. Doing this close work with those who were dying and those who were giving care showed me how serious the costs of suffering can be for patient as well as caregiver, including chaplains. Since that time, I have learned from chaplains, teachers, lawyers, CEOs, human rights workers, and parents that they can experience the same. I was then reminded of something profoundly important and yet completely obvious: that the way out of the storm of suffering, the way back to freedom on the high edge of strength and courage, is through the power of compassion. This is why I took a deep dive into trying to understand what Edge States are and how they can shape our lives and the life of the world.

Cultivating Compassion

In the summer of 2011, a group of research scientists, scholars, and teachers of compassion gathered in Berlin in the studio of Icelandic/Danish artist Olafur Eliasson to explore approaches appropriate to training in compassion. The meeting was a fruitful exploration of a mental and social process that seems to be not well understood in the West. Compassion, for example, is often associated with religion. It is also believed to be at times unhealthy and the cause of distress in those who manifest it. And yet, paradoxically, we are learning that compassion is a source of hardiness, resilience, flourishing, and well-being, from the point of view of research in the fields of contemplative neuroscience and social psychology.

Because compassion is believed to be an important mental and social feature and there seems to be a deficit of it in our society, the research on compassion has taken a quantum leap in recent years.

Earlier in the spring of 2011 prior to this meeting, I had spent several months at the Library of Congress as a Distinguished Visiting Scholar doing research on the development of a heuristic model of compassion. I did not feel that compassion had been sufficiently examined in order to develop effective training approaches.

Compassion has been defined as the emotion one experiences when feeling concern for another's suffering and desiring to enhance that person's welfare. Compassion has two main aspects: the affective feeling of caring for one who is suffering, and the motivation to relieve that suffering. I believe, however, that compassion is also a process that is contingent and emergent. It is grounded in inter-relationality and mutuality; it is also reciprocal and asymmetrical. Thus, compassion is not a discrete quality but an emergent and contingent process that is fundamentally context sensitive, and arises out of the interaction of non-compassion processes with interdependent experiential domains, including: attention and prosocial affect; altruistic intention and insight; and embodied experience giving rise to ethical engagement.

G.R.A.C.E.

The G.R.A.C.E. process was developed to offer chaplains, caregivers, and clinicians a practice to enable them to respond more compassionately and with greater clarity and ethical grounding in their encounter with those who are suffering. The process assists in understanding and integrating specific mental and physical processes that can allow compassion and resilience to emerge in the relationship between chaplain and patient, chaplain and clinician, inter-professional team members, and chaplain and family caregivers.

The G.R.A.C.E. process begins by guiding the chaplain or caregiver to pause briefly in order to focus their attention (Gathering attention) and to briefly recall their intention (Recalling intention). This brief check-in is followed by a rapid self-assessment (Attunement to self) of three interrelated domains of experience: noticing briefly what the body is experiencing; what one's emotional tone is; and what cognitive biases might be present. This is followed by sensing into what the patient might be experiencing (Attuning to other: empathy and perspective taking), and then moving to a short internal prescriptive process (Considering what will serve) before directly engaging in an action that is in service to the patient.

These internal processes might happen very rapidly, even automatically with practice. Yet chaplains often do not take a "reflective pause"; they often immediately assess the client before getting attentionally and ethically grounded, seeing their biases, then sensing into the client's experience before making an assessment. The G.R.A.C.E. process guides a chaplain into that moment (or moments) of reflection that can provide the base for healthy, grounded, and principled compassion. When "engagement" unfolds, there will be a base of integrity and stability to the interaction.

Gathering Attention

G.R.A.C.E. is a mnemonic that is easy to remember when a chaplain is in the midst of a stressful interaction or situation. The "G" in G.R.A.C.E. is a reminder to the chaplain to pause and gather their attention. This can be done through a simple grounding process with attention on the inbreath, or by bringing attention to a particular physical sensation, like the pressure of the feet on the floor, or the sensation of sitz bones on the seat of the chair. Gathering attention can also occur when a chaplain recalls a moment that is experienced as a resource, such as a positive interaction with a client or even a quiet moment at home. What is important in this first phase of G.R.A.C.E. is that the internal processing of the chaplain is gently interrupted so that they can be more of a resource to the self and the client through offering a quality of non-distracted and fresh presence that is stable, discerning, present, and caring. This can involve the re-allocation of attentional resources, briefly, away from the client and into the chaplain's subjective experience, in order to get grounded and focused.

Recalling Intention

Attentional balance supports the next phase of G.R.A.C.E. This is the "R" of G.R.A.C.E., recalling intention. The chaplain, possibly on the exhale, recalls the essential intention of the chaplain's mission, which is to protect and preserve the well-being and integrity of the client. Reifying one's altruistic motivation primes the so-called "narrative self," an aspect of the psyche that is affirmed in the field of meaning and purpose.

Attunement to Self and Other

The "A" of G.R.A.C.E. refers to the process of *attunement* – attunement first to oneself and then attunement to the client, family member, or colleague. Most commonly, a chaplain turns their attention immediately to the client. Not infrequently, perceptual, affective, and cognitive biases are in place, which make it challenging to perceive the client in a relatively unfiltered way. These screens or filters can bias a chaplain's perception of the client. Bringing these biases to the surface allows one to more accurately evaluate the client. For example, a chaplain might be unconsciously triggered by a birthing mother who is addicted to cocaine. The anger toward the mother might affect the chaplain's ability to give care and also be a burden to the mother. Getting in touch with this aversive reaction might allow them to regulate a negative response toward the mother by re-appraising the mother's situation, based on the reflection that drug use is often associated with factors of oppression and lower economic status, and is a sign of deep suffering. This reflective appraisal process can have the effect of shifting a chaplain's attitude and behavior toward the client, and of supporting a compassion-based response.

In the "attunement process," one first brings attention to one's own somatic experience, noticing what the body is experiencing. One aspect of the relevance of being sensitive to one's own bodily experience can be illustrated by research on alexithymia, an autism-related disorder. According to the research, similar neural circuits are activated in the experience of interoceptivity as in the experience of empathy. Findings from these studies on empathic response suggest that the same brain structures that represent an individual's affective state seem to play a role in sharing others' affective states. Researchers propose an interoceptive model of emotions to explain the experience of empathy, suggesting that being mindful of the body might well prime one's capacity for empathy (Mendoza and Foundas, 2008).

Attention is then brought to the affective stream, which can bias attention. There is evidence showing that the representation evoked by observing another person's affective state is biased by one's own affective state – a tendency called *egocentricity bias*.

Then attention rests briefly with the cognitive stream or the thoughts that can bias attitude and behavior. When biases are recognized, a re-appraisal process allows an individual to recognize or reframe the situation or the response to the situation in a non-aversive, non-judgmental way.

This self-attunement is primed by attention, which grounds one's attentional base, characterized by stability, vividness, and duration. It also is primed by intention, where the narrative self is oriented toward concern, care, kindness.

From this base of self-attunement, one attunes to the client. In this model, self-attunement provides the base for empathy or affective resonance, perspective-taking or cognitive attunement, and somatic attunement or sensing into the physical state of one's client.

Considering What Will Serve

The next phase of G.R.A.C.E. involves an internal process that is grounded by attention, intention, and self- and other-attunement. The chaplain can also consider other factors that are woven into the set and setting of the client, including institutional expectations and requirements, the impact of environmental features, such as medical care or academic stressors, the family's expectations, the needs of the inter-professional team, and so forth. All of these threads come together and can prime a discernment process ascertaining what will truly serve this client (or family member, colleague, or team).

Considering what will serve is, from one point of view, a diagnostic process, and it requires that the chaplain engage in a process that is not only based in conventional diagnosis but also supported by intuition and heuristics.

A chaplain is advised not to jump to conclusions too quickly. The discernment process might take time; it certainly requires attentional and affective balance, a deep sense of moral grounding and an ethical imperative, as well as an unbiased attunement into the client's experience and needs.

Enacting, Ending

The "E" of G.R.A.C.E. is focused on two phases of the lived interactional experience of compassion. With the involvement of attention, prosocial affect, self- and other-attunement, and the cognitive process of discernment and consideration, principled, ethical, and compassion-based action can unfold. This is the first part of the "E" of G.R.A.C.E., which is to engage or apply compassion in service to others.

To successfully conclude the interaction, it is also necessary to acknowledge internally and often interpersonally what has transpired in the course of the G.R.A.C.E.-based exchange. This second phase of the "E" of G.R.A.C.E., following engagement, makes it possible to let go of the current interaction and to refresh and move on to the next client-chaplain interaction in a cleaner, clearer manner. It may involve expressions of appreciation and gratitude, asking for forgiveness, or acknowledging what has transpired in the interaction.

To summarize, the elements of G.R.A.C.E. allow a chaplain to slow down and be more mindful and aware in the process of interacting with a client so that compassion can be primed. It is also possible to use G.R.A.C.E. in everyday interactions and allow it to help an individual to cultivate more compassion in life.

Conclusion

Our work as chaplain is never to deny the truth and presence of suffering, impermanence, and death. As we are touched by these realities of existence, we realize that compassion is a moral, social, psychological, and spiritual imperative. That is why one trains in the elements of compassion in order to have the strength and perspective to acknowledge the pain and suffering in others and ourselves and to develop an appropriate and transformative relationship to suffering through insight.

Compassion is central to being fully human. It is a key to reducing systemic oppression and nurturing a culture of respect, civility, and belonging. It is also an element in what makes cultures, organizations, and humans successful. To help us understand the necessity of compassion, science is making a strong case for its benefits and validating the importance of compassion for our survival and fundamental health.

Compassion is also a profound path for those who are in the helping professions. It is the path that the great healers and teachers of the past have walked. And it is a path of sanity that chaplains can discover, step by step. Fortunately, we live in a time when science is validating what humans have known throughout the ages: that compassion is not a luxury; it is a necessity for our well-being, resilience, and survival.

References and Acknowledgements

Baer, R. A., Smith, G.T., Hopkins, J., Krietemeyer, J., & Toney, L. (2006). Using self-report assessment methods to explore facets of mindfulness. *Assessment*, 13(1), 27-45.

Barnes, S., Brown, K.W., Krusemark, E., Campbell, W. K., & Rogge, R. D. (2007). The role of mindfulness in romantic relationship satisfaction and responses to relationship stress. *Journal of marital and family therapy*, 33(4), 482-500.

Batson, C.D., Fultz, J., & Schoenrade, P.A. (1987). Distress and empathy: Two qualitatively distinct vicarious emotions with different motivational consequences. *Journal of Personality*, 55(1), 19-39.

Brown, K.W., & Ryan, R.M. (2003). The benefits of being present: mindfulness and its role in psychological well-being. *Journal of personality and social psychology*, 84(4), 822.

Cameron, C.D., & Payne, B.K. (2012). The cost of callousness: Regulating compassion influences the moral self-concept. *Psychological science*, 23(3), 225-229.

Connelly, J. (1999). Being in the present moment: developing the capacity for mindfulness in medicine. *Academic Medicine: Journal of the Association of American Medical Colleges*, 74(4), 420-424.

Connelly, J.E. (2005). Narrative possibilities: using mindfulness in clinical practice. *Perspectives in Biology and Medicine*, 48(1), 84-94.

Decety, J. (2007). A social cognitive neuroscience model of human empathy. In E. Harmon-Jones & P. Winkelman (Eds.), *Social neuroscience: Integrating biological and psychological explanations of social behavior* (pp. 246-270). New York: Guilford Press.

Epstein, R.M. (1999). Mindful practice. *Jama*, 282(9), 833-839.

Kabat-Zinn, J. (2005). *Coming to our senses: Healing ourselves and the world through mindfulness*. Hachette UK.

Klimecki, O., & Singer, T. (2012). Empathic distress fatigue rather than compassion fatigue? Integrating findings from empathy research in psychology and social neuroscience. In B. Oakley, A. Knafo, G. Madhavan, & D.S. Wilson (Eds.), *Pathological altruism* (pp. 368–383). Oxford University Press.

Konrath, S. (2014). The power of philanthropy and volunteering. *Wellbeing: A complete reference guide*, 1-40.

Lai, C.K., Haidt, J., & Nosek, B.A. (2014). Moral elevation reduces prejudice against gay men. *Cognition & emotion*, 28(5), 781-794.

Lutz, A., Dunne, J. & Davidson, R. (2007). Meditation and the neuroscience of consciousness. In P. Zelazo, M. Moscovitch & E. Thompson, eds., *The Cambridge Handbook of Consciousness*, Cambridge University Press.

Mendoza, John E. and Anne L. Foundas. (2008) *Clinical Neuroanatomy: A Neurobehavioral Approach*. New York: Springer

Schweitzer, A. (1979). *Reverence for life*. Ardent Media.

Seppala, Emma. (2013). "The Compassionate Mind." *Association for Psychological Science - APS*, 30 Apr. 2013, www.psychologicalscience.org/observer/the-compassionate-min

Schopenhauer, A. (1998). *On the basis of morality*. Hackett Publishing.

Gratitude to Dr. Alfred Kaszniak for assistance on the interpretation of neuroscience content in this paper, to Drs. Tony Back and Cynda Rushton for collaboration on the Professional Training Program on Contemplative End-of-Life Care, Mary Remington, Director of Upaya's Buddhist Chaplaincy Training Program, to the Upaya Institute, and the Hershey Family Foundation for funding my work in the end-of-life care field, and Francisco Varela for introducing me to the neuroscience of compassion.

2

Ministry of Presence: Wandering and Street Retreats

Rev. Jitsujo T. Gauthier, PhD

What if you gave up your cell phone, wallet, apartment, car and decided to engage in a practice of wandering? How would it feel to leave home in this way? What if stepping out of habits, routines, preferences, and assumptions that normally bring comfort and safety, actually, reconnect you with what it means – to truly live, and 'be' in the midst of life?

Introduction

Leaving home and wandering from temple to temple is an age-old practice of renunciation in Buddhism. Zen koans record stories of Buddhist practitioners going from one Dharma center to another in search of the true teachings and a true teacher. Similarly, Street Retreats are a practice of wandering and renunciation. This is a foundational practice and core activity of the the Zen Peacemakers. A street retreat is a way to dissolve separation and foster empathy for fellow sentient beings. Pilgrimaging beyond our comfort zone is where growth happens. Part of this street retreat practice is deciding to bear witness to life on the streets for a few days with a small group, the clothes on your back, a blanket, and a water bottle. This is usually a big decision for most people. What if the streets themselves are the true Dharma teacher? What if it's possible to take refuge in the streets? There are many methodologies that integrate mindful practices into daily activities to cultivate a settled body and concentrated mind that naturally foster deep listening, empathy, and a compassionate presence.

Learning outside the classroom provides graduate students with invaluable opportunities to gain practical experience and develop relational, ethical, and critical thinking skills that can enhance their future careers. Activities such as internships, research projects, and work collaborations enable graduate students to apply theoretical knowledge into real-world scenarios, resulting in a deeper understanding of their chosen field. Moreover, engaging in interfaith and intra-religious experiences allow students to experience conflict in a supportive environment. Immersing in learning experiences that go beyond textbooks and lectures, not only enriches education, but also better prepares students for what they will face in the world.

From a Buddhist perspective, the concept of embodied ethics plays a key role, as it emphasizes the importance of practical application in ethical behavior rather than mere theoretical understanding. Buddhists strive to cultivate conduct that is fully embodied and manifested through their thoughts, words, and deeds. This aligns with teachings of non-violence, compassion, and interconnectedness. Embodied ethics foster deep awareness and sensitivity towards oneself and others, leading to more ethical decision-making rooted in nonseparation. Seeing our inherent interdependence can lead to trustworthiness, fairness, and integrity that shape environments to values collaboration over competition, ultimately contributing to the well-being of individuals and society as a whole. This essay will explore ministry of presence, street retreats, engaged compassion, and why getting out of the classroom and onto the streets might be useful.

Ministry of Presence

The concept of "ministry of presence" has Christian roots in the context of chaplaincy. It aims to build relationships based on trust, respect, and empathy through an interpersonal approach of being fully present and attentive to the spiritual, emotional, and psychological needs of others. This worldview sees human connection as crucial for healing and growth. This approach has spread beyond Christianity to permeate various secular fields like healthcare, social work, and education. Professionals who embody this approach demonstrate genuine empathy, active listening, and non-judgmental attitudes, cause those around them to feel valued and understood. Patients often report enhanced satisfaction, reduced anxiety, and improved compliance with treatment plans when they feel a deep connection with their healthcare provider. (Halifax footnote) By incorporating a ministry of presence, a merely medical, professional, academic interaction can transform to a caring, truly holistic, experience.

A Buddhist method for ministry of presence could be viewed as a form of engaged compassion. Buddhist chaplains embody engaged compassion by listening deeply, offering emotional awareness, and providing meaning-making skills to those facing challenges of old age, illness, loss, or trauma. Rooted in the idea of interconnectedness, compassion is developing the capacity to be with the suffering of others and to see this suffering as none other than one's own. Many Buddhist chaplains use the Zen Peacemaker's Three Tenets of not-knowing, bearing witness, and taking action as an approach to compassionate action. In that, they approach care-seekers, or situations, by first emptying the mind of expectations, giving up fix ideas, and being in not-knowing, second by bearing witness and deeply listening to whole person, situation, arising joy and suffering, and third taking action that comes out of the process of not-knowing and bearing witness. Thus, being with the suffering of others is being with the suffering in oneself. This type of sharing in experience can ultimately bring relief to such suffering.

Buddhist chaplaincy has become a growing profession, as people become more interested in Buddhist teachings, tenets, and practices. Many people who are drawn to Buddhist chaplaincy are in search of right livelihood, and wholesome ways to contribute to society. Part of the training is to provide ministry of presence by letting go of their agenda, losing our roles as helper and helpee, allowing a human-to-human connection and shared-wisdom to arise. Aton Boisen, founder of Clinical Pastoral Education (CPE), i.e., hospital internship or residency programs, calls this type of moment – meeting in mutuality. The practice of Buddhist chaplaincy not only contributes to personal growth but also encourages a ministry of wandering within systems, hallways, rooms, and conversations in search of meaning, healing, and connection.

Like the way of the bodhisattva, the way of chaplaincy does not need to be a profession. Anyone can embark on a meaningful journey that includes supporting and guiding individuals through their darkest moments, by sharing in this experience. Sharing in suffering can bring solace and enlightenment to those who meet each other in this sacred of authenticity and mutuality. In social work and community engagement, a ministry of presence can be a tool in facing societal complexities. By genuinely connecting with individuals who face adversity, social workers can gain a deeper understanding of their unique challenges and provide tailored support. When a strong foundation of trust and empathy is established, individuals and communities may become more receptive to empowerment initiatives, which can contribute to resilience and collective action.

Ministries of presence is equally significant in the realm of education. Teachers who cultivate a space of presence create an environment in which students feel safe, respected, and supported. By allowing alive encounters to naturally occur, educators can facilitate meaningful learning experiences, stimulate curiosity, and ignite a passion for learning. Additionally, peer groups and mentor programs that emphasize a ministry of presence may help navigate the academic journey and personal growth more effectively. Embracing a Buddhist ministry of presence as a graduate student implies recognizing its inherent value and consciously integrating practices that develop mindfulness, a settled body and concentrated mind, and a deeper understand of interdependence. This may involve active reflection, self-awareness, and deep listening. It may require taking breaks from your cell phone, social media, limiting the time you look at screens, resisting distractions, and making a commitment to be fully present to yourself and others in every interaction. Incorporating such practices can positively reconnect you with what it means to truly live and 'be' in the midst of this one life we have been given.

Zen Peacemaker Street Retreats

The importance of engaging and being present with unhoused communities cannot be overstated. In a world that often ignores and marginalizes those experiencing homelessness, it is crucial to see people as neighbors and to engage kindly and purposefully. A ministry of presence may serve as a powerful reminder that every human being deserves dignity, respect, and love. It is possible to provide essential support such as food and shelter, but conversation and presence can create a meaningful connection that restores hope and inspires change. A compassionate presence can disrupt narratives of invisibility imposed on unhoused individuals and challenges societal apathy. This can reaffirm worth and acknowledge each person as valuable members of our shared humanity. Through active involvement we can begin to address the immediate needs and underlying causes of homelessness while working towards justice for all individuals left behind by systemic negligence. How do we push against systemic barriers, be advocates of change, and cultivate compassion within ourselves and society at large?

Zen Peacemaker Street Retreats were first introduced by Roshi Bernie Glassman in 1991. These retreats seek to provide a direct encounter with homelessness, poverty, and inequality by immersing participants in urban environments and marginalized communities. The purpose is to foster a deep understanding of societal issues, see our inherent interconnectedness and inspire actions rooted in compassion. By stripping away the comforts and privileges of everyday life, participants are challenged to confront their own biases, assumptions, and prejudices while gaining a genuine sense of empathy and respect for those experiencing hardship. Street Retreats have a profound impact on participants and may emerge as a powerful tool for graduate students to develop personally, cultivate social awareness, and become catalysts for positive change in their communities.

During the street retreat, participants spend several days living on the streets, relying on soup kitchens for sustenance, and seeking safe places to sleep for shelter, e.g., churches, seminaries, synagogues, public buildings, etc. They immerse themselves in a practice of wandering and aimlessness. Participants acknowledge the struggles and realities of all that they encounter. Together, they engage in street meditation, the Way of Council, the Gate of Sweet Nectar ritual, reciting the Zen Peacemaker refuges, precepts and commitments, group decision making, silently walking through city streets, bearing witness, and optional begging practices. These experiences allow participants to dissolve the barriers that traditionally separate observer from observed, truly being in not-knowing, cultivating compassion, and breaking down the dichotomy of "us versus them."

For those new, or skeptical, to a street retreat, the idea is often misconstrued as "pretending to be homeless," or as a form of spiritual tourism. Such ethical concerns are very important to consider, discuss, reflect upon, and articulate within the decision-making process. A street retreat involves actively engaging with individuals experiencing homelessness, listening to their stories, understanding their needs, and finding small ways that serve rather than fix. Participants will inevitably come up against identity barriers, challenge assumptions, deconstruct fears, bear witness to systems that harm, understand renunciation, as well as nurture connections that transcend socioeconomic differences. Those who choose to participate often make an intentional choice to put themselves within the middle of complexity, knowing that they will get muddy in the process. In doing this, they will realize their practice of precepts more deeply – where there is no mud there is no lotus.

How to not fix, yet not turn away, from systemic issues that lead to homelessness, lack of affordable housing, mental health support, employment opportunities, and other effects of capitalism? Without the answers, leaders of street retreats choose to be with participants within such challenges and work together to create containers for mutual learning and reflection. Ultimately, there is potential to awaken bodhicitta, deepen vow, and face complex social issues with greater understanding and authenticity. There is a lot to learn from the unhoused community. Fearless compassion means stepping outside our comfort zones, loosening our identity, and seeing the societal norms that perpetuate barriers that separate individuals and communities.

Engaged Compassion

Engaged Buddhism, as propagated by Vietnamese Zen Master Thich Nhat Hanh, posits that Buddhist teachings go beyond the meditation cushion and temple gates. The Zen Peacemakers, like most engaged Buddhists, believe that genuine liberation involves direct involvement in society's problems through practicing the Three Tenets. Buddhist chaplaincy is also a domain within the broad framework of engaged Buddhism and rooted in Buddhist teachings. Frameworks such as the Four Noble Truths, Eightfold Path, Six *Paramitas*, *Brahmaviharas* and *Way of the Bodhisattva* serve as foundations for chaplains' actions. The Four Noble Truths provide a framework for understanding suffering and its causes, informing the chaplain's approach to addressing the root causes of suffering. The Eightfold Path guides chaplains in cultivating ethical behavior, wisdom, and mental discipline as they navigate complex and challenging situations. The *Brahmaviharas* emphasize developing wholesome qualities and attitudes of loving-kindness (*metta*), compassion (*karuna*), empathetic joy (*mudita*), and equanimity (*upekkha*) towards oneself and others. *The Way of the Bodhisattva* refers to the path taken by those who vow to attain enlightenment not only for their own liberation but also for the benefit of all sentient beings. Within all these frameworks, there are innumerous contemplative practices to help anyone cultivate skills for a ministry of presence that is grounded in compassion and wisdom.

Getting Out of the Comforts of the Classroom

For graduate students, engaged compassion and street retreats can be particularly valuable as it aligns with academic pursuits and career aspirations in a variety of fields. Through direct experiences students can truly understand and address the complex needs of those they serve. They can develop a more nuanced understanding of the root causes of social issues they seek to address. This can invite a sense of authenticity and confidence to their studies, research, initiatives, and potentially create more groundbreaking projects. Experiential opportunities can support students to confront their own biases and assumptions while enhancing their ability to navigate challenging situations with sensitivity to trauma, flexibility, and insightfulness. Such insights can lay the foundation for students to become more effective change agents, equipped with the knowledge, experience, self-awareness, and resilience necessary to create meaningful and sustainable interactions in their respective fields. Moreover, learning outside the classroom allows students to witness firsthand the different ways people engage within various cultural contexts, thus enabling them to form and adapt their own ministry of presence accordingly. In this way, a holistic approach that combines scholarly pursuits with real-world experiences empowers anyone who has the courage to provide compassionate care that goes beyond mere academic knowledge.

By stepping outside of their comfort zone, learning meditative practices, engaging with diverse communities, and participating in such street retreats, students may gain invaluable insights into the human condition. Maintaining healthy boundaries and understanding one's window of tolerance is essential in engaged compassion work. Serving and/or being of service to others can begin to feel like a duty to show empathy and provide unconditional support. However, without appropriate boundaries, there is a risk of harming ourselves, burning out, developing compassion fatigue, and not actually helping others in the process. Helping is giving others the space to exercise their own learning muscles, find their own motivation, and make their own mistakes. Healthy boundaries allow a relational distance without overidentifying with the other person or overextending oneself, while still offering a compassionate presence. Understanding one's window of tolerance can allow us to communicate expectations, limits, self-care, and form trauma-sensitive relationships. By maintaining boundaries and understanding limits, we are better able to sustain compassion work, cultivate a capacity to be in complexity, and ultimately nurture diverse and meaningful relationships.

Conclusion

In a world bustling with technology, a ministry of presence is a timely reminder of the immense value of interconnectedness. A compassionate presence recognizes the inherent dignity and worthiness of all sentient beings and this great earth as it is, without judgment or fixing. As college students refrain from unnecessary use of technology and boldly advocate for direct engagement with social injustice, environmental degradation, and systemic oppression, they will find actions to alleviate suffering grounded in compassion. There is a need for more movements that seek to bridge gaps between spiritual practice and active social change. Hopefully, Buddhist approaches that challenge notions that meditation and isolation from worldly affairs are sufficient for achieving enlightenment will flourish. Perhaps a multitude of forms of resistance will prosper and inspire others to embark on paths of activism rooted a ministry of presence – a truly revolutionary stance.

Innovations outside the classroom, like street retreats, complement theoretical knowledge gained in the classroom with real-world experiences, enabling students to better understand trauma, their window of tolerance, assumptions, and expectations of the world. Whether in engaged Buddhism, chaplaincy, caregiving professions, education, or any professional domain, the ability to embody a ministry of presence that is ardent, attentive, and alert will facilitate transformation and cultivate a world where everyone feels seen and valued. While this may seem like a benevolent gesture, it is also an urgent call to action that demands community of care and a bold sensitivity. A Buddhist ministry of presence acknowledges wholeness and sees each of us as equally responsible for creating a just and equitable society. Being with suffering, working in the cracks, loving our woundedness, and wandering aimlessly is what promotes healing, empowers, and dissolves barriers of separation.

References

Back, Anthony L., Susan M. Bauer-Wu, Cynda H. Rushton, and Joan Halifax. "Compassionate silence in the patient–clinician encounter: a contemplative approach." *Journal of palliative medicine* 12, no. 12 (2009): 1113-1117.

Chappell, David. *Buddhist Peacework*. Wisdom Publication, Somerville MA, 1999.

Cadge, Wendy, and Shelly Rambo, eds. *Chaplaincy and Spiritual Sare in the Twenty-First Century: An introduction*. UNC Press Books, 2022.

Chödrön, Pema, and Helen Berliner. *No Time to Lose: a Timely Guide to the Way of the Bodhisattva*. Boston, Mass: Shambhala, 2007.

Glassman, Bernie. *Bearing Witness*. New York: Random House International, 2000.

Halifax, Joan, and Rebecca Solnit. *Standing at the Edge: finding freedom where fear and courage meet*, 2019.

Hanh, Thich Nhat. Interbeing: *The 14 Mindfulness Trainings of Engaged Buddhism*. Parallax Press, 2020.

Paczyńska, Agnieszka, and Susan F. Hirsch, eds. *Conflict Zone, Comfort Zone: Ethics, Pedagogy, and Effecting Change in Field-based Courses*. Ohio University Press, 2019.

Rahula, Walpola. *What the Buddha Taught*. Open Road+ Grove/Atlantic, 2007.

Rinchen, Geshe Sonam. *The Six Perfections: an oral teaching*. Shambhala Publications, 1998.

Sanford, Monica. *Kalyanamitra: A Model for Buddhist Spiritual Care*, Vol.1. Sumeru Press, 2020.

Thera, Nyanaponika. *The Heart of Buddhist Meditation: Satipaṭṭhāna: A handbook of mental training based on the Buddha's way of mindfulness, with an anthology of relevant texts translated from the Pali and Sanskrit*. Buddhist Publication Society, 2005.

Thera, Nyanaponika. *Brahmaviharas, Four Sublime States* www.buddhanet.net, accessed 01/06/2023: https://www.buddhanet.net/pdf_file/4sublime_states.pdf

Treleaven, David A., and Willoughby Britton. *Trauma-sensitive Mindfulness: practices for safe and transformative healing*, 2018.

3
STAND LIKE A TREE, RELAX AS A FLOWER
Julian Bowers-Brown

A centering practice before *being* with clients/patients

Let go of hundreds of years and relax completely. *Shitou*

1. Find a safe, quiet space in which to practice (I have used a chapel, an unoccupied office and, on occasion, a stall in a public restroom).

2. Begin by standing in a tall and relaxed posture, bringing awareness to your body – your feet flat on the ground and shoulder width apart. Knees, elbows, fingers are slightly bent with hands by your side, palms facing outward. Your head and neck are upright with your chin slightly tucked in, so that your spine is in an extended and natural position. Notice your shoulders, allow them to let go and your chest to feel open, your breath at ease. Allow your eyes to relax in a gentle unfocussed gaze, looking slightly downward. Notice your belly relax as the whole body *stands like a tree* in a gentle breeze –relaxed and alert.

3. Feel your bodily presence – the *tantien* (a point three fingers below your belly button) as your center, a sense of ease, rooted in your stance.

4. With your feet in contact with the ground beneath you, supporting your whole being you can begin now to allow them to lift very slightly, side to side and one at a time, alternating left to right a few times, feeling what it's like to gently move from one foot to the other and how it is to notice as your weight shifts gently in the subtle movement.

5. Now return both feet fully to the ground and a felt sense of stillness as your body centers once again, flexible but stable like a tree and breath moving easily in and out through the nostrils.

6. When you are ready you can again introduce a slight movement but, this time, allowing your body and legs to lengthen, begin to gently shift your weight first to the soles and then to heels of both feet, so that you feel what it's like to gently tilt your posture forward and back, keeping a sense of your center as your weight shifts back and forth.

7. Now return again to a relaxed stillness. A deep felt-sense of ease in your whole body.

8. Take three deep, slow breaths in and out through the nose (if possible). Give your tensions, your concerns, your self-preoccupations to each outbreath.

9. Then simply allow a gentle awareness to accompany your normal, natural, relaxed in and out-breath. Where time allows, rest in this practice of 'silent illumination' for five or more minutes. As your body stills, so too can your heart and mind. As thoughts arise, just like bubbles on the, allow them to drift away each time they emerge.

10. With your body, heart and mind now centered, you can bring this short practice to an end with a longer in-breath and conscious sigh – 'ahhhh'. Follow this with a brief and gentle self-massage. To do this, start by rubbing both palms quickly together to warm the hands and then place them on your forehead and eyes, before massaging your scalp and shoulders and then gently and briskly sweeping your hands over your limbs. Now you can *relax as a flower* in your chaplaincy practice – alert and at ease, open in your heart and mind to what comes. Rain and sunshine.

4
MEAL PRAYER: OFFERING TO THE THREE JEWELS
Adapted by Lama Döndrup Drölma

Tön Pa La Me San Gye Rin Po Che
To the precious Buddha, the highest teacher

Khyob Pa La Me Dam Chö Rin Po Che
To the precious Dharma, the highest protector

Dren Pa La Me Gen Dün Rin Po Che
To the precious sangha, the highest guide

Kyab Ne Kön Chok Sum La Chö Pa Bül
To you, rare and sublime Refuges, I offer this food.

5

ONE HEART GRACE
Zoketsu Norman Fischer

Written at Green Gulch, September 25, 1996

A meal grace originally written for the Zen Hospice Project, but suitable for use in university settings.

As we make ready to eat this food
we remember with gratitude
the many people, tools, animals and plants,
air and water, sky and earth,
turned in the wheel of living and dying,
whose joyful exertion
provide our sustenance this day.
May we with the blessing of this food
join our hearts
to the one heart of the world
in awareness and love,
and may we together with everyone
realize the path of awakening,
and never stop making effort
for the benefit of others.

6
METTA FOR THE BODY
Trudy Goodman, Ph.D.

The first foundation of mindfulness, the ground of our existence where we bring our attention, is the body. The Buddha wanted us to feel the body *in* the body, to feel the breath *in* the breath. What does this mean? It means getting to know the body from within the experience of being this body. Not as a concept or an object that we make 'other' – but from within, from the inside.

Mindfulness is participatory observation – we are both subject and object of loving awareness at the same time. We both witness and experience the emotions and physical sensations that we're having, simultaneously. The word for mindfulness is *Sati*, and it means: remember, don't forget! Don't forget to relax and allow yourself to simply notice and be here, right where you are – present with what's unfolding, willing to see life just as it is. Remember to notice and appreciate life happening, life in the form of *this* breath, *this* sensation, *this* perception, *this* moment!

The Buddha said that within this fathom-long body, this very body that we inhabit, we can awaken to the deepest truths of life – that along with the pleasures and bliss of embodiment, that pain and suffering of embodiment are not a mistake, and can be doorways into impermanence, the dancing, changing, ephemeral nature of this body-based being, the freedom from identity that otherwise determines so much of our destiny, everything that we need to awaken and free our hearts can be known through the body.

The late Indian teacher Nisargadatta Maharaj expressed it this way: discovering "our capacity for empathic, loving awareness." And this is what the following practice can strengthen. He said, "I find that somehow, by shifting the focus of attention, I become the very thing I look at and experience the kind of consciousness it has. I become the inner witness of the thing...I call this love."

So this is the love that we all long for, really. Can you or I truly see, understand, and accept our bodies...? All we need to do is work with our capacity to shift our attention, to direct it in particular ways. This is the good news of the practice: we can develop and train our capacity for *embodied* love right here and now with a practice that can bring ease, well-being, and aliveness to the body.

I am now going to provide detailed directions for this practice that you may use with a college community, or with anyone who would benefit from greater capacity for mindful embodiment.

> Please find a comfortable way to sit or lie down, where you can be relaxed. I'm going to say a few simple words, which you will probably think are simplistic or silly. Please give this practice a try, anyway. Just quietly, silently repeat them to yourself. That's all you have to do. If you're not comfortable closing your eyes in the group, simply lower your eyelids a little bit, so you can still see where you are. Closing your eyes or lowering your gaze is a signal to your body. You can take off your shoes, which is another way of letting your body know this is time to relax. Take

a deep breath to arrive in your own body. Taking three deep conscious breaths brings your mind and body to the same place at the same time.

Now, we will scan very slowly through the body. Bringing attention to the region of your head, simply offer this phrase of well-wishing:

"May my head be happy. May my scalp, my face, my ears, my whole head, be relaxed and happy." And then slowly moving the attention down to the neck, "May my neck be happy. My throat, my neck, may they be at ease."

And now the shoulders: "May my shoulders lower, relax, and be at ease." And moving attention to the arms, "May my arms be happy. My upper arms, elbows, lower arms, forearms. May my arms relax. My wrists and hands, may they be happy, at peace. Fingers, thumbs, palms, back of the hands, my whole arm, both hands, may they be happy."

And bringing attention to the upper back, middle back, lower back: "May my back, my whole spine, be at ease, be well and strong."

And now bringing attention to the chest: May my chest be happy, open, at ease. My belly, my whole abdomen, this whole region that can store so much emotion. May my belly be happy and peaceful. May my bottom, my buttocks, literally the seat of consciousness, be happy, be at ease. And my genitals, may they be content, peaceful. My hips, and this whole pelvic region, may my hips be happy and relaxed. May my thighs be happy, may they be free from judgment, at ease. And my knees, these complex joints, may they be well and happy. And my lower legs, calves, shins, ankles. May my lower legs relax, be at ease. May both of my legs, my whole legs, be happy and well. And my feet, the heels, the soles, the toes, the tops of the feet, the whole foot. May my feet that carry me everywhere, may my feet be happy. May they be appreciated, may they feel loved.

Sense and feel the whole body, from head to toe. Sense the loving awareness, suffusing the whole body with your intention to appreciate, respect, to care for, and love this body. This is feeling a sense of coming home – of finding in this body, your very body – the ground of well-being.

We often end meditations with the sound of a bell, so you can imagine it if you don't have one; when you're ready, open your eyes, make the sound of a bell, "ding." This turning toward our bodies with love can relieve deep loneliness. As a great eighteenth-century Zen monk, Hakuin Zenji, said, "One mouthful of this reality relieves an eternal hunger."

STONE FRUIT: AN INVOCATION
Eli Ryn Brown · 転竹

I invoke the teachers and ancestors and
   lineage elders –
press into my skull and collarbone.
Let the swells of your breath fill my lungs
   with
sweet loving and resistance.
Baptize me in your texts protest expression
ferocity.

I pick a thousand plums and steep the flesh
   into tea,
purple and blue and brilliant,
to serve at the altar of Black futurity.
A prayer for intergenerational embrace
and release from this painful knowing.

My thumb rubs each pit shiny and jewel-like
to be strewn into diadems
atop trans and queer royalty.
If I bow to kiss your feet, I know instead
I will find an uplifted palm.

The meat fills a thousand alms bowls
and I chant into their resonance
until they sing Namo Amida Butsu.
I am you and we are other.

I plant a tree in the backyard
of my parents' house
with seed and mud in my fingertips
and it springs from earth as I from them.

I let the juice be perfume
for each hand that has laid bare on my chest
and hummed warmth into the nape of my
   neck.
Fragrance passes with ephemeral lips
just below the ears,
on the insides of the wrist.

I bathe in the mess of my making
and the beauty of this interdependence.
My hands are streaked with earth and fruit
and the oils of skins.
My mind is a convergence of each thought
we have felt together.

I invoke the teachers and ancestors and
   lineage elders.
I invoke the teachers and ancestors and
   lineage elders.
I call your names into day and night stars
and sing your revolution.

Part II
Spiritual Care Models

Part II: Spiritual Care Models
Introduction

As spiritual care professionals, Buddhist chaplains in college and university settings draw upon models of care (for themselves and for the students and broader university communities they serve) from both traditional Buddhist and contemporary psychospiritual sources. In addressing the diverse needs of 21st century university students who are finding their place in an ever more complex and troubled world, Buddhist chaplains have an imperative: to connect with the deep wisdom of the traditional spiritual care models of their lineages while simultaneously adapting them in ways that align with best practices in the field and rendering them accessible for students of all backgrounds. This section brings together contributors who write on spiritual care models and formation, both in the context of the caregivers (Buddhist chaplains) and the communities they serve.

We open this section with Venerable Priya Rakkhit Sraman's practical advice on nurturing intentional community in one's university sangha through a culture of friendship. Venerable Priya provides us with a grounded perspective born from his years of experience as a Buddhist chaplain at Emory University. He emphasizes the careful and intentional construction of programs and practice sessions, considering one's audience, their needs (spoken and unspoken), and the ways in which one can respond most skillfully. The *Karaniyametta Sutta* serves as a useful framework in bringing a university Buddhist community together, drawing upon ideas of *metta*, mitta, and kalyāṇamitta to foster authentic friendship among students. This spirit naturally flows into spaces that the chaplain creates for group discussions, spiritual practice, art workshops and other creative pursuits, celebrations, and community service. The impact on student intellectual, emotional, and spiritual wellbeing is apparent.

Ernest C.H. Ng then provides us with both theoretical and practical approaches to the formation of Buddhist chaplains in higher education contexts. Exploring the meaning of "formation" as the term has been framed traditionally in the context of Abrahamic religions, Ng examines the Buddhist Threefold Training as a resonant model. He then delves into such frameworks as the Noble Eightfold Path, Four Divine Abodes, Six Perfections, and Four Methods of Pacification as methods through which Buddhist college chaplains undergo spiritual formation both personally and professionally. Through this continuous process of formation, Buddhist chaplains can become increasingly mature in their own practice and thus respond fluidly and skillfully to the dynamic needs of their university communities.

Jonathan Makransky follows upon this illumination of chaplain spiritual development with an exploration of what "self-care" might mean for Buddhist college and university spiritual care professionals. In the course of their work, Buddhist college chaplains encounter unique interpersonal and systemic dynamics that can lead easily to burnout in the absence of deliberate practices of self-care. While practices of care for the individual self (the "self" as conceived on the relative level) are indeed crucial, Makransky argues that these are indelibly situated within broader networks of care grounded in relationships and in the wider universe of Indra's Net in which we are held constantly in love and compassion. In communing with this care, we can ground ourselves in a sustainable source from which to be of benefit to our communities.

Rev. Victor H. Kazanjian Jr. broadens our view of the meaning of spiritual care as he elucidates Wellesley College's groundbreaking systemic spiritual care model. With the inauguration of Wellesley President Diana Chapman Walsh in 1993, the college committed itself to a new multi-faith approach to spiritual life on campus, one that broke with the traditional Protestant Christian model of university chaplaincy in recognition of student needs. Buddhist college chaplains can take note of the ways in which members of the Wellesley community advocated for systemic change to ensure spiritual care for all, including the college's significant Buddhist community. Rev. Kazanjian outlines four principles that guided Wellesley in developing its successful multi-faith program and that can be adapted in other university contexts.

Rebecca Nie's study of Buddhist ceremonies and rituals in higher education settings concludes this section and provides a wealth of information and ideas for any Buddhist spiritual professional working in a diverse university context. Drawing on her experience as the Buddhist chaplain at Stanford University, Nie skillfully examines considerations for adapting traditional ceremonies into contemporary chaplaincy contexts; in doing so, she recognizes the diverse Asian heritage of Buddhist traditions (and those who grew up within them) while maintaining a spirit of welcome for students who are culturally new to Buddhism. Ceremonies of Buddha Bathing, Refuge in Triple Gem, Five Precepts, and Kṣamā (Atonement) are explored in detail, and the chapter concludes with several useful appendices offering ideas for setting up Buddhist ritual spaces, liturgies, and certificate templates.

Nurturing a Culture of Spiritual Friendship and Intentional Community

Ven. Priya Rakkhit Sraman

Introduction

A chaplain plays a significant part in adding to the positive transformation of a campus/university community. As a Buddhist chaplain working in different higher education institutions for almost eight years, I have witnessed the unique potential for positive communal transformation that chaplaincy provides to the community, especially to the student community and to undergraduates in particular. In this chapter I will share my experience of being a university Buddhist chaplain and some of the ways I have engaged and helped nurture the cultivation of an intentional community and its impact.

What is my role?

As a Buddhist chaplain some of my primary tasks include supporting the community in cultivating Buddhist spiritual practice and learning on campus. This happens through regular Buddhist programs such as weekly/bi-weekly meditations, Dharma discussions, book clubs, retreats in addition to regular one-to-one meetings for pastoral and/or spiritual care, grief support as needed, and class presentations as requested. I have also created other programs in addition to the aforementioned such as full-moon events, Vesak (Buddha's birth, enlightenment, and final passing) celebrations, field trips to museums and Buddhist monasteries, and art workshops. The diversity in these programs is intentional, mainly to allow for different ways of engaging with Buddhism, Buddhist traditions, and Buddhist spaces. It is also important as it portrays the richness of Buddhist traditions, cultures, practices, and teachings. On a more pedagogical level, the purpose of such diverse programming is to show the community that Buddhism is accessible in various ways depending on the diverse needs and interests of the participants in the community. This in itself serves as a useful strategy to include members coming with different interests and backgrounds such as heritage Buddhists, non-heritage Buddhists, non-Buddhists, or non-religious, among others. This brings us to the discussion of who comes to the programs.

Who comes to the programs?

I have witnessed participants – mostly undergraduates, but also graduate students, staff and faculty – from vastly different backgrounds in terms of ethnicity, faith, spirituality, sexual orientation, and geographic origin participating in the aforementioned programs. A majority of the participants are usually from non-Buddhist backgrounds. This is not a surprise considering most education institutes, certainly the ones I have served (Tufts University and Emory University), have larger non-Buddhist populations. The strong interest in Buddhist practice in the institutes I have served is undeniable. An average of 20-25 and 30-35 participants in the weekly meditation and Dharma discussion program at Tufts and Emory respectively supports that statement strongly. What makes the space inviting and/or safe for students to participate? What is the need of the community?

What is the need?

College/university is a place where people from various parts of the country and the world come together for education. Coming to a new place brings the challenge of making new friends and building new connections. Finding new friends in a completely new place is not so easy for most, especially if you are a young adult or teenager who has just come out of high school and has left behind the company of friends and family that you have known for years. In spite of the various means the university employs to help make the process of transition easy for new students, it takes time to adjust, adapt and get used to a new place, a new community, a new environment. A meaningful safe community becomes a necessity.

The spaces I have facilitated as the Buddhist chaplain have had as their primary goal a meaningful, safe space for participants who are just getting used to campus and/or are looking for a community to trust. Even if a Buddhist student comes to the Buddhist space looking specifically for a Buddhist community to do Buddhist practices, it is possible that the student might stop coming if that space is unable to provide trust and safety. How do we create a safe space for Buddhist and non-Buddhist students who come to the Buddhist space?

How do we respond to the need?

As the Buddhist chaplain, I create Buddhist spaces to support the community's engagement with Buddhist life and education. In doing so, I do not just present Buddhism to the participants, but while doing so, I also have the responsibility and opportunity to facilitate and guide the audience's engagement with it in terms of its purpose, practice, and relevance. Therefore, for every space I create, I am mindful of its purpose, relevance, and impact with regard to the participants, the content, and the pedagogy of the program. In order for me to make the space inviting to the students, I need to make it relevant to their needs. I need to present the content to the students in a way that not only makes sense to them, but also relates to their positive growth. The pedagogy of the program has to convey the message to the students without making them feel threatened due to their background and experience of Buddhism or lack thereof. To feel safe, the students need to trust the space, and to trust the space they need to believe that the program is for them irrespective of their background and religious/spiritual expertise. How do we convey Buddhism to Buddhists and non-Buddhists alike without risking misrepresentation of the teachings?

This is my duty as a Buddhist chaplain and educator. Luckily for me, there are plenty of Buddhist teachings and practices that do not require a practitioner to identify as a Buddhist in order to practice them, learn them, or cultivate them. I just need to pick the teachings and practices that are relevant to the experience of the audience. The practice of nurturing an intentional community requires purposeful choice of the material used to facilitate the space. What are some examples of the Buddhist teachings and practices that can support the cultivation of an intentional community?

Intentional Community: *Karaniyametta Sutta*

In my regular meditations at both Tufts and Emory, I have used the *Karaniyametta Sutta* for the communal recitation after each meditation. Several students have memorized the text from regularly reciting it. In the early part of the semester, I facilitate discussions based on the Sutta so that students understand its meaning, purpose and relevance.

According to the traditional story, the *Karaniyametta Sutta* is taught to a group of Buddha's disciple monks to help them in adjusting to a new place where they moved to spend the *vassa* – the rains retreat for monastics. The story is that the monks go to spend their retreat at a new location – a wilderness of trees and bushes. As they start their stay, they are disturbed by tree spirits residing in that place. The monks, unable to focus on their practice due to the constant disturbance from the tree spirits, come to request the Buddha for a different location where they could complete the retreat at ease. The Buddha admonishes them that they should return to the very location where the tree spirits reside and complete their retreat there. This time, however, Buddha advises them to recite the *Karaniyametta Sutta* multiple times every day. The monks listen to the Buddha, return to that location and continue their practice, reciting the *Karaniyametta Sutta* every day. Soon after, the disturbance from the tree spirits turns into friendliness and the monks complete their retreat peacefully (Gunaratana, (2017). As we see in this story, the *Karaniyametta Sutta* is a manual on how to conduct oneself if one wishes to cultivate a peaceful relationship. The advice to recite it multiple times per day actually serves as a reminder to the monks of what is needed in order to cultivate themselves so that there is a peaceful, friendly connection amongst themselves and with the tree spirits. A translation of the *Karaniyametta Sutta* is as follows:

> This is what should be done – By one who is skilled in goodness, And who knows the path of peace: Let them be able and upright – Straightforward and gentle in speech. Humble and not conceited – Contented and easily satisfied. Unburdened with duties and frugal in their ways. Peaceful and calm, and wise and skillful – not proud and demanding in nature. Let them not do the slightest thing – that the wise would later reprove. Wishing: in gladness and in safety – may all beings be at ease. Whatever living beings there may be – Whether they are weak or strong, omitting none, The great or the mighty, medium, short or small – The seen and the unseen, Those living near and far away – Those born and to be born, May all beings be happy! Let none deceive another – or despise any being in any state. Let none through anger or ill will – wish harm upon another. Even as a mother protects with her life – her child, her only child, So with a boundless heart – should one cherish all beings, Radiating kindness over the entire world – spreading upwards to the skies, And downwards to the depths – outwards and unbounded, Freed from hatred and ill-will. Whether standing or walking, seated or lying down – free from drowsiness, One should sustain this recollection. This is said to be the sublime abiding. By not holding to fixed views – the pure hearted one, having clarity of vision, Being freed from all sense desires – is not born again into this world.[1]

For those who cannot fathom the idea of tree spirits, you can consider them as residents of the land, just like the residents of a university campus and the surrounding area. This is a way to connect the *Karaniyametta Sutta* to the university community. When students are new to campus, most of them have some difficulty adjusting to the strangeness of the campus and the ways of its residents – other students and locals. Perhaps the same applies to the residents with regard to the newcomers. Just as in the case of the monks and tree spirits, the practices in the *Karaniyametta Sutta* are applicable to the newcomers and old residents of the campus.

It is important to draw attention to such practices of cultivating friendliness in ways that are immediately accessible to students in their campus experience. On the one hand,

---

1 See Gunaratana (2017) for a detailed explanation of *Karaniyametta Sutta* and its translation.

cultivating friendliness provides them practical ways of adjusting to the newness of the campus, giving them some concrete methods making friends. On the other, learning about it in their early encounter with the Buddhist space helps them to realize the wholesome intention of the community – to cultivate a friendly community right from the very beginning. This is a way they can trust the space.

The *Karaniyametta Sutta* involves the cultivation of an intentional community in that it draws attention to the intentionality that drives the practice and cultivation of a harmonious environment; in the very first verse, it says "Those who want to attain peace should practice being upright."[2] If our intention is to cultivate peace, this is a manual with which to work. When reciting it as a group regularly, it can help the community to be reminded of that intentionality. At the very least, students can reconnect with the intentional community once or twice a week when they are in the Buddhist space reciting the text together. Regardless of what they do outside, they can associate the Buddhist space with a safe community that is trying to cultivate a practice of harmony and peace.

As a Buddhist chaplain, this is an opportunity for me to nurture that intentionality by introducing these values and offering such practices to the students who may have not been familiar with them. In my Dharma discussions I take pleasure in lifting up such Buddhist teachings with the hope that students will learn to cultivate them.

But how does one practice the *Karaniyametta Sutta* to cultivate friendship?

Spiritual Friendship:
Metta, Mitta, and *Kalyānamitta*

Metta in the *Karaniyametta Sutta* refers to loving-kindness, friendliness, friendship; and *karaniya* means 'something to/should be done'; meaning: *karaniyametta* – loving-kindness/friendliness to be made. The *Karaniyametta Sutta* thus becomes a guide on creating friendship through acts of love and care. Another word coming from the same root as *metta* is mitta which is a word for friend, companion. With proper cultivation of *metta*, one can become a good mitta. A good *mitta* is a *kalyānamitta* (*kalyāna* means good, wholesome, noble).

Being a good friend – *kalyānamitta* – is of significant importance in the journey of Buddhist spiritual cultivation. Being in the company of a *kalyānamitta* can be the force needed to carry oneself through the entire Buddhist spiritual journey. It is by relying on one's *kalyānamitta* – wholesome/noble/good (spiritual) friend – that a practitioner cultivates virtues and skills to grow spiritually:

> This is the entire spiritual life, Ananda, that is good friendship, good companionship, good comradeship. When a monk has a good friend, a good companion, a good comrade, it is to be expected that he will develop and cultivate the noble eightfold path.[3]

In this text we see the Buddha as the right example of a *kalyānamitta* depending on whom others grow spiritually, intellectualy, emotionally. As Buddhist chaplains, we have the potential to become *kalyānamittas* to our students and to the community. In many ways, our roles force us to become such *kalyānamittas* – the very nature and objective of our presence on campus is to

---

2 Hanh, N.T. *Discourse on Love*. Retrieved (on April 8, 2024) from https://plumvillage.org/library/sutras/discourse-on-love Even though it appears different from Gunaratana's translation, I like Thich Nhat Hanh's phrasing here. It indicates that if someone wishes to achieve peace, here is what they can do. Gunaratana's translation implies that the practitioner already knows the path of peace.

3 See, Bodhi (2016) for discourse on the importance of friendship (p89) and other practices in relation to communal harmony.

uplift and support the spiritual cultivation of the community.

However, there's more to the practice of *kalyāṇamitta* if we are intentional and skillful about it. The "more" is seen when it's not just the chaplain who is the *kalyāṇamitta* to the community, but while being one, inspires and guides the community to become *kalyāṇamittas* themselves. If Buddhist spiritual life flourishes in dependence on *kalyāṇamittas*, then our ideal Buddhist life would be to surround ourselves with them. An intentional community does exactly that by connecting the community through shared values of friendship, harmony, growth.

The *Karaṇīyametta Sutta* is not just a manual for making friends, but rather a practical manual for becoming one. It indicates how we can attend to our own expressions, cultivate peace within, transform ourselves into safe resources so that our presence is not a threat to those around us. When others do not feel threatened by our presence, they will not be hostile to us, they will not be fearful of us. Instead, fearless interaction will lead to curiosity, connection, and friendships. That is when we can engage in meaningful communication to learn with and from each other as a community. In such a community making frineds should not be difficult.

The Buddhist monastic community does this organically. As an ordained monk I often draw relevant examples from my monastic experience to convey Buddhist values to the community. In the Buddhist monastic community, the newly ordained junior monastic has to rely on the seniors for guidance and cultivation on the spiritual path. With experience, the former newcomer becomes skillful enough to guide and share knowledge with others who are junior to them, participating in a continuous cycle of learning and sharing. Thich Nhat Hanh, the famous Vietnamese Zen Master, draws our attention to the urgency of educating and cultivating ourselves as responsible and skillful participants of the wholesome community when he states:

The next Buddha will be Sangha…a community practicing understanding and loving-kindness, a community practicing mindfulness.[4]

Creating Spaces

Group Discussions/Conversations

As an intellectual space, the university makes it easy to have discussions on different ideas and practices. Intellectual engagement is an important means for the community of young students to engage with new ways and practices. It allows for questions and clarifications. I have spent more of my time as a chaplain facilitating discussions than anything else. This creates the opportunity for me to nurture their thought process. More importantly, this is a great way for them to listen to and engage with each other's curiosities, questions, reflections and expressions.

Not all questions need to have the right answer, or an answer at all. Much of the time, we learn a great deal about ourselves and about the topic in question not by focusing on the correct answer to the questions raised but by responding to these questions with further relevant questions. I call this the practice of "sitting with our questions." By doing this we are allowing ourselves to reflect seriously on why we have the questions we have, what other questions do they beg, and what we learn by bringing up those other questions. In this way, through the practice of contemplating our thoughts and specific subjects deeply, we incorporate an important skill into our learning process. Through reflection we can understand the intention behind the question, and the intention behind our participation in the space itself. For example, am I asking a question because I'm used

---

4 Wildtantrika, *Finding Soul Connections in Nature: Walking the Plant Path*. Retrieved (on April 8, 2024) from https://wildtantrika.com/stories/walking-the-plant-path

to asking questions, or because I really care to expand my learning and the learning of those around me? Follow-up questions can be a good way to make everyone in the group actively engaged in the conversation, making them think together instead of relying on one individual to provide the answer. At times, reflective questions can also make other participants interested in responding and thereby engage the whole group in the thought process. This is important because it allows for the diversity of experience in the space to be shared, leading to a corresponding diversity of perspectives, as the *Karaniyametta Sutta* indicates "not to have fixed views," but to allow for various possibilities.

Silent Group Practice

If conversations help us engage with each other's thoughts, silent group practices help us deepen our connections by being attentive to ourselves and those around us. At the very least, it cultivates the skill of observation with attention. Regular weekly group meditations are short silent practice spaces. Guided by the meditation teacher, the shared energy of the space focuses on cultivating attention, kindness, compassion, and other values. Many students enjoy meditating in a group as opposed to doing it alone in their rooms.

Retreats, on the other hand, allow for a longer period of practicing "noble silence." They are a profound way of connecting with oneself and the group. Both at Tufts and at Emory, I have led semesterly off-campus weekend retreats for students to deepen their connection to the practice as well as to the community. Oftentimes students invite their friends to the retreat and/or meet new friends there. At the very beginning of each retreat, I make sure to communicate the expectations regarding respect and safety for each other, creating the intention for the whole retreat experience. While sitting in silence can be awkward, we are mindful and attentive to the awkwardness as we eat, sit, walk, and contemplate next to each other in the same space during the retreat. We recognize and connect with the commonality and safety that we have created for and with each other. We may not be communicating with each other verbally, but we are all aware of the kindness, compassion, and care that we intentionally cultivate for each other during this time. The positive energy in a retreat and at its end is always palpable.

Laughter and Joy

When there is a long period of silence, energy and emotion build up. So, when the time comes for conversation, there is a lot to share. Toward the end of the retreat students have a stronger connection when they return to normal conversation. It always ends with laughter and joy. Reminding our students that fun is part of the cultivation of community is essential. Just because we are in a spiritual space does not mean we cannot laugh and have fun. Authentic spiritual cultivation leads to joy and laughter because we can be at ease with each other.

Art Workshops

Art is another great way to cultivate joy and to have fun. More often than not, Buddhism is thought to be only about mindfulness and meditation, isolated from everything else in life and society. Part of my role as the Buddhist Chaplain is to educate students about the diverse aspects of Buddhism beyond the practice of mindfulness and meditation. Art workshops have been a wonderful means of education and practice for the community. Historically, Buddhists in different cultures have used art as a way to connect with spirituality using such methods as calligraphy, copying Buddhist scripture, drawing Buddhist images, and sculpting. The arts of copying Buddhist images and Buddhist texts, known in Japanese culture as shabutsu and shakyo respectively, form the basis of programs that I have created with the help of a faculty colleague at Emory who is a professor of Japanese culture. As the students use colored pens and pencils to draw along the already printed lines, they engage in mindfulness practice while also learning the meaning and history of the different images and texts that they are copying. Adding a theme to such an event adds to meaningfulness of the discussion. For instance, I collaborated with two students in the Emory Buddhist Club to organize a clay-sculpting workshop titled "Moving Through Impermanence" in which we reflected on the process of impermanence in our lives.

While educational and contemplative, the art workshop is not as serious as a formal meditation session. It is usually a place filled with conversations and laughter. As it is not a formal Buddhist meditation session, those who are unable to or do not prefer to attend meditations get a chance to be part of the community through such a program. Faculty, staff and students who are experienced in art, history, and culture are drawn to these events. They are also often the ones who co-facilitate the workshops, especially if they have experience with Buddhist art and culture. That is another way of expanding community and connection.

Buddhist Celebrations

An important part of community building and connection in traditional Buddhist cultures is the celebration of Buddhist events and ceremonies. While in Western contexts these events may be disregarded as less meaningful cultural practices as compared to meditation, heritage Buddhists have traditionally held such events in high regard especially for the cultivation of spiritual practice and values. Bodhi Day – celebrating Buddha's enlightenment in the Mahayana School, and Vesak – Buddha Day – celebrating Buddha's birth, enlightenment, and final passing in the Theravada School, are two events done at the end of Fall and Spring semesters respectively to connect the community to Buddhist cultural practices. Full moons are also celebrated in relation to different significant events in Buddha's life and Buddhist history.

Community Service

Service is an integral aspect of Buddhist cultivation. *Dāna* – generosity, charity, sharing, service – is the first in the list of *pāramitās* – perfections – which transform the practitioner as they continue to perfect them on their Buddhist spiritual journey.[5] At Emory University, the Emory Buddhist Club has been engaged in meaningful community service through their annual clothing swap program. EBC students distribute boxes around campus for a few weeks for collecting clothes. On specified dates at the end of the collection period, they then gather all of them and put them on display for anyone to exchange clothes, or pick any favorite from the collected items. Whatever remains after that is cleaned and donated to local organizations. This program has had the highest participation (several hundred students) among all Buddhist community programs in which I have participated.

The benefit of diversity in programming is attention to the diverse needs in our community. It is a way of including students of varied backgrounds in the space. It is also useful in expanding the community's understanding of Buddhism. Just as students explore different ways of engaging with Buddhism, they discover new spaces for community and friends.

Diverse programming is especially helpful in educating the student executive boards of Buddhist student organizations on campus. As partners and collaborators in Buddhist programs, these students play a significant role in cultivating the intentional community along with the Buddhist chaplain. Being in close connection with the Buddhist chaplain, their volunteer positions on the executive board give them opportunitites to learn about Buddhist ways more than a regular community member. They are the ones who are consistently with the program in its entirety – planning to execution

---

5 See Rinpoche (2020), for an explanation on *Dāna* and the other perfections.

to completion. A consistent culture provides continuity. After all, they are ones who will continue the legacy of Buddhist life on campus by training new students to join the executive board, much like in the monastic community – the senior trains the junior, who trains their junior newcomers – the legacy of *kalyāṇamitta*. The student executive board is thus a resource allowing for learning to happen naturally through association and involvement. A well-established student board is always good for the larger community. A Buddhist chaplain's role includes nurturing the student board.

Conclusion: Why does it matter?

Why should the intentional practice of building community and friendship matter on a university campus? It matters because of the impact it can have on students' emotional, spiritual, intellectual, and social wellbeing. It creates a safe space for students to belong and feel included. In doing so, it allows for diversity within the space which leads to expanded learning and growth.

As chaplains on university campuses, it is important for us to consider how to make these important Buddhist practices relevant to the diversity of participants in the community, including those who may not be Buddhists and may not even be interested in pursuing Buddhist spiritual goals.

Our programs rarely require a participant to identify as a Buddhist to connect with them. However, there is value in putting in deliberate effort to make sure that the content of programs is relevant to diverse participants. One way I have done so is through check-ins with participants, mostly at the beginning of a program and/or during one-on-one conversations. This helps me to relate the discussion to things brought up during check-ins. As a chaplain, my ministry involves a great deal of interpretation in this way.

As discussed earlier, creating space for curiosity and questioning is also important to connect program content with participants. After all, the purpose of our programs is to benefit the participants, so it is only sensible that their questions should be welcomed. It helps a lot to be a curious companion to the students – to think with them about their curiosities. The point is not to show that Buddhism makes sense, but to explore how Buddhism makes sense (or not) in relation to our experience of life, to remember that it is one of many ways to think about life – not the only way – that is available for exploration.

There are so many ways to argue and debate about the differences and disagreements in our diverse backgrounds. But as chaplains and facilitators we need to focus on what allows us to have a healthy understanding of ourselves and others around us so that we can cultivate harmony in spite of these differences. An intentional (as opposed to accidental) approach to cultivating community in such ways has great benefits.

An important impact of the experience of being in a wholesome community is that students are able to take it beyond campus upon graduation. They can find ways to form intentional communities and wholesome friendships. As they continue through life, they continue to expand their circle of good friends – *kalyāṇamitta* – themselves included.

Bibliography

Bodhi, B. (2016), *The Buddha's Teachings on Social and Communal Harmony – An Anthology of Discourse from the Pali Canon*, Wisdom Publications

Gunaratana, B.H. (2017) *Loving Kindness in Plain English*, Wisdom Publications

———, (2015) *Mindfulness in Plain English*, Wisdom Publications

Sanford, M. Dr. Rev. (2021) *Kalyanamitra – A Model for Buddhist Spiritual Care*, The Sumeru Press Inc

Rinpoche, Z.L. (2020) *The Six Perfections – The Practice of the Bodhisattvas*, Wisdom Publications

8
Traditional Buddhist Healing as Spiritual Care Model
Ji Hyang Padma

In Buddhist spiritual care, contemplative practices that are inherently part of the Buddhist path have served to reenergize the wider fields of pastoral and psychotherapeutic care. To understand the contemplative care model more fully, we will examine it through the paradigm of Buddhist healing, within which the Buddhist teaching is seen as medicine to cure the primary illness caused by the poisons of *raga* (sensual attachment), *dvesha* (anger), and *moha* (ignorance), a cure ultimately achieved through the Middle Way. Buddhism evolved as a relational, community-based healing praxis. While there are significant strengths within the Theravadin healing model, this chapter will focus on Mahayana healing models.

Spiritual Care – The Contemplative Care Model

The root of the Buddhist chaplain's praxis is contemplative care. The gift of deep listening, through the presence of wise teachers, has brought many Dharma students to a place of transformation. The experience of being seen to the core – and being the grateful recipient of compassionate awareness – is life-changing. As we extend a deep listening to ourselves, through meditation, we train in equanimity. We accept the moment, unconditionally, just as it is; we find compassion for every aspect of our body and mind, just as they are. We can then offer genuine compassion to others. When we, as chaplains, extend this deep listening to ourselves and others, we touch a place of wholeness, clarity, and wellbeing. It makes it possible for the other person to sense their own inherent worth and tap into their own inner resources.

This creation of a holding environment and trustworthy relationship is the key responsibility of the chaplain. Relationship heals. It is when our spiritual care is sincerely practiced as a means of expressing connection – and makes contact – that it can create spiritual transformation and healing. This learning how to attend, and how to be with, parallels Winicott's state of unintegration: present as a mother may optimally be with her child, without interfering. The places where counseling psychology, developmental psychology, interpersonal neurology, and meditative practice meet have been very skillfully mapped by Epstein (1999, 2013), Siegel (2007, 2010a, 2010b), and Austin (1999). The centrality of holding space through deep listening, attunement, and entrainment has been well addressed by Giles and Miller (2012) in their seminal work, *The Arts of Contemplative Care*, and by Ellison and Weingast (2016) in *Awake at the Bedside*. This author affirms the centrality of contemplative psychospiritual principles, which are confirmed by ongoing contemplative neuroscience, within Buddhist college chaplaincy.

Buddhist College Chaplaincy as Buddhist Healing

We are well served by placing the practice of contemplative care within a wider context: the paradigm of Buddhist healing, a model that goes back to the times of the historical Buddha. Shakyamuni Buddha was considered the Great Physician, whose medicine healed the original illness of desire, anger, and delusion, and restored wholeness to both individuals and communities. This process is often described as the integration of body and mind, a process achieved through the Middle Way between indulgence and self-mortification; in this regard, healing practices were a natural adjunct to meditation (Tatz, 1985). The words "medicine" and "meditation" share the same root in the Latin *mederi*, which means "to cure," per physicist David Bohm (2005). *Mederi* itself derives from an earlier Indo-European root meaning "to measure." Bohm notes that all things, then, possess their own "right inward measure" that makes them what they are. Meditation can be understood to be a way of taking measure, and realigning with a point of balance that is our right inward measure.

We can understand the mechanism of healing to be the simple law of cause-and-effect described through *paticca samupadda*, which is well described by this canonical verse:

> When this is existing, that comes to be;
> with the arising of this, that arises;
> when this does not exist, that does not exist;
> with the ceasing of this, that ceases.[1]

This teaching expresses a relational ontology, succinctly described by Joanna Macy (1978): "The subject of thought and action is in actuality a dynamic pattern of activity in interaction with its environment and inseparable from existence" (p. 112). When the self is recognized as fluid, and arising interdependently with other beings, this heals the illusion of separation that is at the root of *tanha* – craving, and *dukkha* – suffering. In the *Lotus of the Good Law Sutra*, desire, anger, and ignorance are identified as the causes of illness, like "wind, bile, phlegm" (Clifford, 2006, p. 23). The Four Noble Truths are described as medicine. Through awareness that there is no separate self, afflictive thought patterns are seen as empty and lose their power to afflict the individual.

The remedy of mindful self-insight as medicine is as effective now as it was 2,500 years ago. Chaplains can effectively relieve much college-student distress by teaching students how to work with the mind, providing an ethical foundation, and helping them to break free of the illusion of the isolated, independent self. As noted in Kass (2017), higher education often mirrors humanity's samsaric patterns. Many students feel isolated upon arrival at college; they may also experience higher academic expectations and experience psychological stress. The stressors, combined with less well-developed coping skills and greater HPA axis reactivity (Eiland & Romeo, 2013), contribute to high levels of anxiety and depression, which contribute to patterns of substance abuse among college students. Meditation practice and the ethical framework of Buddhism help rewire the system, supporting the capacity for impulse control, the development of resiliency, and social-emotional learning.

While the promotion of basic sanity and wellness is undoubtedly a high aspiration, there is a deeper level of healing potential we carry as Buddhist college chaplains. There is an opportunity to introduce students to Buddhist ways of knowing – which then shift the center of gravity upon which all life decisions are discerned. The way to understand the Buddha's teaching on mutual causality is described in the Pali Canon with the phrase *yoniso manasikara*.

> *Manasikara* comes from a verb meaning "to ponder" or "to take to heart" and denotes deep attention or attentive pondering. Here this pondering is qualified by yoniso, the ablative of yoni. Yoni, literally, is "womb." By extension it came to mean "origin," "way of being born," and "matrix." ...Such thinking, then...is not a dissecting or categorizing exercise

---

[1] *Majjhima Nikāya* iii. 63.

of the intellect. Synthetic rather than analytic, it involves an awareness of wholeness – an intent openness or attentiveness wherein all factors can be included, their relationships beheld.[2]

The way to understand a relational universe is by seeing with eyes of wholeness: by thinking the world together, and thus entering the web of interdependence ourselves. As we begin to see the web of interbeing within and around us, this can indeed shift the balance of one's life. The mind connects to the heart, and we develop a more ecological awareness – a wise heart, one that actively appreciates difference.

Community-Based Healing and College Sangha

Buddhist monastic communities played an essential role in the development of Indian medicine. The Buddha taught the monks, "Whoever serves the sick, serves me." As the monks, unlike the Brahmin healers, were not bound by caste; through this service they made contact with many communities and were able to bring the Dharma and the healing arts to new places. Out of the teaching of *paticca samudpadda* (dependent origination) and this awareness of interrelationship, a Buddhist ethic of care and concern was developed. Teaching this mutual care – expressed in Korean culture as *jeong*, human warmth – is a significant aspect of Buddhist culture that benefits our student sanghas as well as the larger campus ecosystem in which they dwell. Very often, in temple life, I experienced this through the care that the temple's sangha extended to help me (an American nun) to thrive within the challenging conditions of the *kyol che* long retreat. However, *jeong* is not only experienced by monastics. This natural warmth was evident in the exchanges in the market, and the way that people in the nearby village looked after each other. That awareness that we are always entering into interrelationship, that we have an innate capacity to care for each other and are responsible for each other, is a core value of Buddhist culture.

Diversity of Buddhist Healing Models: Theravadin and Mahayana

While many Buddhist texts underscore the healing potential through realization of *paticca samupadda*, the way that texts describe the dynamics of healing differs across the schools and vehicles of Buddhism. In describing the process of personal liberation from the illness of self-clinging, early Theravadin texts emphasize the medicine of renunciation, which brings freedom from desire. The model of the *bhavana-chakra* (wheel of becoming) is frequently invoked. Mahayana texts emphasize the medicine of *sunyata*, emptiness: cutting through appearance, we see the truth of interconnection. We attain compassion, which cures the poison of anger, and wisdom, which cures ignorance (Clifford, 2006). As Buddhist college chaplains ministering to diverse communities, we need to be familiar with both Theravadin and Mahayana ways of knowing and praxis.

The Upaya of Chaplaincy

While the cultivation of wisdom is an ultimate goal, this practice is balanced by *upaya*, the "application of methods in skillful service to others" (Makransky, 2000, p. 86). *Upaya*, or skillful means, is a core necessity and guiding principle in Buddhist college chaplaincy. Within Mahayana Buddhism,

> Skillful means are the diverse and often subtle activities through which bodhisattvas progress on their path and elicit the wisdom of enlightenment (*prajnaparamita*) in others... in many other scriptures, skillful means includes the infinite scope

---
2 Macy, 1978, p. 53.

of activities and methods through which buddhas and bodhisattvas communicate Dharma in the precise ways appropriate to the capacities of all living beings...the methods that buddhas and bodhisattvas employ to reach beings are as diverse as beings themselves, and are operative through all space and time.[3]

While the term *upaya* is identified with Mahayana Buddhism, this quality of responsivity, adapting the teaching to the person and situation, was undoubtedly practiced by the historical Buddha, who used similes and analytical methods that were familiar to the audience being addressed. College chaplains are continually adapting the teaching to new situations. For instance, this year, the Tufts Sangha student group asked me to provide teaching words for the occasion of their visiting a float tank. The students had a sense that this experience would be a beneficial first-person study of consciousness, and so I met them within that experience. For Buddhist college chaplains, the *upaya* could include a discussion of bell hook's *All About Love*, making fresh spring rolls, watching a Miyazaki film, the offering of a mindfulness study break, an invocation that honors embodiment. The contributions in this volume hint at the vastness of chaplaincy *upaya*.

Mahayana Healing Ritual and College Chaplaincy

As the Mahayana Buddhist tradition continued to develop in the centuries that followed Nagarjuna (c. 150–250 CE), it began to employ diverse methods of teaching, *upaya* that were well suited to the pantheistic cultures of South and East Asia, including sacred images and chanting practice. Within Mahayana traditions, the *Lotus Sutra*, which in Chapter 25 describes the power of calling upon Avalokiteshvara Bodhisattva, has served as the foundation for devotional practices, including chanting meditation. There are also so many other Mahayana ritual practices – in particular, the recitation of the Medicine Buddha mantra, which has been used in many Mahayana lineages to relieve both the existential sickness of separation from innate wholeness and the relative sicknesses of the body and mind (Birnbaum, 1979). The mantra can be recited internally or chanted. In East Asia, the experience of collective chanting is the most common form of meditation. This aspect of meditation practice can be just as transformational as sitting meditation and is less known in the West.

While chanting practice was necessarily sidelined during the pandemic, there is a good argument to be made for its reintroduction to our sanghas. Public health precautions such as good ventilation should be practiced. In addition, it is necessary to give time for the sangha to reach critical mass in learning a chant. However, if these conditions are met, the practice of chanting can be truly transformative.

From a neuropsychological perspective, it has been shown that chanting meditation has an integrative effect upon the nervous system. Melody links separated areas within the cortex, while rhythm connects the limbic system and prefrontal cortex areas of the brain, renewing an innate sense of wholeness (Siegel, 2010a). This could be considered an *upaya*, skillful means. While the motivation for reciting the mantra of the Medicine Buddha may be goal-oriented and dualistic, the actual practice of reciting the mantra thousands of times can bring the mind to a place of stillness and spaciousness. Through that direct experience of making contact with the space that precedes thought, psychospiritual integration and existential healing may take place.

Dharmakaya (Absolute) Healing

The central aspiration of Buddhist chaplain-healers is to bring about awakening: This

---

[3] Makransky, 2000, pp. 116-117.

aspiration and healing is the natural expression of *Dharmakaya*. Mahayana texts within Zen and Tibetan lineages have referenced the need to move beyond the duality of sickness and health, to see a healing wholeness in phenomena just-as-they-are. Vajrayana texts have described this ultimate healing as a process of seeing all phenomena with "pure perception as being inseparable from radiant emptiness and hence a sacred expression of Buddha nature" (Clifford, 2006, p. 29). In the *Vimalakirti Sutra*, Vimalakirti described the essential human ailment: We forget that we are already complete, already pure consciousness. The bodhisattva reenters this realm of duality out of great love, and stays within *Maya*, the play of illusion that is human existence, until all beings are healed. This is a central theme of Buddhist college chaplaincy: supporting students in gaining the capacity to rest the mind in its innate clarity, regardless of situation. Texts that speak to the heart-essence of Buddhist teaching help students awaken to this natural wisdom.

One young Dzogchen practitioner described his flash of insight:

> You're doing it – practicing hard, in and out of airports, and then it happens: you're still where you were, but you're where you are.

Through meditation, one touches into that moment-to-moment awareness that is pure perception, devoid of concept. Even a moment of insight into interdependence can have profound implications. I am reminded of that meditation student who was moved by *tonglen* (giving and receiving) practice to donate a kidney, and by so doing set a chain of 30 organ transplants in motion.

Within the realm of college chaplaincy, this level of healing may manifest as psychospiritual wholeness. As one student responded,

> I was pretty tightly wrapped.... And it's much wider than that now. I kind of let my guard down on all matters and I was able to be honest with myself, about myself, about my relationships…and I'm much more open, I'm much more relaxed, much happier, even though there are sometimes difficult decisions.

Students have also reported that this moment of insight has moved them to social engagement and influenced their vocational choices.

> I'm definitely more involved with taking care of neighbors and working on different sustainable kind of organic food gardening movements in our community, to help out in those practical ways.

> I fell in love with Gaia (the planet). I'm an avid recycler…meditation brings people to an awareness of the earth and a unity of the earth that is very substantial.

Educator and leader Diana Chapman Walsh spoke of this contemplative turn to an ecosystem awareness at a panel discussion I hosted on Buddhism and vocation:

> We need to move into an entirely different consciousness, and social system, in which we follow the rules of nature: we learn, appreciate, follow and understand the laws of nature. That kind of shift in consciousness can happen relatively quickly – only if people find someplace within themselves that is a touchstone for attaining that truth.

As a Buddhist chaplain-educator, one can midwife that inner revolution – a shift in consciousness, which heals consciousness at its root.

Nirmanakaya: Working Within Physical Reality

The Buddhist aspiration to support liberation has always coexisted with a pragmatic willingness to effect change on the relative level. The scholar Atisha, who conveyed essential Buddhist teachings from India to Tibet in the 11th century, also carried with him his work on Ayurvedic healing, *The Heart of Life*. We can see a Buddhist lineage of physical healing carried forth by Kabat-Zinn (1991, 2003, 2005), Borysenko (2007), and Thondup (2013), among others. The capacity of mindfulness practice to effect physical healing, with measurable outcomes, can serve as the beginning of many constructive conversations within university student health and occupational health offices.

There is much work to be done to achieve integrative health for this generation of college students, who have experienced a pandemic tutorial in mind-body health at this critical age. Many of the entering first-year students that I've met already began to learn mindfulness through Calm, Headspace, and other apps that they used to keep themselves mentally grounded during the pandemic. At the same time, these students may be able to find role models within the academy – faculty researchers like Michael Levin at Tufts, B. Alan Wallace at Emory University, Robert Roeser at Penn State – who are modeling the emergent potential for bridging mindfulness practice and psycho-biological research. At Northeastern University, there is now even a Mindfulness minor. As I write this at Omega Institute, a conference on mindfulness and education has convened. While this generation has unparalleled challenges in attaining wellness, it also has unparalleled resources.

The accessibility of mindfulness has made it much easier to have conversations about meditation within the broader college communities. Increasingly, I meet with colleagues in the health and counseling services to discuss overall student wellness, and mindfulness is already part of the students' treatment plans. We can begin to glimpse a new set of quandaries. If every department is offering some variation of mindfulness, is mindfulness being presented devoid of its cultural context? Is it being presented with an ethical framework that extends beyond personal wellness to include collective well-being? Is it being taught with a trauma-sensitive approach? There are so many questions we should be asking.

Yet, at the same time, it is evident that the presence of mindfulness on college campuses is supporting students' wellbeing in ways we would not have considered possible just a couple of decades ago. Research has shown that mindfulness supports physical health and is effective in reducing anxiety and depression, improving self-regulation, and creating a foundation for positive relational outcomes (Roeser et al., 2022).

Sambhogakaya: Subtle-Body Practices for College Students

While the mutual causality between the *Nirmanakaya* and *Dharmakaya* has been charted through contemporary and traditional healing practices described above, there is a third state that is pivotal in traditional Buddhist healing practices: the realm of *Sambhogakaya*, the place of the subtle body. We touch the realm of *Sambhogakaya* through dream states, visualizations, and energy work such as Korean *kido* chanting, *qi gong*, *reiki*, and *Chöd*. While it is difficult to discuss *qi* in an academic context, there are certainly noteworthy pioneers such as William James, James Oschman, Marc Micozzi, Stephan Schwartz, and others who have done so. Schwartz (1998) noted,

> It does not follow that because our house is the one brightly lighted now, that we are the only consequential residence in history's human village. If many observers, over many thousands of years, from many different

cultures, have reported these energetic interactions, and demonstrated their therapeutic usefulness, perhaps our contribution…is to discover exactly what is happening, and how to optimize its effects. (p. 5).

As Buddhist chaplains, we should have sufficient faith in, and knowledge of, first-person studies of consciousness to guide students in this terrain. Many students now enter the path out of curiosity about the consciousness-studies aspects of Buddhist practice. The *trikaya* (three body) model of reality can serve as a framework. Just as the relative and absolute levels of truth are understood as mutually conditioned through healing practices that affect both body and consciousness, the realm of the subtle body is interwoven into our mutual causality. A Buddhist chaplain optimally should encourage students' explorations of consciousness studies through *qi gong*, *kido* chanting, and nonphysical practices such as *reiki*. These are part of our culture and history as Buddhists. In the 21st-century classroom, there are inevitably some questions related to plant medicine and other adventures in consciousness that are beyond our ken. However, the Buddha and lineage-holders offer profound examples of how deeply one can investigate subtle energy with a sober mind.

This motion to include subtle-energy consciousness studies within Buddhist college chaplaincy is congruent with the paradigm proposed by David Bohm – and congruent with Buddhist epistemology and praxis (such as the dream yoga practices utilized in many Buddhist cultures). In essence, Bohm stated that all the explicate order (the world of form, known in a Buddhist trikaya model as *Nirmanakaya*) rests upon an implicate order (emptiness/energy, known as *Dharmakaya*). Embedded within the implicate order is a protointelligence that directs its expression and mediates between these (known as *Sambhogakaya*). For a more detailed synopsis of Bohm's (2005) theory, his text *Wholeness and the Implicate Order* is an excellent resource. Essentially, Bohm's understanding, that this consciousness serves as a bridge between the relative and ultimate realities, can support explorations of the subtle healing technology within Buddhist culture.

We have discussed chanting practice in the previous section as a mind-body integrative praxis. Chanting also opens the door to a direct experience of *Sambhogakaya*. In the Korean Zen tradition and epistemology, *kido* (chanting retreat, literally *ki do*, energy path) are appreciated as an expedient route to experience concentration and *ki*, universal energy. Through the practice of chanting, the mind and body come together in the present moment. In that experience of concentration there is a felt connection with universal energy (*ki*). Then, bringing that quality of attention and energy to the present, it is possible to develop penetrating wisdom that then can support wise and kind action in the world.

Inquiry into the mechanisms through which *kido* chanting brings such a deep sense of wholeness and energy often deepens my faith in meditation practice. On a basic level, the act of chanting together has the effect of unifying a sangha and bringing about a greater attunement to each other. Chanting meditation reconnects us with the oral tradition at the root of Buddhism. It teaches the Dharma in a way that can more easily be committed to heart. In addition, chanting brings about body-mind integration and a change of consciousness. The research on those mechanisms of this change has, in many cases, already been done by the anthropologists who have researched shamanism and indigenous practices. There is existing research on synchronized resonation. The use of temple instruments to induce a nonordinary state of consciousness through the entrainment of the cerebral cortex with the limbic system has been documented to cause changes in brain waves and to increase immune health (Bittman et al., 2001). If we look closely, we can find scientific support for the use of rhythm in our Buddhist ritual – whether it is the Korean *moktak*, Tibetan *rnga*, Japanese *taiko* drumming, or simply the spoken word, as is practiced in Theravadin ritual. These practices help effect a change of consciousness that brings us into body-mind synchronization on an individual level, into resonance with each other as a collective, and helps unlock neuro-spiritual pathways that catalyze awakening. More research is needed to discern the neuropsychological differences in effect produced by different liturgies and practice traditions. Further research, based on leads from consciousness studies and shamanic studies, will help guide the chaplain and practitioner to use the most efficacious melody and percussion based on their disposition and purpose, and serve to develop Buddhist healing praxis.

College-Student *Sambhogakaya*

Currently, there are many college students who inquire about the nature of consciousness, seeking techniques for navigating altered states of consciousness and dreamwork. While teaching at a holistic graduate school, I found many students had questions about psychedelics, and some found holotropic breathwork to be a valuable technique for cleansing the lens of perception. At Tufts, some Buddhist students decided to explore sensory deprivation immersion therapy (float tank) to observe their own consciousness. There is an explosion of curiosity with regards to *Sambhogakaya* within college student communities, and more generally within our culture. We can support students' first-person consciousness studies by providing them access to Buddhist lucid dream practices, Buddhist *qi gong*, and other subtle energy work.

Within Buddhist lucid dream practices, it is specifically understood that the purpose for navigating this realm of *Sambhogakaya* is to see all waking reality as illusion, all phenomena as empty of essential self (Sumegi, 2008). Dream yoga practitioners utilize this knowledge of emptiness and dependent arising to navigate the dream worlds of subtle energy to bring about healing (Sumegi, 2008). Through practice navigating the dream worlds of *Sambhogakaya* during life, the Buddhist practitioner would then be well prepared to navigate the *bardo* of *Sambhogakaya* after death (Sumegi, 2008). Therefore, within Buddhist college chaplain contexts, the practices of working with the subtle body, performing healings using visionary work, and offering *bardo* instructions can be seen as skillful means to guide students towards the ultimate attainment of *bodhicitta*, awakened heart-mind.

Within the perceptual state of *Sambhogakaya*, the realm of subtle energy, and dreamtime, cause-and-effect is described as *tendrel*, a Tibetan term that implies a direct experience of the all-pervasive nature of dependent origination, in which the connections between cause and effect may not be visible on the surface. Sumegi (2008) has described the function of *tendrel* on the level of *Sambhogakaya*:

> In Buddhist theory, just as a particular experience is not constituted merely of a given set of external conditions but is also influenced by the subjective mind, so the omen or the tendrel becomes what it is through the mental attention and attitude of the experiencer. Crows cry in the trees all day, but when the mind pays attention to a particular event, and a particular feeling arises because of it, then one can speak of tendrel. (p. 108)

Thus, dreams, intuition and the subtle body can be seen as part of a spiritual, mental, and physical continuum of consciousness, and reflecting on the interdependence of these phenomena can be a valuable pathway for looking into the self. While this continuum of consciousness is beginning to be described through psychoneuroimmunology and related Western medicine, it has long been understood through traditional Buddhist medicine. Additionally, there are parallels both within Western psychology and quantum physics, through Jung's theory of synchronicity and *unus mundus*, a theory that consciousness and matter are two aspects of one reality. Both Carl Jung and his colleague-correspondent, physicist Wolfgang Pauli, believed that synchronistic events reveal an underlying unity of mind and matter, and that study of these phenomena would help us effect healing on the deepest level (Jung & Pauli, 1955).

That connection between consciousness and matter, between mind and the physical body, is described in Tibetan Buddhist medicine through the mediating principle, which is the subtle body, the meridians and energy centers that govern health and spiritual wellbeing. Experiential knowledge of the subtle body can be conveyed within the framework of college chaplaincy through the healing arts of *qi gong* exercises, *tsa lung* (Tibetan breathwork), *soen yu* (Korean Buddhist *qi gong*), *reiki*, and/or dreamwork. This aspect of Buddhist praxis benefits college students by extending their knowledge of cultural Buddhism.

In addition, teaching these practices connected to the *Sambhogakaya* principle is an effective way to bring home the perspective of the Mahayana sutras – that of the *Diamond Sutra*, which teaches nonattachment to phenomena; the *Heart Sutra*, which teaches the emptiness of phenomena; and the *Lankavatara Sutra*, which teaches that phenomena are projections of mind. To really grasp these, we need an experiential basis. Undoubtedly, observation of one's own mind through meditation provides one route into this experience. However, it is this writer's perspective that subtle energy practices provide the most vivid example of consciousness as a causal factor in our mutually arising world.

In the subtle energy practice of *reiki* healing, for example, one receives an empowerment to work with *reiki* by receiving sacred symbols representing the seed syllables *Hum* and *Hrih*, as found in Tendai Buddhism, through the transmission of a teacher. Like a note sounded to help a musician tune their instrument, the *reiki* attunement is given so that the student can attune their mind to access the healing resonance of *reiki* and the *reiki* lineage: It supports the student's spiritual growth. As the student studies the symbol and practices sending *reiki* to themselves and others, their innate capacity to connect with *ki* (universal energy) becomes empirically evident through the feedback received from the healing practice. The metaphysical understanding that underlies the practice of *reiki* is based in Japanese Buddhist culture, which itself is influenced by Chinese Buddhism, as well as Buddhism's South Asian roots. Thus, while *reiki* is sometimes characterized as "new age" or is thought to have originated in Christianity, the principles and techniques it employs are in fact classically Mahayana Buddhist.

Contemporary Approaches

As Jon Kabat Zinn (2003) noted,

> Mederi itself derives from an earlier Indo-European root meaning "to measure...all things have, in Bohm's words, their own "right inward measure" that makes them what they are.... "Meditation", by the same token, is the process of perceiving directly the right inward measure of one's being through careful, non-judgmental self observation. (pp. 163–164)

The model of Buddhist chaplain as healer is easily aligned with Kabat-Zinn's (2003) view of the Buddha as a natural "scientist and physician" (p. 145). The act of bringing mindful attention to our moment-to-moment experience restores the body-mind to a sense of wholeness. Zen Master Thich Nhat Hanh also often spoke of mindfulness as medicine. In a visit to Google, he described the ways that mindfulness could help Google staff reduce stress, improve resiliency, and center their lives in wellness.

> If we walk mindfully and reverently
>   on the earth,
> we will generate the energies of
>   mindfulness,
> of peace and of compassion
> in both body and mind . . .
> With each step the earth heals us,
> and with each step we heal the earth.[4]

Just as mindfulness helps the individual mind-body system to find a point of balance, so mindfulness may also benefit the wider ecosystem of the university, and the body politic. This can be discussed through pathways such as relational neuropsychology.

Through the skillful adaptation of these ancient teachings on mindfulness to the campus context, something is transformed. Students are healed in body and spirit. They may also glimpse the potential of a healing wholeness within our shared lives.

Conclusion

In this chapter, we have examined the contemplative care model through the paradigm of Buddhist healing, which dates back to the historical Buddha. The medical etiology can be understood to be the simple law of cause-and-effect described through *paticca samupadda*, and the healing mechanism, mindful self-insight as medicine. Meditation practice and the ethical framework of Buddhism support the development of resiliency and enhances social-emotional learning.

While many Buddhist texts underscore the healing potential through realization of *paticca samupadda*, the way that texts describe the dynamics of healing differs across the schools and vehicles of Buddhism. As Buddhist college chaplains ministering to diverse communities, we need to be familiar with both Theravadin and Mahayana ways of knowing and praxis. In this article, we have used the Mahayana term *upaya*, to refer to a quality of responsivity, adapting the teaching to the person and situation. Responsivity and adaptability, however, is not exclusive to that tradition; that quality is evident in the teaching of the historical Buddha. Buddhist college chaplaincy is an ongoing exercise in skillful adaptation. As the Mahayana Buddhist tradition continued to develop in the centuries that followed Nagarjuna, it began to employ diverse methods of teaching, *upaya* that were well suited to the pantheistic cultures of South and East Asia, including sacred images and chanting practice. In East Asia, the experience of collective chanting is the most common form of meditation. This aspect of meditation practice can be just as transformational as sitting meditation and is less known in the West.

While chanting practice was necessarily sidelined during the pandemic, there is a good argument to be made for its reintroduction to our sanghas. From a neuropsychological perspective, it has been shown that chanting meditation has an integrative effect upon the nervous system: Through that direct experience within chanting practice of contacting the space that precedes thought, psychospiritual integration and existential healing may take place. The central aspiration of Buddhist chaplain-healers is to bring about awakening; this aspiration and healing is the natural expression of *Dharmakaya*. As a Buddhist chaplain-educator, one can midwife that shift in consciousness, which heals consciousness at its root.

The Buddhist aspiration to support liberation has always coexisted with a pragmatic willingness to effect change on the relative level. Within the *trikaya* model, we know that as the sphere of *Nirmanakaya*. The capacity of mindfulness practice to effect physical healing,

---

[4] Thich Nhat Hanh, 2023, "If we sit mindfully" section.

with measurable outcomes, can serve as the beginning of many constructive conversations within university student health and occupational health offices. There is much work to be done to achieve integrative health for this generation of college students, who have experienced a pandemic tutorial in mind-body health at this critical age. While this generation has unparalleled challenges in attaining wellness, it also has unparalleled resources. The accessibility of mindfulness has made it much easier to have conversations about meditation within the broader college communities.

While the mutual causality between the *Nirmanakaya* and *Dharmakaya* has been charted through contemporary and traditional healing practices described above, there is a third state that is pivotal in traditional Buddhist healing practices: the realm of *Sambhogakaya*, the place of the subtle body. As Buddhist chaplains, we should have sufficient faith in, and knowledge of, first-person studies of consciousness to guide students in this terrain. The stories of the Buddha and lineage-holders offer profound examples of how deeply one can investigate subtle energy with a sober mind. This motion to include subtle-energy consciousness studies within Buddhist college chaplaincy is also congruent with the quantum-physicist Bohm's paradigm and congruent with Buddhist epistemology and praxis, such as the dream yoga practices utilized in many Buddhist cultures. Essentially, Bohm's understanding that that consciousness serves as a bridge between the relative and ultimate realities can support explorations of the subtle healing technology within Buddhist culture. We have discussed chanting practice in the previous section as a mind-body integrative praxis. Further research, based on leads from consciousness studies, will help guide the chaplain and practitioner to use the most efficacious melody and percussion based on their disposition and purpose, and serve to further develop Buddhist healing praxis. Just in this way, all of the texts and practices of the Mahayana tradition can be studied and refined, as remedies for our avidya, to be applied to help all students of the way to find the true measure of their own wholeness.

The integration of relational ontologies and practices embedded within the lineages of Mahayana healing practices may therefore be a valuable gift to the twenty-first-century Buddhist chaplain, who is expected to draw in an ecumenical way from the full canon to serve their students. As we make use of these resources, the field of spiritual care will benefit from the deeper potentials of intersubjectivity, which support the development of relational, contextual, holistic, and sociocentric skills and knowledges needed to resolve the challenges that face our increasingly diverse and interconnected world. We are fortunate to live in this transitional time, when this wisdom from the ancient past may illuminate our future. May these practices illuminate our shared path to wholeness.

REFERENCES

Armstrong, K. (2004). *Buddha*. Penguin.

Austin, J.H. (1999). *Zen and the brain: Toward an understanding of meditation and consciousness*. MIT Press.

Birnbaum, R. (1979). *The healing Buddha*. Shambhala.

Bittman, B.B., Berk, L.S., Felten, D.L., & Westengard, J. (2001). Composite effects of group drumming music therapy on modulation of neuroendocrine-immune parameters in normal subjects. *Alternative Therapies in Health and Medicine, 7*(1), 38.

Bohm, D. (2005). *Wholeness and the implicate order*. Routledge.

Borysenko, J. (2007). *Minding the body, mending the mind*. Da Capo Press.

Clifford, T. (2006). *Tibetan Buddhist medicine and psychiatry*. Motilal Banarisidass.

Eiland, L., & Romeo, R.D. (2013). Stress and the developing adolescent brain. *Neuroscience, 249*, 162-171.

Ellison, K.P., & Weingast, M. (Eds.). (2016). *Awake at the bedside: Contemplative teachings on palliative and end-of-life care.* Simon and Schuster.

Epstein, M. (1999). *Going to pieces without falling apart: A Buddhist perspective on wholeness.* Broadway Books.

_____. (2013). *Thoughts without a thinker: Psychotherapy from a Buddhist perspective.* Basic Books.

Giles, C.A., & Miller, W.B. (Eds.). (2012). *The arts of contemplative care: Pioneering voices in Buddhist chaplaincy and pastoral work.* Simon and Schuster.

Jung, C.G., & Pauli, W. (1955). *The interpretation of nature and the psyche. synchronicity: An acausal connecting principle.* Pantheon Books.

Kabat-Zinn, J. (2003). Mindfulness-based interventions in context: Past, present, and future. *Clinical Psychology: Science and Practice, 10*(Summer), 144-156.

_____. (2005). *Coming to our senses.* New York, NY: Hyperion.

_____. (1991). *Full catastrophe living: Using the wisdom of your body and mind to face stress, pain, and illness.* New York, NY: Dell.

Kass, J.D. (2017). *A person-centered approach to psychospiritual maturation: Mentoring psychological resilience and inclusive community in higher education.* Springer International Publishing.

Macy, J.R. (1978). *Interdependence: Mutual causality in early Buddhist teachings and general systems theory* (UMI No. 7908553) [Doctoral dissertation]. ProQuest Dissertations and Theses.

Makransky, J. (2000). Historical consciousness as an offering to the trans-historical Buddha. In J. Makransky & R. Jackson (Eds.), *Buddhist theology: Critical reflections by contemporary Buddhist scholars* (pp. 111-135). Routledge.

Roeser, R.W., Galla, B., & Baelen, R.N. (2022). *Mindfulness in schools: Evidence on the impacts of school-based mindfulness programs on student outcomes in P–12 educational settings.* Pennsylvania State University.

Schwartz, S.A. (1998). Therapeutic intent and the art of observation. *Subtle Energies, 1,* ii-viii.

Siegel, D. (2007). *The mindful brain.* Norton.

_____. (2010a). *Mindsight.* Bantam.

_____. (2010b). *The mindful therapist.* Norton.

Sumegi, A. (2008). *Dreamworlds of shamanism and Tibetan Buddhism: The third place.* SUNY Press.

Tatz, M. (Trans.). (1985). *Buddhism and healing: Demieville's article "Byo" from Hobogirin.* University Press of America.

Thich Nhat Hanh. (2023, July 17). *Thich Nhat Hanh's walking meditation.* Lion's Roar. https://www.lionsroar.com/how-to-meditate-thich-nhat-hanh-on-walking-meditation/

Thondup, T. (2013). *Boundless healing: Meditation exercises to enlighten the mind and heal the body.* Boston, MA: Shambhala.

9
Chaplain Formation for Buddhist College Chaplaincy

Ernest C.H. Ng, PhD

Introduction

Chaplain formation is a well-established concept in chaplaincy from Abrahamic traditions but not necessarily in the context of Buddhist chaplaincy. This chapter first briefly explores the meaning of chaplain formation in Abrahamic traditions as a framework to elucidate what it could mean in the Buddhist context. It hopes to clarify the contribution of the Threefold Training, i.e., moral discipline, mental concentration, and wisdom in the formation of a Buddhist chaplain. The unique identity of Buddhist chaplaincy, embodied with the wisdom of impermanence, suffering, and non-self, is then explained and further expanded with the introduction of the Noble Eightfold Path. For Buddhist college chaplains, the practices of four divine abodes (Pāli: *Brahmavihāra*), Six Perfections, and four methods of pacification (Skt.: *catvāri saṃgraha vastun*) are core building blocks in chaplain formation. These practices are introduced in detail in the context of college chaplaincy.

Defining Chaplain Formation

Chaplain formation is inseparable from spiritual formation but there is more to it. Chaplain formation refers to how a chaplain is formed, while spiritual formation refers to how the spirit is formed for a chaplain. Chaplains are known as clergy "in charge of" or "officially attached" (Merriam-Webster, 2024) to a certain place and community of worship – chapels, hospitals, hospices, local communities, colleges, prisons, senior care homes, branches of the military, and so forth. A chaplain is "a person chosen to conduct religious exercises," or "appointed to assist a bishop." A chaplain is "an official who is responsible for the religious needs of an organization" (Cambridge, 2024a). This signifies a certain level of religious authority, leadership, responsibility, religious sanctification, endorsement, and pedigree. Even though the term chaplain originates from the Christian faith, many other religions or practice groups adopt it for their respective leaders, e.g., Humanist chaplains, Buddhist chaplains, Muslim chaplains, Jewish chaplains, Eco-chaplains, and so forth.

According to the competencies rubrics of the Board of Chaplaincy Certification Inc. (BCCI, 2024) in the United States, professional chaplains should demonstrate competencies in the areas of: 1) integration of theory and practice; 2) professional identities and conduct competencies; 3) professional practice skills; 4) organizational leadership. They are also required to fulfill additional general requirements on: 1) education in relevant fields of Theology, Philosophy or Psychology; 2) faith group endorsement or recognition; 3) practicum and pastoral education through Clinical Pastoral/Psychospiritual Education ("CPE"); 4) work experience; and 5) professional competence as demonstrated in writing and the certification interview. In addition, professional chaplains are also required to adhere to the Common Code of Ethics (BCCI, 2024). Spiritual care professionals in other countries such as those in Canada under the Canadian Association of Spiritual Care follow similar competencies requirements with slightly different emphasis (CASC, 2019). This suggests that chaplains in the contemporary world are expected to obtain formal academic training at the Master's degree level, develop a deep foundation of theology, philosophy and psychology, and integrate such understanding into their personal practices and services. Even though there is no direct reference to spiritual formation for most of these rubrics, it is embedded and integrated in all aspects of the professional competencies. Professional chaplains must attempt to manifest the impact of religions and traditions on them, and then integrate these experiences in their professional practices.

Like chaplaincy in other areas of practice, Buddhist college chaplaincy as a specialized field of practice is an emerging one with limited professionalization including accreditation, education, training, and research (Sanford, 2021, pp. 66-68). It is in this context of growth, learning, and exploration that this chapter hopes to invite deeper reflection and development to strengthen recognition within the field and among other stakeholders. The term "College" is adopted herein to refer generally to "Higher Education" institutions for adults beyond high school. The target groups of college chaplains are primarily young adults but also cover a broad community at the University including post-graduates, teaching, administrative, and managerial staff, family and other community members in the "College". These groups cover a wide range of social location[1] as represented in society but may also offer a different dynamic because of visiting and exchange students, teachers, administrators, family members, and so forth, from other cities or countries overseas. In this chapter, I use the term "students" to represent the dominant target of care for college chaplains. The term "careseekers" is also used interchangeably with "students" to include those who interact with the chaplains, realizing that they may connect and interact in a more casual and general context without formally "seeking care."

Spiritual Formation from Abrahamic Traditions

In Abrahamic traditions (Brague, 2015; Cambridge, 2024b), there has been much research, practice and study on spiritual formation but not chaplain formation per se. Spiritual formation for Simuț (2022, p. 1) is "almost synonymous with sanctification" in practice. Its purpose is holiness building upon a "continuous awareness about God's sovereignty" through "a wide range of spiritual realities…[focusing] on god with a view to our radical transformation." It is an integrative and experiential process visible "in every aspect of our lives" (2022, p. 2) in worship, fellowship, preaching, service, work, and so forth. It is therefore purposeful with the goal of metamorphosis or transformation. Simuț also quotes Nelson (2010) in suggesting that it is "nothing but life in conversation with God." In relation to ministry, the ultimate goal is not only self-transformation but facilitating the transformation of those within the ministry. In the rest of his book, Simuț further introduces spiritual formation as perceived by other theologians.

For example, Origen presented spiritual formation in terms of a continuous cooperation between the human will and God's will, a journey of changed mind and renewed soul through faith, and focused on God with reflection and contemplation; or according to Evagrius, as a process of incessant development through deep understanding of the Scripture which leads us to the divine contemplation of God as Trinity. It could also be a divine embodiment, according to Augustine, who proclaimed that spiritual formation is "a journey towards our inner reality, our inner man…." (Simuț, 2022, p. 19). Kempis believed that spiritual formation begins when we become aware of our weakness against the sinful influence of Satan

---

[1] An individual's social location is defined as the combination of factors including gender, race, social class, age, ability, religion, sexual orientation, and geographic location.

and turn our hearts to Christ, following him to fight the devil. Similarly, Owen proposes that spiritual formation begins when we begin to "kill sin" in a "lifelong war" (p. 49). Edwards shares the same awareness of hell and heaven with heaven as the final destination characterized by love and faith (p. 71). In Luther, it is the reading of Scripture through which Christ stays within our hearts, guiding us to live a life of joy and happiness through faith in Christ (p. 35). For Calvin, spiritual formation is "spiritual life through the knowledge of Christ which leads to our mystical union with God" (p. 43). It is the full acceptance that we are created by God in a personal father and son relationship. In Pascal, it is "an attempt to move towards God by allowing Christ to supernaturally dwell within us as real presence and prefect love" with total submission (p. 55). Wesley considers spiritual formation as a dedicated development of "a character and a behavior which is as close as possible to Christ's" by reading the Bible, praying for the illumination of our reason, and by growing in Christ's character. Spurgeon also upholds the significance of the Bible but emphasizes deep understanding through prayers (p. 77). For Packer, spiritual formation is not accomplished without submitting ourselves to God "as disciples but also as slaves." It is considered as a "healthy obsession with Christ" (p. 77). Overall, spiritual formation according to these theologians relies on God's power but also requires our devotion, submission, and discernment (p. 91).

For the Islamic faith, Abu-Shamsieh (2013) identifies that spiritual formation involves "deep reflection on various verses in the Quran and the examination of the Sunnah." He regards "the Lordship of God and the institution of prophethood that support the concept of Tawhid or oneness of God" as the theological foundation. He feels close to God and that "God is with us" physically and spiritually. Spiritual formation relies on the entrustment of God to establish faith and guide humanity. It is a deep relationship with God based on love – a deep understanding that "God is approachable and loves to be approached." He invites chaplains to cultivate "communication skills, awareness of [their] acceptance and respect for people, and empowerment through engagement and consultation for this ministry." Spiritual formation emphasizes "better speech," "better action," "intentional balance between body, mind and heart," the practice of "soft-spoken speech and kindness." Abu-Shamsieh also highlights the importance of conscious engagement and consultation, "providing services according to each individual's needs" while maintaining strong integrity with one's own faith. The role of the chaplain, accordingly, is to be available and present and explore with the community what God's love means, reflecting together the quality of peacefulness, contentment and tranquility of being with God. Muslim chaplains also empower patients to enter into deep reflection and practice patience amidst hardship.

Horowitz et al. (2023) elucidates in a recent study that many Jewish chaplains are ordained as rabbis or cantors, with three quarters of the paid Jewish chaplains in their survey also having completed at least one unit of CPE; some of these are board certified. In the college or higher education setting, Jewish chaplains "connect with students' spiritual and existential needs" and support them in their search for meaning in life, integrating different aspects of their academic, personal, and career lives in the past, present, and future. Some of the qualities of Jewish college chaplains include "an approachable and comfortable presence," "holding" those they serve with "flexibility to move with them." Chaplaincy is thus like a "spiritual hammock" which offers those in need "time, space and strength to rejuvenate and to prepare" for the future. Horowitz's research also highlights the ability to "hyper-listen," not trying to solve problems unless necessary but offering companionship to process things together. Jewish chaplains also serve as a voice or representative of the Jewish community and interact closely with chaplains from other traditions or members of the college community. They serve not only the Jewish community but also the entire university-wide community.

From Skillsets to Mindsets

The survey above offers a cursory review of what spiritual formation means in Abrahamic traditions but does not mean to serve as a comprehensive analysis nor a comparative study. However, it allows for a better understanding of how chaplain formation and spiritual formation is perceived, leading to more clarity for Buddhist traditions in the college setting. Buddhist college chaplaincy is an emerging field and hence its formation process is still evolving. The formation of Buddhist college chaplaincy as a field could draw on the experiences of its peers while identifying its own distinctive qualities and contributions. Similar to other traditions, Master level academic training in Buddhist ministry, Buddhist counselling, Buddhist spiritual care or related fields is highly recommended. Even though Buddhist college chaplains are not only scholars, clergy, counsellors, or spiritual care practitioners, chaplains undergo these trainings drawing upon the contributions of different care approaches and methodologies (Kinst, 2021). Particularly in the college setting, formal academic training offers a shared language through which chaplains can connect with students, faculty, and the administrative teams at their institutions. Academic education also offers the theoretical and theological foundation for chaplain candidates to further their practicum training. In fact, many Master level programs incorporate at least one unit of CPE through which students engage with the day-to-day experience of chaplaincy in action under the guidance of a field preceptor and an individual supervisor.

Post CPE work experience is also necessary for chaplains to accumulate experience managing different case situations. As in other traditions, professional skills such as communication, leadership, and organizational management are valuable for Buddhist chaplains to work closely with the communities they serve. Chaplains should be comfortable in leading common religious services, practices, and programs for community members who could benefit from religious life on campus. They should also ably embody professional ethics which meet the moral expectations of the Buddhist chaplaincy field and society more broadly. It is also important to develop a deep humility regarding our professional boundaries and limitations as chaplains. The capacity to identify resources within Buddhist communities and other professions to attend to the needs of careseekers is perhaps more important than acquiring these skills ourselves. We are far from being *Bodhisattas* with a thousand hands, but we can bring in support from other professionals such as counselors, physicians, parents, student advisors, police, and so forth, to offer the best possible support for careseekers. Professional "skills" or "techniques" are skillful means which should be properly guided by the qualities of our "heart" and "mindset." The following sections further elaborate on these underlying qualities of spiritual formation.

Taking Refuge in the Triple Gem

It seems needless to say that a Buddhist chaplain must take refuge in the Triple Gem including the *Buddha*, *dhamma*, and *saṅgha* (Ng, 2020, p. 4). Nonetheless, as Buddhism emphasizes that all humans can embark on the path of Buddhahood and eventually become Buddhas, some chaplains may over time lean toward parts of the Triple Gem instead of all three of them. This may become apparent as a chaplain evolves from overly humble and dependent at the beginning of their career to overly confident and authoritative over time. The *Buddha* as the Enlightened One and the Blessed One is a teacher and a healer. He is neither the creator nor a savior. He is the embodiment of ultimate compassion and wisdom and full accomplishment of the Six Perfections (Pāli: *pāramitā*). Spiritual formation in Buddhist chaplaincy is not so much about being obedient or submissive to the authority of the *Buddha* but more to follow his path of enlightenment. *Dhamma* is the righteous living "well proclaimed" by the *Buddha* but also "inviting inspection" and "to be experienced by the wise for themselves." It is not meant to be dogmatic. Just as the *Buddha* is one who has arrived in suchness, the *"Tathāgata,"* the *dhamma* is the nature of reality not invented by the *Buddha* but also experienced by all noble spiritual practitioners in the past, present, and the future. The *saṅgha* is the community of practitioners practicing the good, straight, true, proper way who are worthy of gifts, hospitality, offerings, reverential salutation. It is the "unsurpassed field of merit for the world" (Ng, 2020, p. 4). This confidence and faith in the Triple Gem is a core part of spiritual formation but often misinterpreted by practitioners.

For Buddhists, confidence and faith in the Triple Gem is built upon a deep understanding on the law of karma, the doctrine of dependent arising, and the Noble Eightfold Path. It is not blind faith or blind hope because it is built upon effort and clarity. The Buddha invites us to "come and see" these practices and principles ourselves. The Four Noble Truths explaining the cause, origin, cessation, and the path leading to the cessation of suffering are Truths because they are essentially the same observations and realizations experienced by all accomplished practitioners (Ng, 2020). The *Buddha* facilitates our understanding of the path leading to the cessation of suffering, but we have to walk through it. As he taught in the *Kālāma Sutta* (AN 3.65), we should not follow views blindly but actively discern what is skillful or unskillful to our welfare and happiness. Spiritual formation for a Buddhist chaplain (and for all Buddhists) involves personal transformation arising from a deep understanding of the suffering caused by afflictions and defilements in our mental activities, speeches, and bodily actions originating from the three poisons of greed, hatred, and ignorance. The Noble Eightfold Path is an integrated path based on Buddhist understanding of human psychology and behaviors to address the three poisons and their expressions, through the Threefold Training of moral discipline (Pāli: *sīla*), mental concentration (Pāli: *samādhi*) and wisdom (Pāli: *paññā*). The Buddha explained that this path of moral life is supported by mental concentration and wisdom, a graduated discipline (Pāli: *anupubba-sikkhā*), a graduated course of conduct (Pāli: *anupubba-cariyā*), and a graduated mode of progress (Pāli: *anupubba-paṭipadā*) of our mind and bodily actions (Ng, 2020, p. 161).

This perspective is essential because it is a valuable but challenging balance of humility and confidence in self and other transformation. Spiritual formation for Buddhist chaplains is a long path from the most challenging realm of existence in the hungry ghost realms to the ultimate realization of compassion and wisdom as the *Bodhisattas* and *Buddhas*. Until we practice to the point of non-recursion like the *Bodhisattas*, even the blessed heavenly beings are subject to fall and unskillful rebirth. It is indeed a long and graduated path of cultivation and extended practice to change our habitual inclination (Pāli: *prāvṛti abhyāsa*). Yet we are hopeful for spiritual formation and transformation because the three marks of phenomenal existence (Pāli: *tilakkhaṇa*) (1) impermanence (Pāli: *anicca*), 2) suffering (Pāli: *dukkha*), and 3) non-self (Pāli: *anattā*) (Karunadasa, 2015)) promise the possibility of transcendence (as well as descendance). The Buddha proclaimed that even if a portion as small as a pinch of dust defies change in the psychophysical personality of a human being, then practicing the higher life is of no avail (Karunadasa, 2015). Therefore, Buddhist chaplains should be trained to hold the duality of hope and despair by understanding our own and others' vulnerabilities and fallibilities, as well as potentialities and *buddha* nature. We are all on this path and we are still humans aspiring to be *Bodhisattas* and *Buddhas*.

As chaplains, we have not perfected our compassion and wisdom. We are bound to make many bad decisions and are entangled with difficult thoughts, feelings, and emotions. We may encounter moral dilemmas as we may not have sufficient compassion and wisdom to fully comprehend reality and make proper decisions. Understanding our own limitations is to fully embrace our own humanness, seeing the impermanence, suffering, emptiness, and non-self in us and those we care for. We take refuge in the Triple Gem, meaning that we are not alone in this journey. We are witnessed and supported by the *Buddha*, guided by his teachings, and accompanied by a strong community of practice. The Triple Gem serves as a guide, a supervisor, and a mirror in our chaplaincy. For chaplains in the contemporary world, our presence and modes of delivery could be adapted as skillful means to alleviate the suffering of others. However, the core essence of Threefold Training is the same. As we gain confidence, authority, and respect as chaplains, we must remember that even chaplain authority is merely a skillful means. In chaplain formation, taking refuge in the saṅgha could be achieved through faith group endorsement or recognition. Since finding the right community can be challenging at times, chaplains may find this requirement either a checking-the-box process or an uncomfortable exercise which subjects an individual's free will to a particular collective or tradition. Recent research suggests that securing faith group endorsement is a meaningful obstacle for potential chaplain candidates. Despite this risk, I still argue for the importance of endorsement as well as affiliation with an ongoing community of practice. This could ensure that chaplains receive required supervision, spiritual guidance, and peer support. It also offers a line of accountability and responsibility beyond a secular work or volunteering relationship. Chaplaincy is too spiritually demanding and challenging to go-it-alone. From my own experience, chaplains would benefit from regular meet-ups with peers within or outside of the their organizations in the format of traditional repentance and reflection, Interpersonal Relationships Group ("IPR"), council, and so forth, to facilitate time and space for one-on-one or group reflections.

Threefold Training and the Noble Eightfold Path

In Buddhist spiritual formation, the Threefold Training can be considered as a three-in-one practice also intertwined with the Noble Eightfold Path. Ng (2020, pp. 34-36) illustrates their relationship together with their detailed practices. For example, wisdom in the Threefold Training comprises the Right View and Right Intention of the Noble Eightfold Path, which are supported by the understanding of the Four Noble Truths and the right intentions of renunciation, good will, and harmlessness respectively. While Buddhism has been associated with a well-established religious and philosophical structure and system, it is better appreciated not as a "religion of ideals and philosophy" but a "religion of practice" (Payutto, 1998). Through the lens of spirituality, Buddhism is a "system of training in conduct, meditation, and wisdom" (Gethin, 1998), with a deep wisdom of interconnectedness and a transcendental aspiration of the cessation of suffering (Ng, 2022, pp. 258-259). As explained by Karunadasa (2015), the Threefold Training comprises three stages of moral development corresponding to the three levels of unskillful moral qualities of greed, hatred, and ignorance: (1) moral discipline, to restrain our behaviors, expressed in vocal and physical actions; (2) mental concentration, to still the mind in turbulence, although it cannot remove unskillful qualities lying below surface-consciousness; and (3) wisdom, to uproot all unskillful qualities which have sunk to the "bottom" of the mind when the mind becomes still. That is why the components of this practice are threefold – mutually supportive of the others.

Mental Concentration

In most of the Buddhist Chaplaincy Training programs surveyed, including Upaya Zen Center, New York Zen Center, Naropa, Sati Center/Institute of Buddhist Studies, and University of the West, Buddhist meditation is an integral part of the chaplaincy training. One should not however reduce Buddhist meditative practices to secular conceptions of mindfulness. Buddhist meditative practices comprise more than sitting meditation but also include other contemplative practices such as those introduced in the *Path of Purification* (Pāli: *Visuddhimagga*) (Ñāóamoli, 2010) which may not be as well-known. Even though Buddhist chaplains may not know all meditative methods, it is important for them to realize that different meditative methods are developed to meet different individuals' characters and needs. There is no one-size-fits-all method, and some meditative objects could be more effective or more trauma triggering than others because each of us has different sensitivities.

While CPE and modern psychology may put a stronger focus on feelings than mind, Buddhist teachings may appear to focus more on the mind. This impression has become even more prevalent due to the growth of secular mindfulness and its associated cognitive behavioral therapy and stress reduction models, which have become more well-known and popular in the past few decades. Bodhi (2024) suggests that humans participate in three major domains of life: transcendent, social, and natural. The transcendental domain is the aspiration of classical contemplative spirituality, whereas the social domain includes our interpersonal as well as political, social, and economic relations. The third domain is the natural domain covering our physical bodies, other sentient beings, and the natural environment. Bodhi (2024) argues that spirituality tends to "privilege the transcendental and devalues the social and natural domains." He challenges this tendency, arguing that it overlooks that "social and natural domains are integral parts of the path to truth and happiness." He advocates for the integration of "ascending spiritual movement with a descending movement." The realization of love and grace from above should connect with and nourish every aspect of our mundane lives.

While Bodhi (2024) acknowledges the transcendental, social and natural domains as an integral part of our spirituality, Welwood (2002, p. xvii) identifies personal practice as consisting of three other domains: 1) meditation for the super-personal dimension; 2) psychological work for the personal; and 3) conscious relationship for the interpersonal. He attributes psychology and psychotherapy to the purpose of self-integration while spiritual work through meditation pertains to the purpose of self-transcendence. Welwood subsequently defines spiritual bypassing as ignoring self-integration in order to avoid dealing with what needs to be sensed, felt, acknowledged, or reflected in spiritual ideas and practices. To address the risk of spiritual bypassing, Buddhist chaplains should expand their awareness with the practice of the Four Foundations of Mindfulness (Pāli: *satipaṭṭhāna*) which cover the mindfulness of the body, feelings, mind, and dhammā (the hindrances and awakening factors) (Anālayo, 2018).

It is crucial for Buddhist chaplains to maintain a regular practice of mental concentration as the gateway to mental stability and serenity (Pāli: *samatha*) together with access to insight (Pāli: *vipassanā*). Practices of mental concentration allow for chaplains to stay undisturbed despite all the uncertainties and chaos outside. The practice of mental concentration should not be minimized as a relaxation nor a productivity technique. It is an anchor in a rough sea, an oasis in the desert, a lighthouse amidst darkness, offering a shelter of compassion and wisdom for Buddhist chaplains and everyone they care for. As argued below, Buddhist meditative practices with proper guidance and adherence to moral discipline and wisdom are consistent with trauma-sensitive and trauma-informed care (Anderson, 2021). Nonetheless, trauma sensitivity in chaplaincy cannot be taken for granted as chaplains continuously progress in their Threefold Training. Buddhist chaplains are equipped with various "portable" anchors, oases, and lighthouses for themselves and others to support their wellbeing in normal and crisis situations. With deeper levels of awareness within oneself and toward the external world, meditative practices are also the foundations and the accelerators of moral discipline and wisdom (Ng, 2020, pp. 165-167).

Moral Discipline and Precepts

Moral discipline is an integral part of the Threefold Training and spiritual formation, but it has not been explored extensively in the context of Buddhist chaplaincy. All Buddhist chaplains must adhere to the Professional Ethics code applicable to where they serve, e.g., in colleges, hospitals, senior care homes, hospices, and so forth. However, Buddhist moral discipline is observed not as a professional obligation but as bodily action, speech, and thought that are "enriching and rewarding" for oneself and others (Harvey, 2000). The Buddha taught his students in the *Kālāma Sutta* (AN 3.65) not to follow authority, customs, or popular views blindly, but actively discern what is skillful or unskillful to our welfare and happiness. Moral wrongdoing is determined as such because it is characterized by the three poisons of greed, hatred, and ignorance. They are the reasons why our minds are captive to suffering. Observation of moral discipline does not restrict us but sets us truly free. In fact, it is the building block of the virtue of non-violence or non-harming (Pāli: *ahiṃsā*) principle shared by Buddhists and many other traditions. To see this through the lens of contemporary trauma theory, chaplains observing moral discipline not only protect themselves from suffering but also cultivate a trauma-sensitive and perhaps even a trauma-safe field of care. With the support of a deep mental concentration practice, chaplains can establish not only strong self-awareness of their own identifies but also their moral presence; they can better appreciate how they have impacted their careseekers and vice versa. Chaplains must also constantly observe any transference or countertransference in their chaplaincy relationships.

Buddhist chaplains may observe different moral disciplines or precepts depending on their traditions. Most Buddhists share the core five precept of: 1) no taking life; 2) no stealing; 3) no sexual misconduct; 4) no lying; 5) no intoxicants (Ng 2020, p. 163). These moral disciplines are observed by Early Buddhism, Mahayana Buddhism, and Vajrayana Buddhism as the foundation for inner moral cultivation and the gateway to self-liberation. Thich (2009) offers a contemporary adaptation of these precepts by introducing more secular and relatable descriptions to daily life in the Five Mindfulness Trainings. Buddhist chaplains engaging in the world observe the ideal of the Buddha and Bodhisatta to liberate all beings from suffering. In the process, we are learning and practicing the path with compassion and wisdom, but we are nowhere near perfection. That is why most Buddhist chaplains also take on various Bodhisattva precepts or the path of engaged Buddhism. For example, students of the Upaya Buddhist Chaplaincy Training Program could elect to receive the Sixteen Practices of a Zen Peacemaker (Upaya, 2024) which comprise the Three Refuges, the Three Tenets of a Zen Peacemaker, and Ten Practices of a Zen Peacemaker. Students of the San Francisco Zen Center observe the Sixteen Bodhisattva Precepts (SFZC, 2024) which also comprise the Three Refuges, Three Pure Precepts, and Ten Grave Precepts. For Plum Village, members of the Order of Interbeing observe the Fourteen Mindfulness Trainings (Thich, 2012) as part of their Engaged Buddhism practice. The Yogacara Mahayana Bodhisattva Precepts have four major precepts and forty-one minor precepts (Dharmaksema, 2011; Chiu, 2019), focusing on tearing down our ego-centric perspectives.

These precepts have different details, but they are in essence trainings of compassion and wisdom directing aspects of bodily actions, speech, and thoughts. There are different precepts for different traditions and for lay and monastic practitioners. Fully ordained monks observe nearly 250 precepts and nuns observe more than 300 (Chiu, 2019; SZBA, 2008). In the Early Buddhist practices, these precepts focus on individual liberation (the *Pratimoksha*). In the Mahayana Bodhisattva precepts, there are three dimensions of pure precepts (Skt.: *trividhani silani*) including: 1) the precepts to upkeep (Skt.: *samvara sila*) similar to the Early Buddhist precepts of individual liberation; 2) precepts to perform good actions (Skt.: *kushaladharma sila*); and 3) precepts to benefit all living beings (Skt.: *sattvarthakriya sila*) (Plum Village, 2022). As Thich (2004) reminds us, these three dimensions are interconnected with one another: "This is the spirit of the Vinaya. In it there is the way of the *Bodhisatta*, the awakened person who is animated by compassion." For Buddhist chaplains embarking on their journey to serve, they do not directly receive a calling from the *Buddhas* or the *Bodhisattas*. However, their aspirations of compassion and wisdom (Pāli: *bodhicitta*) are kindled through a vertical transcendence with the compassion and wisdom of the *Buddhas* and *Bodhisattas* and a horizontal transcendence with those they care for by resonating with the suffering and aspiration for happiness of all beings.

Wisdom and Compassion

Wisdom (Pāli: *paññā*) in Buddhism is the ability to understand everything in this world, both internal and external, truly, as it is. Wisdom is a proper understanding of phenomenal existence as impermanence (Pāli: *anicca*), suffering (Pāli: *dukkha*), and selflessness (Pāli: *anatta*). In the context of Buddhist chaplain formation, it is both inner chaplaincy and outer chaplaincy, understanding who we are, deeply connecting with and supporting others in their difficult moments. It guides us on our own path of liberation and that of others. It is a deep understanding of the Doctrine of Dependent Arising and the true nature of our "self". The *Buddha* taught in the *Anaṅgaṇa Sutta* (MLDB. MN 5) that the "self" is the "mother of all blemishes" because we have an erroneous fixation on it. This fixation can be addressed through seeing whatever unwholesome qualities are in us as they are in others, seeing sufferings of others as ours. This is an effective way of practice because we are getting rid of the idea of "self" by seeing our "self" in "others". Through chaplain formation, we begin to realize the nature of suffering and that chaplains may just be a day away from the suffering of those in front of us. When we see that we were once students and we are still learning, we can appreciate the happiness and suffering students are going through with an open mind (Fisher, 2021).

Buddhist chaplains serve through human-to-human relationships as well as spirit-to-spirit connections. They must realize how they are being present, how they are perceiving others, and how they are impacting others. Unlike the Western schools of psychology and psychotherapy, the field of Buddhist spiritual care, counselling and chaplaincy has a relatively short history. Nonetheless, the *Buddhas*, *Bodhisattas*, and grand masters in the past have demonstrated how they healed, inspired, and taught others. They are depicted as the embodiment of profound compassion and wisdom, meaning that they are living compassion and wisdom to perfection. They are authentically and fully integrating the practice into every part of their life. Though their healing and supporting models are not presented in the familiar helping processes of 1) establishing a working relationship, 2) assessing or defining present problems, 3) identifying and setting goals, 4) choosing and initiating interventions, and 5) planning and introducing termination and follow-up (Corey, 2014), the *Buddha* taught the Four Noble Truths which invite us to face the difficulties of suffering (Pāli: *dukkha*) head-on

(Epstein 2014), realizing the nature of suffering, its origin, cessation, and the path to cessation.

A unique contribution of Buddhist teachings and practices in spiritual formation is the wisdom of "self" which is in essence non-self. Non-self does not mean the negation of self-identity but that there is "no independent self-identity, mental or material, which is impervious to change" (Karunadasa 2001, p. 3). Karunadasa (2015) argues that cessation of a wrong interpretation and construction of the world "through the lens of our ego-centric perspectives," or a wrong view coming from a wrong understanding of self, is in fact the "cessation of suffering. This is the core foundation for the *Bodhisatta*'s cultivation of the Six Perfections" (*pāramitā*): 1) generosity, 2) virtue, 3) patience, 4) vigor, 5) meditation, and 6) wisdom, together with another four methods of pacification (Skt.: *catvāri saṃgraha vastun*): 1) generosity, 2) loving speech, 3) beneficial conduct and action, 4) being with others. Using the terminology of CPE, Buddhist chaplains make "effective use of self" with the realization that the true self is free from attachment to any identity or view. This is also a manifestation of the Three Tenets in the Sixteen Practices of "Not Knowing", "Bearing Witness", and "Healing" in the Zen traditions (Upaya, 2024).

As implied in the *Sallatha Sutta* (SN 36.6), Buddhist chaplains do not resist any feelings, pleasant, unpleasant, or neutral, in themselves or in others. They can be truly present with the joy and suffering of the world by feeling together up-close – not just participating. In the *Diamond Sutra*, (Dhammajoti, 2013; Thich, 1997) the Buddha taught Subhūti that a *Bodhisattva* could not be truly compassionate and generous unless he truly transcends his own self-ideation, being-ideation, living-soul-ideation, or person-ideation. The *Bodhisattva* is the ideal and role model of chaplains in the Mahayana tradition, someone who is enlightened but stays in *Saṃsāra* because they vow to serve all sentient beings in suffering (Ng, 2020, p. 169). Without ideation, compassion and wisdom arise in the *Bodhisatta* freely. That explains why the four divine abodes (Pāli: *brahmavihāra*) of loving kindness (Pāli: *mettā*), compassion (Pāli: *karuṇā*), altruistic joy (Pāli: *muditā*), and equanimity (Pāli: *upekkhā*) were taught by the Buddha and practiced by all Buddhist traditions (Ng, 2020, p. 172). These practices are, respectively, the hope that all sentient beings be well and happy, be free from suffering, be rejoicing in all of our happiness and virtues, and be free from duality. If the Buddha was fixated on his body, he would not be ready to give his body to a tiger or cut off his flesh to feed an eagle as he did in his past lives. Without truly realizing the interdependent nature of his own identity, he would not be enlightened! (Dhammajoti, 2013; Thich, 1997). As the *Heart Sūtra* proclaims, when "there are no more obstacles in [the *Bodhisattva*'s] mind, they can overcome all fear, destroy all wrong perceptions and realize Perfect Nirvana" (Thich, 2014). Without obstacles in their mind and without fixation on an erroneous ego, *Bodhisattas* benefit all beings without hinderance. They are selflessly generous, offering loving speech by expressing their compassion in the ways care-seekers need. They are "being with others" by offering their full "self". Inspired by the Threefold Training, Ng (2020, p. 188) proposes a six "I"s transformation strategy which is also applicable to chaplain formation: from *individual* to *integral*, offering a full self without biases, from *independence* to *interdependence*, breaking through the boundary of self and others, and from *ignorance* to *insight*, realizing the wisdom of impermanence, non-self, and suffering.

Chaplain Image of Non-self

Many aspects of Buddhist chaplain formation noted above are applicable across various fields of chaplaincy. Buddhist chaplains serving in colleges must understand the challenges their target groups are facing. As mentioned earlier, members of the college community are often quite diverse, and they may come from different locations. A community of shared Buddhist practice may offer a familiar environment for strong religious support but each of the members may have their own stories very different from the dominant college culture. College youths are transitioning from adolescence and growing into independence as young adults. Sanford (2021, p. 66) reminds us that entering college could be their very first experience of "dislocation" from families and religious communities. Tanaka, Kasbekar and Negru (2022) list out ten common problems for this age group: 1) losing a match in sports; 2) being with strict parents; 3) breaking up; 4) grieving the death of a family member; 5) feeling envious of successful friends; 6) being uneasy as a Buddhist; 7) experiencing bullying and prejudice; 8) feeling uncertain about the future; 9) being afraid of death; and 10) experiencing inferiority complexes. Their own identities are constantly changing when holding the duality of immaturity and maturity, dependence and independence, obedience and rebellion, submission and aggression, thoughts and feelings, hope and despair, and so forth. In summary, there is no simple identifier for them and there is no one-size-fits-all solution.

On some occasions, college chaplains have to be more assertive and authoritative, while in others they have to be gentle and friendly. They may show up as a coach, a mentor, a friend, a parental figure, a guide, a celebrant, a supervisor, and so forth. In the *Lotus Sūtra*, the practice of the *Bodhisattva Avalokiteśvara* (Skt.) is acclaimed by the Buddha as the "Universal Gateway" because "[i]n all the worlds of the ten directions, there is no place where [the *Bodhisattva Avalokiteśvara*] will not manifest himself" (Kubo & Yuyama, 2007, p. 301). It is the not knowing and the bearing witness of the *Bodhisatta* which opens many gateways and allows for deep healing to happen. If chaplains maintain strong attachments to their views, identities, and work, they will not be able to see the nature of those they are interacting with. They will see the careseekers' "otherness" instead of interbeing. The concept of *Bodhisattas* is inseparable from those who are suffering; and the concept of *Buddha* is irrelevant if everyone is enlightened. Buddhist chaplains should follow the footsteps of the *Bodhisattas* to connect with careseekers freely without biases from their own identities, views, personalities, social locations, preferences, and so forth.

Sanford (2021, p. 122) comments that many well-known frameworks of chaplaincy have strong Judeo-Christian roots, such as those compiled by Dykstra (2005): 1) living human document, 2) living human web, 3) solicitous shepherd, 3) courageous shepherd, 4) self-differentiated Samaritan, 5) wounded healer, 6) circus clown, 7) wise fool, 8) intimate stranger, 9) ascetic witness, 10) diagnostician, 11) moral coach and counselor, 12) indigenous storyteller, 13) agent of hope, 14) midwife, 15) gardener, 16) reticent outlaw, etc. In the *Lotus Sūtra* (Kubo & Yuyama, 2007, pp. 297-298), the Buddha explains that *Bodhisattva Avalokiteśvara* teaches the dharma by changing himself into various forms if sentient beings anywhere are to be saved by that particular form: a *buddha*, a *pratyekabuddha*, *Brahma*, *Śakra*, *Īśvara*, *Maheśvara*, great commander of the *devas*, *Vaiśravaṇa*, a minor king, wealthy man, householder, state official, brahman, monk, nun, layman, laywoman, a wife, a boy or a girl, a human, nonhuman, *Vajrapāṇi*. The sutra provides a long list of sufferings to which the *Bodhisattva Avalokiteśvara* will respond (pp. 299-302).

Just like the *Bodhisattas*, Buddhist college chaplains should show up in different chaplain forms depending on what really serves the students. The Four Methods of Pacification mentioned above – generosity, loving speech, beneficial conduct and action, and being with others – are crucial to building rapport, trust, and connection. Chaplains serve by offering connection instead of helping or fixing (Remem, 1999). As we hold "bare witness" with careseekers in such a way that we are connecting with the feelings and bodily sensations in ourselves and others, resonance and healing are possible. Careseekers know that we are present and available when they need guidance and support. By practicing "not knowing" we are not fixated on our views nor asserting them on students, even when we "know" that they are on the "wrong" path or doing wrong. Halifax (2018a) offers a scientifically grounded G.R.A.C.E. training model for cultivating compassion-based interactions which is essential to Buddhist chaplain formation. G.R.A.C.E. model comprises five components of Gather attention, Recall intention, Attune to self/other, Consider what will serve, Engage and end. It draws from the insights of neuroscience, social psychology, ethics, and contemplative perspectives to support our practice and services. This model is described in more detail by Halifax in Chapter 1 of this volume. The notion of pastoral authority of chaplaincy in other traditions may not apply well in Buddhist chaplaincy because the *Buddha* and *Bodhisattas* offer their leadership, compassion, and wisdom without any concept of being the leaders or carers (Ng, 2019). The moral authority and leadership of the *Buddha* is not established through charisma or power but through his perfection in wisdom and practice. The teaching of the *Buddha* has been more "persuasive instead of coercive, and more descriptive than prescriptive" (Karunadasa, 2015). Even if Buddhist college chaplains exert authority, it is meant for the benefit of those we care for, not for the sake of our own egos. Chaplains serve the community by facilitating good conditions in flourishing with plenty of space and patience. They must be aware of their own influence and authority over those they serve, particularly when the careseekers are vulnerable.

Sanford (2021) proposes that Buddhist chaplains operate in a Three *Prajñās* framework for spiritual care. In this framework, chaplains gain wisdom by "listening, contemplating, and practicing in successively more refined ways" with four iterative stages of self, student, chaplain, and spiritual friend (Skt.: *kalyāṇamitra*), each with different intentions, tasks, and outcomes. I agree with Sanford that the path of chaplain formation for Buddhist chaplains is to become a good spiritual friend as exemplified by the *Buddha*. Just as Neufeld and Maté (2013) argue that parents need to matter more than peers by offering a stable and reliable attachment instead of providing skills, Buddhist college chaplains also need to develop a reliable spiritual friendship with students. No doubt we are no substitute for the love and care of parents to students, yet we have the spiritual stability and maturity to accompany them in their journey. This is particularly true in the modern age of social media in which many college students are subject to in-person or cyberbullying, developmental trauma, as well as other problems such as suicide, substance use, eating disorders, attention-deficit/hyperactivity disorder, anxiety and depression (Neufield and Maté 2013; Pedrelli, et al. 2015; Lipson et al. 2022; ACHA, 2024). Students ultimately have to make their own choices and take their own steps. They would, however, benefit from spiritually mature chaplains who can hold space for them and stay with them in good and difficult times, experiencing a glimpse of compassion and wisdom as manifested by the *Buddhas* and *Bodhisattas*.

Guide of Hope in *Saṃsāra*

Buddhist college chaplains working with young adults must also demonstrate strong confidence (faith) and hope even when the real world is dark. Hope here is not blind, but rather nurtured by moral discipline, wisdom, and mindfulness. Chaplains are in the business of offering hope, particularly in colleges. In college, students may experience many life "firsts" – first love, first job, first break up, first death, etc. These first encounters could be exciting, anxious, devastating, and even life-threatening. Looking back, we may find these first encounters no longer that important, but they were overwhelming when we were young. Buddhism is permeated with hope for personal development and for caring for others. King (2013) argues that hope is "confidence in the possibility of change in situations of hopelessness, poverty and oppression" because with the right practice, change is possible for oneself and the external world and therefore offers the possibility of hope. According to Macy and Johnstone (2022, p. 4), active hope is a practice. In the Work That Reconnects model, hope can be developed through a spiral of four stages: 1) Coming from Gratitude; 2) Honoring Our Pain for the World; 3) Seeing with New Eyes; and 3) Going Forth. In what Halifax (2018b) calls "wise hope," cultivation that "requires that we open ourselves to what we do not know, what we cannot know...and this is the space in which we can engage." It is realistic and fathomable to hope for a world of healing and peace. "We need to show up" no matter what. As Thich (2022) taught, "with mindfulness we are no longer afraid of pain. We can even go further and make good use of suffering to generate the energy of understanding."

As Ng (2016) argues, hope is essential in an individual's own cultivation, as well as in facilitating others' transformation in the context of pastoral services. It is linked with our respect for the "Buddha-nature in oneself and in others, with gratitude for the Buddha and the Buddha's compassion, and with the courage that strengthens people to go on living in the midst of catastrophe." It is therefore possible to cultivate hope and offer hope – not offering a false and blind wish but the deep understanding and practice to "face reality in all its contradiction, to help people to wait, to realize that love has a cost and a cross." It is also about facilitating situations where "concrete experience of hope can be somehow anticipated." Buddhist college chaplains may learn from Thich's message to the Youth (Wake Up Community, 2016). He argues that true practitioners are rebels in a force of resistance. We "rebel against the forces that lead to a meaningless and illusionary life.... There are ways of rebelling which only create more bondage and suffering...and there are ways of rebelling that can offer us real freedom." Thich suggests that initial change from within is important, working on our inner confusion and suffering. As Buddhist college chaplains, we can support the deeper needs of students for love and connection. We can facilitate them in connecting with the dreams already in them, instead of the dream(s) out there, properly applying their time, energy, passion, intelligence, talent, and resources. We accompany them in their search for connection and growth. This trust and connection is indeed the foundation of horizontal transcendence between students and chaplains, as well as the foundation for vertical transcendence between students and divine through the support of the chaplains.

Conclusion

Community members in college settings benefit from the support of Buddhist chaplains as much as Buddhist communities benefit from the participation of college community members. This is because Buddhist college chaplains connect with students in support of their spiritual and social needs. Engagement with youth also ensures that Buddhist teachings and practices address the needs of society at present and in the future. The spread of Buddhism depends on practitioners from all social locations regardless of age, gender, employment, education, wealth, etc. In the *Flower Ornament Sutra* (Skt.: *Avataṃsaka Sūtra*) (Cleary, 1993), *Bodhisattva Mañjuśrī* is depicted as a charismatic young prince and *Sudhanakumāra* as a youth. *Sudhanakumāra* was instructed by *Bodhisattva Mañjuśrī* to embark on a pilgrimage to visit fifty-three "good friends", including *Bodhisattva Samantabhadra* in the last visit for guidance toward liberation. An eight-year-old girl called *Sumati* demonstrated profound wisdom worthy of a deep bow from *Bodhisattva Mañjuśrī* regardless of age. As Hsingyin (1987) reminds us, *Buddha* was in his early thirties when he was enlightened, and Master Xuanzang was only twenty-six when he decided to travel to India to bring back many valuable Buddhist scriptures. The college community is a vibrant one with many energetic, courageous, and motivated members who have great potential to make significant positive changes in themselves and others. Buddhist college chaplains with the necessary chaplain formation and development serve pivotal roles on the path. It is my sincere wish that this chapter invites further study on the research, training, and development of Buddhist chaplains serving in college settings and other fields.

Abbreviations

AN   *Aṅguttara Nikāya*, the "numerical" discourses.
NDB   *The numerical discourses of the Buddha* (translation of AN; see Bodhi (2012)).
SN   *Saṃyutta Nikāya*, the "connected" discourses.
MLDB   *The Middle Length Discourses of the Buddha* (translation of MN; see Ñanamoli and Bodhi (1995))
MN   *Majjhima Nikāya*, the "middle-length" discourses.

References

Abu-Shamsieh, K. (2013). The spiritual formation of a chaplain: An Islamic perspective. *Reflective practice: Formation and supervision in ministry.* https://journals.sfu.ca/rpfs/index.php/rpfs/article/download/287/286/573

ACHA. (2024). Reference group executive summary. Fall 2023. *National college health assessment IIIb.* American College Health Association. https://www.acha.org/documents/ncha/NCHA-IIIb_FALL_2023_REFERENCE_GROUP_EXECUTIVE_SUMMARY_03.19.24.pdf

AN 3.65. Kesaputtiya. In NDB, 279-283. Wisdom Publications.

Anālayo, B. (2018). *Satipaṭṭhāna meditation: A practice guide.* Windhorse Publications

Anderson, R. (2021). *Being upright: Zen meditation and the Bodhisattva Precepts.* Shambhala Publications.

BCCI. (2024). Requirements and definitions for Board Certified & Associate Certified Chaplains. https://www.apchaplains.org/bcci-site/becoming-certified/

Bodhi, B. (2012). *The numerical discourses of the Buddha: A translation of the Aṅguttara Nikāya.* Translated by from the Pali by Bhikkhu Bodhi. Wisdom Publications.

Bodhi, B. (2024, March 1) *Bridging the spiritual and mundane.* Awakin.org. https://www.awakin.org/v2/read/view.php?tid=942

Brague, R. (2015). The concept of the Abrahamic religions, problems and pitfalls, in Silverstein, A. J. and Stroumsa, G. G. (eds), *The Oxford Handbook of the Abrahamic Religions* (2015; online edn, Oxford Academic) https://doi.org/10.1093/oxfordhb/9780199697762.013.5, accessed 25 July 2024.

Cambridge. (2024a, March 1). Chaplain. *Cambridge Dictionaries Online.* https://dictionary.cambridge.org/dictionary/english/chaplain

Cambridge. (2024b, March 1). Abrahamic. *Cambridge Dictionaries Online.* https://dictionary.cambridge.org/dictionary/english/abrahamic

CASC. (2019). Competencies of CASC/ACSS Certified Professional. CASC/ACSS. https://www.spiritualcare.ca/uploads/1/3/9/8/139872819/competencies-of-casc-acss-certified-professionals-june-2019.pdf

Chiu, T. (2019). Bodhisattva Precepts and their compatibility with vinaya in contemporary Chinese Buddhism: A cross-straits comparative study. *Journal of the Oxford Center for Buddhist Studies*, 17: 193-224

Cleary, T. (trans. 1993). *The Flower Ornament Scripture: A translation of the Avatamsaka Sutra.* Shambhala Publications.

Corey, G. (2014). *Theory and practice of group counseling*. Cengage. Learning Custom Publishing.

Dharmaksema. (trans. 2011, December). *The book of Bodhisattva Precepts*. https://www.sutrasmantras.info/sutra31.html

Dhammajoti, K.L. (2013). *Reading Buddhist Sanskrit texts: An elementary grammatical guide*, 2nd ed., The Buddha-dharma Centre of Hong Kong.

Dykstra, R.C. (2005). *Images of pastoral care: Classic readings*. Challis Press.

Epstein, M. (2014). *The trauma of everyday life*. Penguin Press.

Fisher, D. (2012). May you always be a student. In Giles, G.A. & Miller, W. B. (eds.) *The arts of contemplative care: Pioneering voices in Buddhist chaplaincy and pastoral work*. Wisdom Publications.

Gethin, R. (1998). Four Truths: The disease, the cause, the cure, the medicine. In *The Foundations of Buddhism*, 59-79, Oxford University Press.

Halifax, J. (2018a). *Standing at the edge: Finding freedom where fear and courage meet*. Flatiron Books.

Halifax, J. (2018b). A case for wise hope in dark times. Keynote speech at Contemplation by Design 2018. https://www.scienceandnonduality.com/video/a-case-for-wise-hope-in-dark-times

Harvey, P. (2000). Economic ethics. In *An Introduction to Buddhist Ethics: Foundations, values and issues*, 187-197. Cambridge University Press.

Horowitz, B., Cadge, W. & Weisberg, J. (2023). American Jewish chaplains: Adopting an American form. *Contemporary Jewry*, 43: 683-709. https://doi.org/10.1007/s12397-023-09507-9

Hsingyun. (1987). The prospect for Buddhist youth: talk delivered at the Neng Ren Society, Taipei, January 1, 1978. Fo kuang Publisher.

Karunadasa, Y. (2001). The early Buddhist teaching on the practice of the moral life. The Numata Yehan lecture in Buddhism fall 2001, University of Calgary.

Karunadasa, Y. (2015). *Early Buddhist teachings: The middle position in theory and practice*. Hong Kong: Centre of Buddhist Studies, University of Hong Kong.

King, S.B. (2013). Hope in engaged Buddhism. In *Hope: A form of delusion?* ed. Elizabeth Harris, Sankt Ottilien, 166-167.

Kinst, D.J. (2012). Cultivating an appropriate response: Educational foundations for Buddhist chaplains and pastoral care providers. In Giles, G.A. & Miller, W.B. (eds.) *The arts of contemplative care: Pioneering voices in Buddhist chaplaincy and pastoral work*. Wisdom Publications.

Kubo, T. & Yuyama, A., (trans. 2007). "The gateway to every direction [Manifested by Bodhisattva Avalokiteśvara]." In *The Lotus Sutra* (translated from the Chinese of Taishō Volume 9, Number 262 of Kumārajiva), 2nd ed., 301. Berkeley: Numata Center for Buddhist Translation and Research.

Kumar, P.P. (2010). Introducing Hinduism: The master narrative – a critical review of textbooks on Hinduism. *Religious Studies Review*, Vol. 36. No. 2, June 2010. 115-124.

Lipson S.K., Zhou, S., Abelson, S., Heinze, J., Jirsa, M., Morigney, J., Patterson, A., Singh, M. & Eisenberg, D. (2022). Trends in college student mental health and help-seeking by race/ethnicity: Findings from the national healthy minds study, 2013–2021. *Journal of Affective Disorders*, 306, 138-147. https://doi.org/10.1016/j.jad.2022.03.038

Macy, J. & Johnstone C. (2022). *Active hope: How to face the mess we're in with unexpected Resilience and Creative Power*. New World Library.

Merriam-Webster. (2024, July 24). Chaplain. In *Merriam-Webster.com dictionary*. https://www.merriam-webster.com/dictionary/chaplain

MLDB. MN 5. *Anaṅgaṇa Sutta: Without blemishes*. In MLDB, 108-114, Wisdom Publications.

Nyanamoli, B. & Bhikkhu, B. (1995). *The Middle length discourses of the Buddha: A translation of the Majjhima Nikaya (Teachings of the Buddha)*. Wisdom Publications.

Nyanamoli, B. (trans. 2010). *The path of purification (Visuddhimagga) by Bhadantácariya Buddhaghosa*. Buddhist Publication Society. https://www.accesstoinsight.org/lib/authors/nanamoli/PathofPurification2011.pdf

Nelson, P. K. (2010). *Spiritual formation: Ever forming, never formed*. InterVarsity Press.

Neufeld, G. & Maté, G. (2013). *Hold on to your kids: Why parents need to matter more than peers*. Vintage Canada.

Ng, C.H., E. (2019). Servant leadership beyond servant and leader: A Buddhist perspective on the theory and practice of servant leadership. In Bouckaert, L. & van den Heuvel, S. (eds) *Servant leadership, social entrepreneurship and the will to serve*. Cham: Palgrave Macmillan. https://doi.org/10.1007/978-3-030-29936-1_3

Ng, C.H., E. (2020). *Introduction to Buddhist Economics: The relevance of Buddhist values in contemporary economy and society*. Palgrave studies series in Buddhist economics, management, and policy, edited by Clair Brown and László Zsolnai. Cham: Palgrave Macmillan.

Ng, C.H., E. (2022). "Embodying morality in management theory and practice: A Buddhist perspective." *Journal of Management, Spirituality & Religion*, 19 (3), 258-274. https://doi.org/10.51327/TMXQ5830

Ng, C.H., E. (2016) *Buddhism and Cultural Studies: A profession of faith*. London: Palgrave Macmillan.

Payutto, P.A. (1998). *Buddhist Economics, A middle way for the market place*. Buddhadhamma Foundation.

Pedrelli, P., Nyer, M., Yeung, A., Zulauf, C. & Wilens, T. (2015). College students: Mental health problems and treatment considerations. *Acad Psychiatry*, 39, 503-511. https://doi.org/10.1007/s40596-014-0205-9

Plum Village. (2022). Thich Nhat Hanh on the deeper meaning behind monastic rules. *Plum Village*. https://plumvillage.org/articles/the-deeper-meaning-behind-monastic-rules.

Remem, R. (1999). Helping, fixing or serving? https://www.mentalhealthsf.org/wp-content/uploads/2020/01/HelpingFixingServing-by-Rachel-Remen.pdf

Sanford, M. (2021). What do Buddhist chaplains do? *Kalyāṇamitra: A model for Buddhist spiritual care*. Sumeru Press.

Simuţ, C.C. (2022). *Spiritual formation, a concise introduction and guide*. Palgrave Macmillan. https://doi.org/10.1007/978-3-030-97447-3

SN 36.6. *Sallatha Sutta: The Arrow*. Translated from the Pāli by Thanissaro Bhikkhu. Access to Insight (BCBS Edition), 30 November 2013, http://www.accesstoinsight.org/tipitaka/sn/sn36/sn36.006.than.html

SFZC (2024). The Sixteen Bodhisattva Precepts. *San Francisco Zen Center*. https://www.sfzc.org/offerings/establishing-practice/sixteen-bodhisattva-precepts

SZBA (2008). The evolution of the precepts. *Study material for the 2008 national conference of Soto Zen Buddhist Association*. https://terebess.hu/zen/szoto/Precepts_Study.pdf

Tanaka, K.K., Kasbekar, D., Negru, J.H. (2022). *GEMS: An introduction to Canadian Buddhism for young people and the young at heart*. Sumeru Press.

Thich, N.H. (1997). *The Diamond Sutra.* Transcript of the dharma talk given by Thich Nhat Hanh. 14 December 1997 in Plum Village. http://www.abuddhistlibrary.com/Buddhism/G%20-%20TNH/TNH/The%20Diamond%20Sutra/Dharma%20Talk%20given%20by%20Thich%20Nhat%20Hanh%20on%20December%2014%20IV.htm

Thich, N.H. (2004). *Freedom wherever we go: A Buddhist monastic code for the 21st Century.*

Thich, N.H. (2009). *The Five Mindfulness Trainings.* http://plumvillage.org/mindfulness-practice/the-5-mindfulness-trainings/

Thich, N.H. (2012). *The Fourteen Mindfulness Trainings.* http://plumvillage.org/mindfulness-practice/the-14-mindfulness-training

Thich, N.H. (2014). *The Heart Sūtra.* http://plumvillage.org/wp-content/uploads/2014/09/2014-Thich-Nhat-Hanh-New-Heart-Sutra-letter-cc.pdf

Upaya. (2024). *The Sixteen Practices of a Zen Peacemaker.* Upaya Zen Center. https://www.upaya.org/zen/liturgy/peacemaking/

Wake Up Community. (2016). Thich Nhat Hanh's message to the youth. Wake Up. https://wkup.org/thich-nhat-hanh-message-youth/

Welwood, (2002). *Toward a Psychology of Awakening.* Shambhala.

10
What Is Self-Care for Buddhist College and University Chaplains?

Jonathan Makransky

Introduction

It was 9:00 pm on a Friday, and I had reached the end of an approximately 60-hour work week, packed with leading student supervisory meetings and meditation sessions; staffing weekly religious services; supporting High Holiday planning for my Jewish colleagues; and strategizing on the Ramadan *iftar* schedule with my Muslim colleagues, not to mention pushing our department cart precariously loaded with catering trays across campus countless times. As I walked from my office to the campus gate across a largely deserted quad, I contemplated whether to spend an hour on the bus and subway to get home to my apartment, or cave and spend the money on a ride share. Deciding to splurge and spend the extra $20 in this case, I ordered a Lyft. I texted my girlfriend (who lived 500 miles away, unable to relocate to the city where I was serendipitously able to find a university spiritual life job after grad school) that I was on my way home and would probably be too tired to spend much time on the phone with her when I got there. Arriving back at my apartment, I scooped myself a generous bowl of Ben and Jerry's ice cream, poured a glass of cheap red wine, and climbed into bed to watch a couple of episodes of some show or another on Netflix before drifting off to sleep in a vague state of anxiety and loneliness. Friday nights like this one were frequent occurrences for me in the course of this job. I was becoming burnt out and did not have a clear idea of how to hold myself in care.

Fellow Buddhist spiritual care professionals in higher education might find the tenor of that evening familiar (and if you don't, I rejoice in your healthy sense of work-life balance!). While we are able to be present to burnt-out students and staff and present them with gentle reminders about rest, relaxation, and spiritual practice, we may find it challenging to integrate those practices into our own lives. Like other chaplains and chaplain-adjacent professionals in higher education contexts, and indeed those in caring professions more broadly, Buddhist campus chaplains are called upon to support the community both broadly and deeply, and often in ways that fall outside what we may have thought would be our purview when we entered the field. Program design and administration; budgeting and strategic planning; interreligious engagement work (the lion's share of which, in higher ed contexts, often seems to fall to those who do not fit easily within the predominant Christian-centric frameworks generally found in campus spiritual life offices); supporting students in organizing for racial and economic justice; facilitating meditation sessions, Dharma talks, and rituals; mentoring student groups; and counseling students in distress – all of these activities form a vocation that is extraordinarily joyful, fulfilling, and in line with our spiritual values, but also profoundly exhausting at times.

Studies have shown that among the factors leading to burnout in chaplains and other caring professionals, the most predictive are organizational elements, such as feeling bogged down in bureaucratic systems (i.e., those found at universities) and high caseloads of patients/clients in need, coupled with the secondary traumatic stress that can emerge in chaplain-client relationships (Hotchkiss and Lesher, 2018; Beaumont et al., 2016). The unique challenges and opportunities found in higher education chaplaincy, particularly for chaplains ministering to traditionally marginalized populations, resonate with this analysis. On many college and university campuses, a Buddhist chaplain may be one of the very few non-Judeo-Christian spiritual care professionals present, or perhaps the only one – a position that can be isolating in the face of expansive and often byzantine university administrative systems that must be navigated with skill. For this reason, in addition to students who identify as Buddhist or Buddhist-curious of all backgrounds, many students who fall outside the traditional "religious/spiritual box" (humanists, religious nones, general seekers, those with multiple spiritual belongings, and so on) may also approach a Buddhist campus chaplain instead of other spiritual care colleagues. While this can result in extraordinarily rich and fruitful community-building and spiritual care relationships, it can also substantially increase the chaplain's caseload and add complexity to the work that must be discerned and integrated carefully. Throw in strapped program budgets, understaffing, and an increasingly fraught climate of discourse on many college campuses, and we can begin to see the contours of the waves on samsara's ocean! And yet, if you're like me, you probably feel that despite all of these challenges, you feel called to this work in some way, that you find it lifegiving and meaningful despite its challenges, that you love the students and community in which you practice, and perhaps that showing up for them authentically is a way of embodying bodhicitta, the mind of enlightenment, in the world.

In her chapter in *The Arts of Contemplative Care*, Rev. Dr. Daijaku Kinst reminds us that "chaplaincy is taxing; understanding self-care and knowing how to address one's needs intelligently are integral parts of the successful chaplain's life" (Kinst, 2012, p. 15). But how can we, as Buddhist spiritual care professionals skilled in embodying compassion and wisdom for others, come to embody it equally skillfully for ourselves when we are used to practicing in the context of anattā, the lack of a solid self? What does "self-care" mean in this context, and how does it differ from the popular notions of self-care that permeate the self-help sphere? How can we integrate the importance of self-care into the more expansive ethic of the bodhisattva, one who makes the aspiration again and again to practice until all beings are free? As I have wrestled with my own experiences of anxiety and burnout in campus spiritual care settings, I have come to realize that deliberate, deeply grounded care for myself (even as I practice recognizing that my "self" is not a solid entity) can be a radical tool to tap back into my underlying motivations of care for those in my university communities, and of all beings ultimately.

This chapter is an initial attempt to address some of these core self-care questions facing Buddhist chaplains and other spiritual care professionals in higher education settings. It stems from the deep wisdom of my teachers and mentors and, subsequently, from my spiritual practice and discernment processes, scriptural study, and engagement with the wonderful students, faculty, and staff with whom I've worked at universities over the years. The chapter will begin with an exploration of self-care in the context of the individual chaplain; it will then flow into how this grounded self-care is actualized in relationships with others, both those from whom we receive care and those to whom we extend care. It will culminate in the natural merging of self-care into the radical interconnectedness of systemic care, the care found in the deep recognition of the spacious, luminous nature of all beings and our ultimate inseparability. I argue that "self-care" for the Buddhist campus chaplain cannot be understood or realized fully outside of this context, but rather as a natural, mutual outflowing of care within our vast network of wisdom and compassion. Rather than writing a primarily theoretical academic piece, I have attempted a practical theological approach in putting into words some of the ideas and practices that would have been helpful for me as I was starting on this path. As such, though it is far from comprehensive, I hope this work may be a helpful starting point to engage frameworks of self-care in our own contexts, even as we all form a larger community of care: a sangha of campus catering cart pushers!

Self-Care in the Context of Oneself

While many Buddhist schools, particularly those situated within the Mahāyāna tradition, refer to the ultimate view as infinitely spacious, sky-like, the union of emptiness and luminosity, entirely unconditioned by labels such as "self," "other," "friend," "enemy," and so on, all acknowledge beings' more limited perception of reality on the relative level. The great tantric Buddhist master Padmasambhava once said, "Though the view should be as vast as the sky, keep your conduct as fine as barley flour." The importance of attention to the relative truth of our own conduct, and thus the relative truth of our own needs, is particularly salient for Buddhist university chaplains who must maintain our own sense of groundedness in order to be effective in our caregiving roles with young people. When actualized as self-care, this attention to our own needs involves nurturing ourselves with rest and replenishing practices, as well as honest self-inquiry about our limitations and areas of growth, our "shadow work." In this way, our conduct toward ourselves becomes as fine as barley flour, and we can become compassionately present to our own body, speech, and mind in ways that are at once loving and appropriately challenging.

A simple yet fruitful starting point in deliberately engaging our own self-care practices can take the form of a basic assessment of our patterns. As Buddhist spiritual care professionals, we can become skilled in couching our thoughts and actions in lofty philosophical and religious frameworks focusing on ultimate liberation from suffering, which are indeed critical; sometimes, however, we can lose sight of our basic needs on the relative level in that process. Checklists like Lisa D. Butler's adaptation of a self-care assessment can be helpful tools on this front (Butler, accessed May 20, 2024). Are we making time to cook healthy, nourishing meals? Are we getting enough sleep? Are we taking enough time off (when possible) for vacation or retreats? Are we devoting enough time to our relationships with our partners, families, and friends? Are we making space for our own spiritual practice and to be in community with our *sangha*? I have found that when I discount the importance of basic elements like these in favor of more "urgent" tasks, all other aspects of my life and work feel more constricted and less fruitful as a result. Just as the Buddha did not achieve enlightenment until he embodied the Middle Way, abandoning both extreme ascetic practice and laziness, so too must we recognize that we cannot be of ultimate benefit to our students and communities if we are sleep-deprived and strung out.

Boundaries are essential tools in supporting self-care. One might object (as I have in the past) that spiritual care professionals must be present for community members whenever and however needed, particularly in campus settings where mental health crises have become increasingly acute in recent years; for Buddhist practitioners, in particular, our vows to be of benefit to all sentient beings may spur us to work tirelessly. Sohaib Sultan, the late beloved Muslim chaplain at Princeton University, reminds fellow chaplains of the importance of boundaries even in the face of urgent need:

> It is hard for me to turn away from commitments, especially when it involves meeting the urgent needs of other people or my community as a whole. Though it is hard for me to place limits on the time I give others, I've seen…that constant activity

is not a sustainable way of being, for myself, for my family, for my students, or for my community. Even as I struggle to establish a balance, the process itself has been illuminating.[1]

Sultan further develops this point in describing his relationship-building with students, noting that he can model ways to maintain a relationship with God and be present with students more fully as they struggle with the workload and time management imperatives of 21st-century university life. In maintaining self-care through boundaries, we thus embody compassionate presence both for students and for ourselves.

Through such acts of self-nurturance, we allow for the space to engage in deliberate spiritual practices that get at the core meaning of self-care, practices that enable us to hold our bodies, voices, and minds in care to the extent that we can begin to release our habitual patterns that prevent us from being fully present to other beings. In describing the importance of spiritual practices of self-care in fostering a ministry of presence, Buddhist chaplain Micka Moto-Sanchez asserts that "it is through the right understanding of the self that one can release the self to enter into another's world without injury" (Moto-Sanchez, 2016, p.22). Framing the issue even more radically in his recently published book *The New Saints*, Lama Rod Owens reminds us that initial focus on individual practice is essential, as "there is no collective liberation without individual liberation" (Owens, 2023, p. 55). Such modes of spiritual practice are numerous and flow from the lineages in which we are situated as practitioners and caregivers.

The Buddha is said to have taught 84,000 different methods for the myriad inclinations and dispositions of sentient beings, and it is essential for budding Buddhist campus chaplains to explore the practice paths that are most fruitful for them with the guidance of their spiritual friends and *sanghas*. While a full exploration of Buddhist practice lineages is beyond the scope of this chapter, I have found on a personal level that integrating many moments of calm abiding (*samatha*) and insight (*vipassanā*) meditation throughout the day on campus (in addition to any dedicated time to sit on the cushion that I set aside) is vital in maintaining a sense of openness and care for myself. For example, taking a few minutes in my desk chair to meditate on my bodily sensations can be an excellent reminder that I am constantly grounded in the compassionate spaciousness of the nature of my mind through my body's rootedness in the Earth (see Lama Willa Blythe Baker's recent work *The Wakeful Body* for a profound exploration of such practices). Focusing on my breath for ten counts, looking out my office window to merge my mind with the openness of the sky for a couple of minutes, or quietly chanting a few repetitions of a mantra are all practices that I incorporate into my work.

Insight practices of noticing and exploring the root of difficult emotions and perceptions as they arise have also become important for me. They form a core component of my "shadow work," the process of working with my own obstructions, biases, and other aspects of myself that I'm more comfortable not thinking about but that I must acknowledge and integrate into my practice, particularly as someone who works among students of all backgrounds and is embodied as a white, cisgender male (in this lifetime, at least). Such insight work, Cheryl Giles asserts, allows us to compassionately see our prejudices in the context of our full humanity, and we can thus embody this understanding to "open up and learn, heal, and grow from our experience rather than habitually react[ing] from conditioning" (Giles, 2012, p. 47). In this way, one can be conscious of and avoid the dangerous trap of spiritual bypassing (which is particularly treacherous for chaplains and other spiritual care professionals), in which spiritual practice is used as a distraction from difficult

---

[1] Sultan, 2013, pp. 43-44.

emotions and trauma rather than a means to work with and metabolize them. Continuous cultivation in techniques of calm abiding and insight like these grounds us increasingly profoundly in the nature of our experience in our work with students and colleagues and helps us to integrate our practice on the cushion and in retreat into our daily lives more broadly.

Self-Care and Other-Care

As these individual self-care practices (both mundane and spiritual, though all activities can be spiritual) shift us into healthier relationship with ourselves, they naturally expand our frames of reference to include those around us, both those from whom we receive care and those to whom we extend care in our work. In doing so, they begin to deconstruct some of the notions of the self's solidity that contribute to burnout. Kristin Neff notes that self-compassion inevitably leads to greater feelings of care for others, as "self-compassion entails seeing one's own experience in light of the common human experience, acknowledging that suffering, failure, and inadequacies are part of the human condition and that all people – oneself included – are worthy of compassion" (Neff, 2003, p. 87). Self-care is thus also intimately connected to care that we have received from those who have helped us to see that our "suffering, failure, and inadequacies" cannot touch our inherent deep worth as beings, those who have mirrored to us the love, compassion, joy, and equanimity that we embody for ourselves and others in our spiritual care roles. After all, those who provide spiritual care need spiritual care, too.

The process of recognizing the deep care we receive throughout our personal and professional lives appears differently for each person, but in my experience, perhaps the most effective way of accessing it is being in the presence of my spiritual friends and mentors (either physically or through bringing them into my meditation practice). Our community of mentors, spiritual teachers, and ancestors holds us in care constantly, even in times when we have trouble practicing care for ourselves; we can call upon them at any moment and in any place, whether in a pastoral conversation with a student or on our commute home at the end of a long day. Indeed, through the lens of the Buddha's teachings, there is no self-care separate from the care of our circles of connection. My father, John Makransky, has written extensively on the power of recognizing and communing with benefactors, those who have wished us to be deeply well, happy, whole, and free of suffering (Makransky, 2007, p. 22). Our benefactors may be family members, sangha members, ancestors, friends, professional mentors, teachers, Buddhas, bodhisattvas, or even pets; the more frequently we bring them to mind, whether in formal meditation practices of receiving loving energy from them or in brief moments of our daily lives, the more deeply we can feel their caring presence and the wider their circles become.

For example, from time to time, the sun shining through my office window in the morning reminds me of the way my grandmother smiled at me as the sun shone on her face through the window by her armchair. I take a moment to allow the energy of her care to flow into every aspect of my body and mind, resting in it and trusting in it more than any anxieties I may have about myself and my work. I then allow it to infuse into my interactions with students and colleagues throughout the rest of the day. I also keep photos of my Buddhist spiritual teachers, Chökyi Nyima Rinpoche and Phakchok Rinpoche, near my desk, along with an image of Tara, the mother of all the Buddhas (according to the Vajrayana tradition) and the compassionate presence with whom I work most closely in my daily spiritual practice. Whenever I look at them, I allow myself to be drawn into their enlightened care like iron being drawn toward a magnet, and I am reminded that any self-care in which I engage is in communion with the blessings of my spiritual ancestors and is ultimately inseparable from them.

This constant care from our community of benefactors flows into and through us in union with our practices of self-care. It thus extends to those with whom we are in relationship personally and professionally, holding all within its spacious responsiveness. When a student comes to the spiritual life office in distress or when an event attendee is frustrated that a program is starting late, I often pause for a moment to feel the loving energy of my own benefactors flowing into me and then through me into the person in front of me, infusing our interaction. In conjunction with the shadow work referenced above, this received care can also aid us in compassionately acknowledging and releasing difficult thoughts and emotions that may arise in transference-countertransference dynamics in spiritual counseling. If I am in touch with my benefactors, when a student says something that triggers me based on my own experiences, I can notice my emotional and embodied response as it arises, allow it to be bathed in their caring energy, and let it pass as I reground myself to listen deeply and respond skillfully to the student in front of me. In this way, I am able to gently acknowledge the truth of my inner experience while holding it lightly, rather than allowing it to harden into a pattern that may ultimately lead to frustration and burnout with time. Of course, this can be easier said than done, particularly for those who have experienced trauma or who come from marginalized groups; thus, we must be gentle with ourselves and call upon our benefactors to be present with us, and rely on our regular spiritual practice and guidance from our communities.

In addition to practices of receiving and extending love and compassion like these, on a more ordinary note, building strong relationships with colleagues and professional mentors can be an essential aspect of self-care for campus chaplains. Even though most campus spiritual care offices do not have multiple chaplains who consider themselves Buddhist, investing in lifegiving relationships with fellow staff members of all backgrounds is crucial in providing space for reflection, solidarity building, or even simply venting from time to time. Colleagues and supervisors act as important sounding boards and checks when issues arise in student counseling and group dynamics, not to mention navigating complex administrative processes inherent to higher education, like strategic planning and budget reconciliation. This teamwork can be crucial in advocating for student and staff needs in the face of limited resources. It alleviates some of the stress that arises when doing this difficult work in isolation. Writing in the context of her interreligious work with colleagues at Wellesley College, Ji Hyang Padma asserts that "what we are most deeply called to do is to return to the deepest, pure elements of our practice and our ministry – listening, openness, trust" (Padma, 2012, p. 190). Some of my most fruitful professional relationships have developed in open and trusting partnerships with Hindu, Jewish, Muslim, Latter Day Saint, Catholic, and Humanist colleagues; even as our differences are apparent, many university student anxieties, heartbreaks, and joys are the same across traditions.

In addition to promoting teamwork and solidarity in the professional context of campus chaplaincy, these relationships can foster joy. During the grind of the semester, our interactions with colleagues can remind us that we have fellow travelers in this work, that we are part of a wider network of relationships, and that we must not lose sight of the beauty of working with young people in a vibrant community. In the months after I completed graduate school and moved to a new city for my first job in campus spiritual life, for example, my supervisor would invite a few colleagues (many of whom were navigating similar transitions) and me to her on-campus apartment where she served as a resident minister. We drank tea, did creative writing exercises, and reflected together on the challenges and triumphs of adapting to our work at a new university in a new city. This group of colleagues and mentors, many of whom I still talk with regularly, were instrumental in reminding me of the care we all are held and with which we hold others.

Self-Care and the Threads of Indra's Net

Deep practices of care for ourselves and receiving and extending care, in turn, lead us to recognize over time that the networks of care in which we are embedded are vast and deeply, inextricably interconnected. As we recognize this on increasingly more profound levels, self-care becomes inseparable from the spaciousness and luminosity of this "systemic" care. In her recent work *Casting Indra's Net*, Pamela Ayo Yetunde draws a connection between Martin Luther King Jr.'s evocation of "the inescapable network of our mutuality" and Indra's Net in ancient Indian cosmology, the net that encompasses the entirety of the universe and that symbolizes *pratītyasamutpāda*, dependent origination; all beings are "mirrors, diamonds, and pearls in this flowing, universal net" (Yetunde, 2023, p. 4). Thus, as a Buddhist campus chaplain and as a sentient being in general, "my body is part of a bigger body, the bigger body is part of me. Taking care of my body, I take care of the bigger body. Taking care of the bigger body, I take care of my body" (Yetunde, 2023, p. 150). In this way, when we engage in care for our body, speech, and mind, receive this care from our benefactors, and extend it to others, we are ultimately recognizing the luminous, shifting interplay of all phenomena, the interconnection of beings beyond labels of "self" and "other," "friend" and "enemy." The implications of Indra's Net are profound, both for our spiritual practice and our chaplaincy work within our university communities.

We can come to a deeper recognition of the interdependence symbolized in Indra's Net as we open ourselves to receiving and extending care in broader circles and ultimately commune with the boundless awareness of the nature of our mind that underlies this care. Several spiritual practices can help us in this journey, in community with our teachers and sanghas, but we can also incorporate this consciousness into life on campus. As I write this chapter in the spring of 2024, campuses across the country have been rocked by the brutal conflict in Gaza as students have mobilized in protest and university administrations have struggled to respond effectively, with some authorizing brutal police crackdowns on protestors. Deeply embedded systemic injustices surrounding race, class, sexuality, and gender identity persist both in higher education and in society writ large, and impending environmental catastrophe looms in the background; all of these dynamics weigh heavily upon the minds of the students we encounter in our work, and they cause us deep distress as well. There are no easy answers that we can give to students when they come to us with these concerns as they look toward graduation and the start of their post-college lives. However, grounding ourselves in the endless networks of care within Indra's Net can enable us to embody wisdom and compassion skillfully in facing such vast and systemic injustices and thus show up for our students as an example of deep listening, presence, solidarity, and responsiveness.

Recognition of the interconnected web of phenomena illuminates the hatred, grasping, and ignorance we experience in the world as ultimately illusory, even as these forces have extraordinarily damaging consequences in our relative reality. Thus, rather than succumbing to numbness and overwhelm, we can tap into our deep wells of care to recognize all around us as sacred manifestations of Indra's Net and act skillfully to address suffering. Rather than acting out of reactivity, we can embody grounded responsiveness for our communities. Here, we arrive at the ethic for which deep self-care prepares us. In Lama Rod's words,

I am trying to achieve complete personal liberation from suffering to help as many beings as possible get free…. My intention then becomes an expression of awakened care, which is the need for all beings to be free from suffering…. It is also intentions that begin to shape the reality of karma, creating the energetic causes and conditions of what I experience.[2]

As campus chaplains, while we cannot solve the systemic violence that impacts our students and wider communities, we can integrate self-care for personal liberation in expressing awakened care for the beings around us in our thoughts, words, and actions. Thus, we shape causes and conditions in measurable and immeasurable ways to tilt the balance toward liberation for all. This way of being allows us to serve those suffering in front of us in a mode that cuts through the clouds, obscuring the sun of our awakened nature, including the clouds of burnout. Bodhicitta, the mind of awakening, shines as we push our cart full of catering trays across the quad to our next program.

References

Baker, W.B. (2021). *The Wakeful Body: Somatic Mindfulness as a Path to Freedom*. Boulder: Shambhala.

Beaumont, E., Durkin, M., Hollins Martin, C.J., & Carson, J. (2016). Measuring relationships between self-compassion, compassion fatigue, burnout and well-being in student counsellors and student cognitive behavioural psychotherapists: a quantitative survey. *Counselling and Psychotherapy Research*, 16(1), 15-23. doi: 10.1002/capr.12054.

Butler, L.D. (2010, August). *Self-Care Assessment*. Retrieved from University at Buffalo School of Social Work: https://socialwork.buffalo.edu/content/dam/socialwork/home/self-care-kit/self-care-assessment.pdf

Giles, C. (2012). Beyond the Color Line: Cultivating Fearlessness in Contemplative Care. In C.A. Giles, & W.B. Miller (Eds.), *The Arts of Contemplative Care: Pioneering Voices in Buddhist Chaplaincy and Pastoral Work* (pp. 41-52). Boston: Wisdom Publications.

Hotchkiss, J.T., & Lesher, R. (2018). Factors Predicting Burnout Among Chaplains: Compassion Satisfaction, Organizational Factors, and the Mediators of Mindful Self-Care and Secondary Traumatic Stress. *Journal of Pastoral Care and Counseling*, 72(2), 86-98. doi: 10.1177/1542305018780655

Kinst, D.J. (2012). Cultivating an Appropriate Response: Educational Foundations for Buddhist Chaplains and Pastoral Care Providers. In C. A. Giles, & W. B. Miller (Eds.), *The Arts of Contemplative Care: Pioneering Voices in Buddhist Chaplaincy and Pastoral Work* (pp. 9-16). Boston: Wisdom Publications.

Makransky, J. (2007). *Awakening Through Love: Unveiling Your Deepest Goodness*. Boston: Wisdom Publications.

Moto-Sanchez, M. (2016). Ministry of Presence. In N.J. Michon, & D. C. Fisher (Eds.), *A Thousand Hands: A Guidebook to Caring for Your Buddhist Community* (pp. 17-24). Richmond Hill, ON: Sumeru Press.

Neff, K. (2003). Self-Compassion: An Alternative Conceptualization of a Healthy Attitude Toward Oneself. *Self and Identity*, 2, 85-101. doi: 10.1080/15298860390129863.

Owens, R. (2023). *The New Saints: From Broken Hearts to Spiritual Warriors*. Boulder: Sounds True.

---

2 Owens, 2023, p. 80.

Padma, J.H. (2012). Changing Our Mind, Transforming Our World. In C. A. Giles, & W. B. Miller (Eds.), *The Arts of Contemplative Care: Pioneering Voices in Buddhist Chaplaincy and Pastoral Work* (pp. 185-191). Boston: Wisdom Publications.

Sultan, S.N. (2013). A Muslim Chaplain on Finding His Way. In L.A. Forster-Smith (Ed.), *College and University Chaplaincy in the 21st Century* (pp. 35-44). Woodstock, VT: Skylight Paths Publishing.

Yetunde, P.A. (2023). *Casting Indra's Net: Fostering Spiritual Kinship and Community*. Boulder: Shambhala.

11
Towards a Multi-faith Community at Wellesley College

Rev. Victor H. Kazanjian Jr.

First published in *Building the Interfaith Youth Movement*, 2005, Alta Mira Press, ed. Patrice Brodeur and Eboo Patel.

Perhaps it was the opening words of welcome from Baha'i, Buddhist, Christian, Hindu, Jain, Jewish, Muslim, Sikh and Unitartian Univeralist students; or the call to worship by Native African drumming offered by the Yanvalou African Drum and Dance Ensemble; or the mystical singing of a Zoltan Kodaly piece by the College Choir; or the scripture read by Buddhist, Catholic, Jewish, Muslim and Protestant Chaplains; or the classical Indian song and dance performed by Hindu students; or the inspirational reflections on the theme "Education as a Spiritual Journey" by writer/teacher Parker Palmer; or the echoes of a Hebrew song sung in round; or the prayers for a new president, spoken in seven different languages; perhaps it was one of these things or the inter-wovenness of all of these things elements of the service that moved those gathered at the Inaugural Multi-faith Celebration to realize that something different was happening at Wellesley College, when Diana Chapman Walsh was inaugurated as Wellesley's 12th President in the fall of 1993.

This celebration was the most visible manifestation of a revolution in religious and spiritual life taking place at Wellesley College, a revolution that has evolved during the past decade to a comprehensive exploration of the role of religion and spirituality in higher education. In 1993, the Wellesley College community was introduced to an exciting new model of religious and spiritual life. At a time when most colleges and universities, confused by the conflict between a mono-religious institutional history and a multi-religious contemporary college community, were de-emphasizing the religious and spiritual dimensions of their institutions, Wellesley set out on a journey in the opposite direction. Determined to continue to value the role of religion and spirituality in the educational experience which has been so much a part of her past, Wellesley created a new and largely untraveled path for an academic community (or perhaps any community), the exploration of multi-faith community.

How did this happen? First a bit of context.

The Wellesley College that you may think you know, or at least that I thought I knew before arriving at Wellesley, is not the Wellesley that I found in February of 1993 when I walked onto campus for the first time. The college whose name conjures up for many images of white New England debutantes, (as evidenced by the recently released Hollywood film, *Mona Lisa Smile*) is, in fact, one of the most racially and ethnically diverse colleges in the United States. Due to its commitment to need-blind admissions, which enables Wellesley to admit students without regard to financial status, and to an equally strong commitment to multiculturalism as an essential context in which excellent global education takes place, Wellesley College's student body is a microcosm of human diversity. What had not changed as rapidly by 1992, were the institutional structures that were born out of Wellesley's history as a more homogeneous community in which the cultural norms of wealthy, white, Western Protestant Christian society were dominant. One such outdated institutional structure was the college chaplaincy that was a reflection of both Wellesley's history and reflected a much broader history of religion and higher education.

The history of religious and spiritual life in higher education has been complicated at best. It was religiously-inspired motivation that led to the founding of many of the earliest colleges and universities in this country and shaped early educational philosophy and pedagogy. The relationship between religion and education persisted, over the growing objections of many scholars who found their academic freedoms restricted by theological principles rather than educational ones. This continued until the mid-20th century when secular scholarship won out and most colleges and universities severed ties with organized religion or relegated it to the extreme margins of the educational enterprise. In non-religiously-affiliated institutions, chaplaincy programs continued to exist either on the margins of academe quietly serving their communities or in a few remaining places like Duke, Harvard, and Stanford – historically powerful religious programs clinging to larger roles within institutions, but in increasingly ceremonial ways.

Wellesley College's religious history was in some ways no different (and in a few very important ways completely different). Like many similar institutions, by 1993 Wellesley had a College chaplaincy program which was a slightly modified version of its earlier Christian chaplaincy. Religious life at Wellesley was led by a full-time College Chaplain, who was the Protestant Chaplain. The Protestant Chaplain was first and foremost responsible for the Protestant Christian majority on campus and then, only by her own inspiration rather than by design of her role, concerned with the spiritual lives of all students. (In fact, Wellesley's two previous College Chaplains, Paul Santmire and Connie Chandler-Ward, were outstanding examples of spiritual leaders serving all members of the community in spite of their institutional roles.) In addition to the College Chaplain, a part-time Hillel Director/Campus Rabbi and a Roman Catholic Priest (both funded for the most part by their own religious communities) served Jewish and Roman Catholic communities on the margins of campus life. In the face of the dissonance between this model and the college's diverse student population, College Chaplain Connie Chandler Ward, in her final letter to the community in 1991, pleaded with the College to move beyond this outdated model of religious life that failed to respond to the reality of the diversity of the contemporary college community, but rather simply perpetuated the outdated culture of the past.

The religious context of the Wellesley College culture is indeed similar to many New England schools and yet different enough to be fertile ground for experimentation. Founded in 1875 by Henry Durant, a self-proclaimed evangelical Christian and friend of evangelist/educator Dwight Moody who served on Wellesley Board of Trustees in the early years, the language of Wellesley's founding documents is filled with calls for the radical necessity of women's education as a Christian imperative. Listen to the language of Durant's opening address to the college: "The Higher Education of Women is one of the great world battle cries for freedom.... I believe that God's hand is in it; that it is one of the great ocean currents of Christian civilization; that He is calling to womanhood to come up higher, to prepare herself for great conflicts, for vast reforms in social life, for noblest usefullness."[1] Although clearly Christian in context, the language of Wellesley's mission called from the beginning for the education of women for full participation in the world. One point to which I will return later in this chapter is that although explicitly Christian, Wellesley was from the beginning also fervently non-denominational

---

1 Glasscock, Jean, *Wellesley College: 1875-1975 – A Century of Women*, (Wellesley College, Wellesley, MA 1975) p. 1.

and therefore not attached to any organized religion, a fact that has been significant to its multi-faith development. Through the years, the Christian context of the College's mission gave way to the values of secular liberal arts education. What did not fall away, however, were the institutional structures that carried the cultural norms of Wellesley's Protestant Christian past. These structures remained largely invisible to those who shared the dominant culture (wealthy, white, western and Protestant Christian) and yet painfully obvious to those who did not fit this cultural profile. Community members were reminded of the dominant culture through the words in the Wellesley logo (*Non ministrare, sed ministrare,* "not to be served but to serve," from Christian scripture), Christian images in stained glass windows across the campus, and college rituals such as convocation and baccalaureate which followed Christian liturgical forms. Each of these things served as subtle (and not so subtle) reminders not only of the historical culture of Wellesley, but created a sense that Wellesley's contemporary culture is Christian and that all others may be welcome, but are welcomed guests. The college which I discovered in 1993 is best described by Diana Eck in her extraordinary book *Encountering God* in which she presents three forms of inter-religious relationship: exclusivist, inclusivist, and pluralist. Wellesley was according to this analysis an inclusive community in which "the diversity of peoples and traditions is included in a single worldview that embraces, explains, and supersedes them all."[2] What I found particularly ironic in my first year at Wellesley was to discover that this secular college was unknowingly perpetuating institutional structures that proclaimed Protestant Christian hegemony. My first big challenge was to attempt to bring this factor to light as we tried to move from an inclusivist community to a pluralistic one in which different cultures, traditions and perspectives are equally valued in a grand experiment of educational encounter among different peoples of the world.

In contemplating this process of change, I discovered certain aspects of Wellesley's history that stood apart from these dominant cultural norms and other peer institutions. As it turned out, these historical realities played a crucial role in laying a foundation for the creation of the multi-faith religious and spiritual life program. As mentioned above, Wellesley was founded as a women's college in defiance of a male-dominated culture. The memory of such a revolutionary spirit of equality through challenging cultural norms remains a part of Wellesley's stated institutional values. This initial value of gender equity has been extended over the years at Wellesley to include those racial, ethnic, and religious groups that have historically been excluded from full participation in shaping the culture in institutions of higher education. Wellesley's seventh President, Mildred McAfee Horton, illustrated such revolutionary thinking in her farewell address to the College in 1949. When talking about the importance of including all students into the Wellesley community she said, "Because she is a student at Wellesley, that rich girl, that poor girl, that Catholic, Protestant, Jew, Muslim, Hindu, American, Egyptian, Chinese, Iranian [girl]...is entitled to all the 'rights, dignities and responsibilities' of this College." At another occasion she added, "The day we learn as a people that differences do not necessarily involve discriminatory evaluations, vast problems of human relations will be solvable."[3] It became clear after a brief introduction to Wellesley's history that the value of equality and the goal of Wellesley as a diverse educational community would play a positive role in the development of a multi-faith model.

A second factor that enabled us to build a case for the importance of a multi-faith model

---

2 Eck, Diana, *Encountering God*, (Boston, Beacon Press, 1993) p. 179.

3 Horton, Mildred McAfee, Presidential Addresses provided by the Wellesley College Archives.

of religious and spiritual life at Wellesley College was Wellesley's defiantly non-denominational religious beginnings. While the founders of Wellesley were certainly devout Christians, they refused to be attached to any Christian denomination. This meant that, from the beginning, the religious and spiritual life of the College was entrusted to the president and the faculty rather than an external religious institution. Although this led to the rapid secularization of the College in the mid-1960s, I found that it also enabled me to call upon these early ecumenical roots when suggesting that a multi-faith community which included people of all traditions was a better reflection of Wellesley's educational values than a community in which one tradition was privileged over another (the old College Chaplaincy model.) The principles underlying Wellesley's ecumenical roots have been translated a century later from inter Christian ecumenism to multi-faith ecumenism.

And finally, in the early 1990's while many colleges and universities faced with fiscal challenges were downsizing or curtailing support for their outdated chaplaincy programs, Wellesley chose a different route. Convening a consultation on the religious and spiritual life of the college, involving trustees, students, faculty, and senior administrators, the college devised a plan to renew its commitment to religious and spiritual life through a multi-faith program. The first act of the college in this direction was to create the new position of Dean of Religious and Spiritual Life, the role of which was not to represent any one religious community, but to design and oversee a new structure that would meet the religious and spiritual needs of students, faculty, and staff, and consider the role of religion and spirituality in the college's overall educational mission. The second part of this charge proved to be especially important, in that it opened a door to reconsider the relationship between religion/spirituality and education, a process that ultimately moved religious and spiritual life from the margins of the institution to a seat at the table in defining how to implement the college's core educational goals.

In my opening address to the College as Wellesley's first Dean of Religious and Spiritual Life, I offered the following words:

> I believe that it is the awakening of a desire for wholeness, in one's self, in one's relationships, among humanity and in all of creation that is the essential task of all spirituality and religion and the essential work of education. In my first few months at Wellesley, I have been truly inspired by the desire of so many people here to incorporate a spiritual component into their lives in this community: students who seek the support of familiar religious experience, other students who explore the possibilities of spirituality beyond institutionalized religion; faculty who see the educating of the mind as inseparable from the nurturing of the spirit; and staff for whom the place in which they work holds the possibility for the development of community. In these first months, I have experienced a genuine commitment to include religion and spirituality in the life and learning of this College.
>
> Now for some, the thought of a College embracing any sort of religious or spiritual component in this day and age strikes fear in their hearts and raises critical not to mention constitutional concerns...and I might say not without good reason, for in the past the mingling of religion and academia has often meant the establishing of a normative religious perspective centered around a single religious tradition. But we are up to something new at Wellesley, something which springs forth from the

rich religious and spiritual traditions of this College and yet something which truly reflects the magnificent montage of religious and spiritual beliefs represented in today's Wellesley College community.

It is my hope that in the years ahead, we will, through the Religious and Spiritual Life Program, nurture a multi-faith environment which truly responds to this rich diversity of religious tradition and experience represented in the Wellesley College community among students, staff and faculty. This means striving to support the spiritual, educational, and worship needs of each religious group on campus, while establishing new ways in which people of all religious and spiritual beliefs can learn about and from one another and thereby begin to discover the common threads which bind us together as people of faith. This I might mention is very different from past interfaith efforts where the goal was most often to establish a kind of common, neutral language and practice, which offended no one but which also quickly became unrecognizable to any person of faith. Our hope is to affirm the integrity of each religious tradition while challenging people to see their own experience as simply a part of some greater whole....

But there is more to this challenge than the support of the religious and spiritual lives of people at this College, for I believe that spirituality far transcends the boundaries of institutionalized religion and is a part of the intellectual, moral and personal development of all people. As an academic institution charged with the task of educating women to fully engage in society, the incorporation of a spiritual dimension to this educational process seems essential. What that means...how that becomes manifest in this community, is the work of discovery that lies before us. There is much in the recent and past history of this College that will inform us in this process. Some of what has come before, we will incorporate into the future. While some things, we will necessarily need to leave behind. For we are attempting something new and yet something old as well. For the roots of this movement towards spiritual wholeness hearken back to the beginning, the beginning of creation...and that which we create here at Wellesley in our day, will, if we do it well, awaken in us the desire for wholeness and help us rediscover a very essential aspect of our common humanity.

And with these words, we began a process of experimentation as to the role of religious and spiritual life in higher education that continues to this day. At the inauguration of Diana Chapman Walsh as Wellesley President in 1993, two ceremonies signified the beginning of a new era of religious and spiritual life at Wellesley. The first was the multi-faith celebration held the evening before the inauguration. Months in the planning by a team that included students from the Baha'i, Buddhist, Christian (Evangelical, Orthodox, Protestant, and Roman Catholic), Hindu, Jain, Jewish, Muslim, Native African, Pagan, Sikh, Unitarian Universalist, and Zoroastrian religious communities, this celebration introduced the community to the implications of the inspiration to multi-faith ecumenism that they had followed. For some, it was the realization of a dream, for others perhaps more of a nightmare, for the door was now opened to deconstruct one hundred years of Protestant Christian-defined college culture and rebuild a new multi-faith community. The next day, at the inauguration ceremonies, President Walsh was presented with the "keys to the College," an historic Wellesley ritual unearthed for this occasion. The three keys, to the library, the dormitory, and the chapel, represent the three historic areas of educational development central to a Wellesley education, the intellectual, the social, and the spiritual. The implication of this ritual embraced by President Walsh was clear. Wellesley was seeking to reclaim its historic values of a holistic education for women that included the spiritual dimension. At that moment, none of us had any idea how significant this process would become for Wellesley and for those outside of Wellesley concerned about the role of religious and spiritual life in higher education.

Space does not permit me to adequately tell the story of the past decade of multi-faith work at Wellesley. Several years ago I attempted this in a chapter in the book Education as Transformation: Religious Pluralism, Spirituality and a New Vision for Higher Education in America.[4] For this chapter, rather than retell the tale in narrative form, I would like to highlight a series of principles that guided our process and in doing so hopefully provide insights that can be used to develop multi-faith programs in different contexts.

1. Ultimately this is about education, not religion.

One of the principles that we discovered only by making many mistakes over many years, was that ultimately questions about the role of religion and spirituality in higher education must start and end with the question "How does religion and spirituality enhance the education of our students?" not the question, "How do we support religion on our campuses?" This is a principle that religious folk often find hard to swallow. But if you can't get past this question, stop! because your efforts will most likely lead to the perpetuating of old dysfunctional processes, not the birth of new constructive ones. For too long, religious professionals working in higher education have spent inordinate amounts of time bemoaning the fact that they feel marginalized on campuses, voicing frustration that faculty members have all the power and nostalgically reflecting back on the good old days when "religion really mattered." Having wasted far too much time participating in these musings myself, I learned my lesson one fall day when a faculty friend clearly tired of listening to my whining about the marginalized state of religion on campus said, "Did you ever consider that maybe it is your job to think about how religion and spirituality fit into education, not ours?" Oops. I sat silent. Fifty years after secular colleges and universities rejected religious control over their educational institutions, I was still carrying the notion that religion and spirituality should be assumed to be an important part of the educational process. This gentle confrontation early in my time at Wellesley changed my entire orientation to the work of religious and spiritual life on campus. What became clear was that a new dialogue was needed as to why religion and spirituality are relevant to education. The first step for us was to initiate a conversation about this question so that we could explore the possibility of a partnership between academics and religious folks working together to enhance our students learning. We found it useful to start such a conversation by reflecting on questions that students are asking about religion, spirituality and education. For example, in a survey of Wellesley students in 1995 these questions emerged.

> "I am a scholar and I am spiritual. Are these two parts of one person? Or I am two people separated from myself by the split in education between mind and spirit?"

---

[4] Kazanjian, Victor and Laurence, Peter, *Education as Transformation: Religious Diversity, Spirituality and a New Vision of Higher Education for America*, (New York: Peter Lang Press. 1999).

"Why must I leave the religious part of myself outside the door of my classes, only to enter and encounter writings of those who were inspired by their religious faith?"

"How can I understand the role that religion plays in the world around me, if I do not have the opportunity to understand the role that religion plays in the life of my classmates?"

"In terms of my religion, I am invisible. My professors, they look at me, see the color of my skin and think they know my story. I am African-American and I am Jewish. How can they see me, if they do not know me? and how can they teach me, if they do not see me?"

To adequately take up questions such as these, educators and religious professionals must come together with students and talk about the relationship between religious/spiritual identity and intellectual development. Academics have long recognized the philosophies and practices of the world's religious traditions as formative in the establishment of various systems upon which societies are organized, including systems of law, governance, education, and other dimensions of the total complex of human relations. However, in most of our colleges and universities the influence of these same philosophies and practices on the formation of individual students has gone largely unrecognized by educators. The role of religious identity in students' lives has most often been separated from the education of students and relegated to religious communities who have set up outposts, (called chaplaincies) on college and university campuses. Often these programs have little relationship to the educational program of their institutions. They are seen by many faculty as vestiges of a past entanglement between institutional religion and institutions of higher education and therefore are looked at as either irrelevant or antithetical to contemporary secular education. While issues of racial and cultural identity are finally being seen as central to a comprehensive understanding of the intellectual development of students, by and large religious/spiritual identity has not been included in these discussions. This, however, is beginning to change.

Researchers and writers such as Beverly Daniel Tatum and Daryl Smith, who work on the impact of identity on intellectual development, have begun to include religion as a significant category of identity relevant to education. In the Spring 98 issue of *Diversity Digest*, Daryl Smith includes religion in her analysis of campus diversity. "...diversity on campus encompasses complex differences within the campus community and also the individuals who compose that community. It includes such important and intersecting dimensions of human identity as race, ethnicity, national origin, religion, gender, sexual orientation, class, age and ability. These dimensions do not determine or predict any one person's values, orientation, or life choices. But they are by definition closely related patterns of societal experience, socialization and affiliation. They influence ways of understanding and interpreting the world." If this is so, if religious identity impacts the way a student understands and interprets the world, then religious/spiritual identity is an educational issue and needs to be taken up as such. Other resources for the discussion of religion, spirituality and education include the work of the Education as Transformation Project based at Wellesley College [www.educationastransformation.org] and the Higher Education Research Institute and specifically their Spirituality in Higher Education project. [www.spirituality.ucla.edu] The first step then to developing multi-faith campus programs is to locate this effort in the larger discourse of enhancing education. This means new conversations among faculty, religious professionals and students.

In 1998 we attempted one such conversation at Wellesley. We gathered a group of Wellesley students and asked them to share stories of "moments of meaning" that they had experienced in their classes. At the time I was searching for a way to make the connection between religion/spirituality and education and struggling with the language to use. As I sat with these students and listened to their stories, their words provided a new language for our discussions. The students told of moments of meaning, inspiration, connection, wonder, and awe in the classroom, and many spoke of these moments as having a religious or spiritual dimension. The classes in which these moments occurred cut across the entire curriculum, from biology to history, from sociology to theater, from ethnic studies to mathematics – story after story of moments when they were awakened to a deeper understanding of themselves, of others around them, and of the world which they described as transformational in some way. One student told of a moment in molecular biology when during a lab when she suddenly made the connection between the smallest forms of life and the largest living ecosystems of the planet. Another student related an experience of working on a psychology project with her mentor in which the faculty member's encouragement of the student's research resulted in them co-authoring a paper and in the students having a sense of herself as being able to have original thoughts. Still another student shared her experience of her political science studies (and her own understanding of the world) coming alive during a winter-session trip to Mexico. Students spoke about transformational moments coming through collaborative work with other students, through service-learning opportunities associated with a course, through an encounter with particular texts, through the mentoring of a faculty member.

The next step was to approach faculty members with the stories told by their students. I e-mailed faculty members telling them that a student in their class had described having a transformational experience, a moment of meaning in their class. I then invited these faculty members to a discussion about such moments in the learning and teaching process. Over the course of the next month, 55 faculty members met to discuss transformational moments in the classroom and shared similar stories with one another about such moments from their own learning and teaching. Eventually the discussion centered on the reasons for their original choice to become a scholar and a teacher. Some spoke of a passion for seeking truth, others of a desire to kindle a fire within their students, many told stories of having been affirmed as a person whose ideas were of value by a faculty mentor in their own life. Many spoke of the joy of watching students come alive in their classes as connections between self and world began to be made.

A meeting between students and faculty to process the experience led to the formulation of central questions that they felt bring religion and spirituality together with education. These questions included: What is the purpose of our learning? What does it mean to be an educated person? What does my learning/teaching have to do with my living? How is my learning relevant to the lives of others? Embedded in the stories told by students and faculty and in their questions is a vocabulary that seems to bridge the chasm between the language of religion/spirituality and the language of scholarship.

2. You've got to be willing to move beyond tolerance.

Perhaps the most profound lesson that we have learned at Wellesley is that tolerance is not the goal that we should seek in forming pluralistic community. In the face of a world punctuated by acts of intolerance, how could tolerance possibly be an unworthy goal for which to strive? After all, throughout history has not tolerance been the goal towards which forward thinking people have worked in seeking to respond to conflict? At a time when tolerance has often been replaced by overt acts of intolerance on our campuses, a little tolerance seems a worthy goal. Our experience (and numerous historical examples) tells us otherwise. Tolerance, as often practiced in our communities, is little more than conflict arrested. While it is a harness applied to the destructive forces of ignorance, fear, and prejudice, and provides a kind of wall between warring parties, at best this is a glass wall where protected people can see one another going about parallel lives. In this condition, people exist less able to harm each other, but also unable to interact, due to the wall of tolerance dividing them from each another. As such, tolerance is not a basis for healthy human relationship nor will it ever lead to pluralistic community, for tolerance does not allow for learning or growth or transformation, but rather ultimately keeps people in a state of suspended ignorance and conflict. Rather than tolerance as a goal, we choose to speak about tolerance as only a first step to interdependence.

A program with tolerance as its ultimate goal is satisfied with tinkering with existing models so that previously disenfranchised students feel a little less disenfranchised. While this may serve to mollify students for a while, it fails to examine both the structural ways in which religious life programs were created to serve particular groups of students (and not others,) and that inter-religious dialogue may be one of the most significant skills that students learn at college in preparation for work in today's multi-religious realities.

The multi-faith program at Wellesley College is entitled Beyond Tolerance. For us this means that in moving beyond tolerance we seek ways in which religious diversity can be a resource rather than a barrier to building multi-faith community. In developing this program, we started with the assumption that to move from a mono-religious community to a multi-religious community would take people from all traditions building new relationships and providing leadership for the college as a whole. This required building two leadership teams: The Religious Life Team of chaplains and advisors: and the Multi-faith Student Council. The Religious Life Team at Wellesley College is now comprised of a Buddhist Advisor, Catholic Chaplain, Hillel Director, Hindu Advisor, Muslim Advisor, Protestant Christian Chaplain, and Unitarian Universalist Chaplain. This team meets weekly with the Dean, not simply to coordinate our work but also to examine together issues of religious and spiritual life that affect the lives and learning of our students. The religious life team meets regularly with other religious advisors on campus such as the advisors to Intervarsity Christian Fellowship, Real Life, and the Mormon student group, so that all religious professionals on campus are in touch and working collaboratively. The group also works regularly in partnership with student life professionals (including residence life staff, counseling services, and cultural advisors) and faculty members interested in supporting the whole lives of students as they go through their college years.

The multi-faith student council is a second leadership group in the beyond Tolerance Program. This group is comprised of students from the various religious traditions on campus. Representation is based on equity of voice not proportional representation (more like the US Senate than the House of Representative.) There may be two Bahai's on campus and 1000 Roman Catholic Christians on campus, but both groups have an equal number of representatives on the council. The goals of the council are as follows:

- to engage in an exploration of the possibility of religious pluralism at Wellesley College as women from different religious and spiritual traditions.

  Religious pluralism in this context is nurturing and celebrating all particular religious traditions and spiritual practices represented in the Wellesley College community and actively engaging this

diversity in ways that build community by exploring the principles that bind us together in a common life.
- to serve as an advisory council for the Dean of Religious and Spiritual Life.
  The council meets regularly with the Dean of Religious and Spiritual Life and convene in times of community crisis.
- to serve as a leadership team, along with the Religious Life Team and the Dean of Religious and Spiritual Life, nurturing the religious and spiritual life of the College. To do this the council should:
  o meet periodically with Religious Life team;
  o participate in the planning of multi-faith community worship;
  o participate in the development of the Religious and Spiritual Life program;
  o plan programs relating to religious, spiritual, ethical issues for the college community; and
  o seek ways to engage communities outside of Wellesley in this work of religious pluralism.
- to act as a liaison between the sending religious community on campus and this multi-faith work. It is essential that each member of multi-faith council have an active and engaged relationship with their own community and its leadership.
- to provide advice on issues related to student religious activities by advising on complaints filed under the code for religious organizations and serving as liaison with College Government and Senate.

The religious life team and the multi-faith student council are the heart of the religious life program at Wellesley College. The relationships that are built and the conflicts that are engaged among members of these groups provide the insight and inspiration for the work that we do. My job is always to facilitate this process and remind them that just sitting in a room together engaging in creative dialogue is a radical act in and of itself.

3. The Protestants are not going to be happy. In fact, no one may really be happy at first. (i.e., This isn't about making people happy!)

When dismantling century-old culturally embedded structures and replacing them with new pluralistic ones, it is likely that no one is going to be particularly happy, (at first and probably for a long time.) When we began the process of restructuring religious life at Wellesley, it soon became clear that everyone was being asked to reconsider their identity in the system. For Protestant Christians this meant giving up privileged status, much of which was invisible to them until it was taken away. Very much like the process of becoming conscious of issues of race, those with privilege are often unaware of their status until it is challenged. Over the years, I have found myself spending a lot of time helping Protestants grieve the loss of their status of being the normative tradition of the college. A few are outraged at the loss of their "Christian College," but quite frankly for most it is a subtler change, a sense of loss of the familiar, a slight disorientation from "so much change." Attending to the very real grief process of this community while at the same time not allowing this to slow down the process of transformation is a role that somebody needs to take up, if this issue is to be addressed.

The second part of this principle is in many ways the most unexpected. One would think that a group that has been marginalized for decades, if not centuries, would heap praises on a process that changes these unjust structures. However, the reality of having a seat at the decision-making table presents new challenges for groups whose identity has been forged as being outsiders for years. Many non-dominant culture groups on our campuses have organized themselves around their marginalized identity (understandably so). It takes time for this to change.

More than a decade after starting this process at Wellesley, we are just now beginning to see real change in terms of people's sense of identity within the community. In part, this has to do with the transitory nature of student populations, but culture change takes time and we have found it best to remind everyone of that a lot. (Another reason why people can find this work frustrating.)

While I am delivering the "bad news" (or perhaps most challenging aspects) about this work, let me offer another principle.

4. Including everyone at the table means more food.

Most of our religious life programs have spaces on our campuses and hold spaces in the budget that reflect old models that serve only particular groups of students. Questions about dividing existing resources or designating new resources can unravel efforts to develop new programs before they get off the ground. Rather than pitting communities against each other over limited resources, we have found it better (although not always successful) to start by considering examples of institutional change within higher education that are somewhat analogous. For example, there was a time when Greek and Latin were the only languages taught in universities. Then a strong case was made to expand opportunities for students to take additional languages because it would enhance their education. German, French, and Spanish were added, then Russian, Hebrew, and Hindi. At no point in the process was the Latin department asked to teach Hindi, nor the Greek department French. We do not ask sociologists to provide the foundations of chemistry in their classes, nor do we ask academic deans to provide psychological counseling for students. In addition, we create spaces in classroom buildings and dormitories that meet the needs of the students in those settings. Therefore, once we have established that religious and spiritual life is in fact an important part of the educational goals of the institution (see principle #1) then providing resources for the staffing and space needs of religious groups on campus should be no different.

Under the leadership of President Walsh, Wellesley College has found creative ways to support religious and spiritual life on campus. From consistent organizational support from senior administrators to fundraising initiatives including the most recent College Campaign in which religious and spiritual life was a priority, Wellesley has stood behind its vision of a decade ago for a renewed religious and spiritual life program through times of conflict as well as celebration.

This leads me to a final comment about our journey towards multi-faith community at Wellesley College that has to with celebration. During the past 12 years, many of the significant moments in people's lives that relate to the religious and spiritual life programs are moments of community ritual and celebration. For some religious and spiritual celebration, it is that small gathering of Muslim or Jewish students gathering for weekly prayer, or the morning Buddhist meditations, or Christian or Hindu scripture study that they will remember as a meaningful part of their overall educational experience. For others, perhaps most, religious and spiritual celebration will be a time when students, faculty, and staff came together to mark a moment of joy or struggle. It is in these gatherings led by the college's spiritual leaders, where people find comfort and community. It is in moments like these, the memorial service for a student or service marking a tragic world event, the multi-faith convocation, or baccalaureate service that celebrate the beginning and ending of a school year, that questions about the importance of religious and spiritual life vanish and we are reminded of the kind of ways in which the search for meaning through our learning and in our lives is a task that requires all forms of seeking.

Take a look at the mission statements of any college or university in the country. Somewhere therein you will find reference to the highest vision of education that enables each student to find creative expression for their thoughts and actions in ways that positively contribute to one's community and the world. This is a goal around which scholars and religious folks alike can rally. The search for meaning in this moment in history needs to be a search that draws upon the diversity of human experience and wisdom. As such, it needs to be a multi-faith search in which the depth of all religious and spiritual understanding is brought together with the breadth of scholarly inquiry. Perhaps then, by forging a new partnership between these two worlds can we adequately engage the internal and external struggles that face our world.

There is a second inscription that is part of Wellesley College's motto. The words are Incipit Vita Novae, translated as "Here begins new life," a motto worthy of the highest vision for the spiritual and the scholarly. In our journey towards multi-faith community, we have begun to sense the creative possibilities that might be born from a new partnership between these two worlds. It has been a good beginning and we are excited about what our second decade of multi-faith community will hold.

12
Buddhist Ceremonies for Higher Education and Related Considerations

Rebecca Nie

Keywords

ceremonies, multifaith, heritage, diversity, precepts.

Abstract

This chapter details the research, adaptation, and officiation of classical Buddhist ceremonies for higher education based on the author's chaplaincy serving the highly diverse Buddhist community at Stanford University. The chapter delves into four key Buddhist ceremonies in shared multifaith spaces and the thought process behind them. It also provides manual-style steps for the ceremonies' programs.

Introduction

Ceremonies are essential for creating a sense of belonging, marking personal spiritual growth, and uplifting a community. The unique needs of college *sanghas* call for rituals distinct from those in congregational settings. This chapter explicates four key Buddhist ceremonies and other high-level considerations for initiating and officiating traditional Buddhist ceremonies for a high-diversity postsecondary institution. The members of postsecondary communities often practice various lineages of Buddhism, and their cultural backgrounds can range from expatriates from traditional Buddhist societies to curious spiritual seekers. Higher education Buddhist chaplaincy is currently at its beginning stages, and many details are still to be hammered out. This chapter serves as one of the early attempts to bring traditional Buddhist ceremonies into higher education chaplaincy. It is natural to expect many changes and adaptations to the ceremonies outlined in this chapter as our collective efforts in postsecondary Buddhist chaplaincy evolve and grow.

The Buddhist ceremonies in English-speaking countries' congregational *sanghas* inherit tremendous diversity in form and historical roots. Buddhists in the U.S., U.K., Australia, and Canada draw from a wide range of racial, ethnic, and socioeconomic backgrounds (Seager, 2012). Some of the earliest traditional Buddhist ceremonies were likely performed at the historical Tam Kung Miao, founded in 1877 in Canada by Chinese expats (Placzek et al., 2006) or with roots in Jōdo Shinshū, founded as the Japanese immigrants began to arrive in the U.S. in the 1870s. Meanwhile, the Theosophical Society's healing ceremonies are just as meaningful for its members, whether or not similar forms have been maintained since its founding in the 1870s by H. Olcott and H. Blavatsky, who took Refuge in Triple Gem in Sri Lanka (Seager, 2012). Continuing in the more recent century, Buddhist temples constantly broke new ground throughout the 1950s (Koppedrayer et al., 2006). *Sanghas* with diverse relationships to ceremonies sprang forth with momentum in Australia (Rocha & Baker, 2011), Great Britain (Bluck, 2006), and all over North America in the nineteen-sixties, fueled by the counterculture movement (Seager, 2012). Buddhist practices and their corresponding ritual landscape in the English-speaking world continued to evolve dynamically throughout the 1990s and into the 21st Century. Much of this history and growth is fueled by dialogues and creative forces from congregational *sanghas* with their roots in traditional Buddhist cultures and those with majority membership departing from their childhood traditions. As members from these communities attend higher education, often joined by international students from traditional Buddhist cultures, the spiritual growth and explosion of practices become even more complex and exciting.

The Buddhist rituals developed in the Western congregational Dharma centers can be of great value when adapted for a college community. As Japanese Soto Zen priest and teacher Peg Syverson explains, "Ceremonies have profound, complex, and mysterious dimensions, and serve many purposes, both in the lives of individuals and the life of a community. Without them, the immense transformational moments of our lives go unrecognized, uncelebrated, unwitnessed, and unappreciated, and a spiritual community can become just a club of interested individuals." After detailing high-level considerations, this chapter explores offering the traditional ceremonies by diving into Buddha Bathing, Refuge in Triple Gem, Five Precepts, and *Kṣamā* (Atonement). Of the four ceremonies, the first two are intended to be welcoming and inclusive of witnesses and participants from other faiths, and they all take place in shared multifaith spaces. The readers will receive a first-hand account of how to adapt generic spaces for Buddhist ritual use and a version of the iconography and liturgical language that is both faithful to heritage and welcoming in the broader cultural context of secular institutions.

The four classical ceremonies have been the cornerstone of Buddhist rituals all over Asia. Many Western *sanghas* also offer them for celebration, initiation, leadership conferral, crisis resolution, and so on. The scopes of these four ceremonies in classical Buddhism are broader than their current applications in many congregational centers. Their teachings all have lesser-known aspects that make them particularly suitable for higher education. The author carefully selects and respectfully adapts these ceremonies to meet the needs of a university community. The chapter provides a comprehensive account of the thoughts and efforts involved in amplifying aspects of these timeless ceremonies to serve higher education organizations.

Planning and executing programs and rituals that connect with the multitude of Asian heritage in a higher education community while remaining welcoming and accessible to those culturally new to Buddhism is a prevalent challenge. The chapter explicates how the Stanford Buddhist community navigates these demands while upholding multifaith pluralism. It provides insights into adapting and facilitating public rituals that honor the spiritual depth of classical Buddhism while being relevant and meaningful within our evidence-based contemporary worldview. It probes into ways to communicate Buddhism's profound compassion and wisdom beyond language at the core of these ceremonies, bridging the gap between their cultural roots and the needs of a generation grappling with pressing issues such as climate change, globalized career paths, and artificial intelligence. While this chapter is based on the particularity of the author's work at Stanford University, drawing on her access to the commentaries of the Chinese Vinaya and training in Korean Zen, it intentionally addresses the broader issues and experiences of ritual in a university context for chaplains with other cultural and lineage background.

This chapter's exploration starts with high-level considerations and guides the readers into ceremony-specific discussions. It devotes one-third of the article to a manual on how to prepare for and conduct these ceremonies. In the appendices, the readers will find lists of material and action items for setting up Buddhist ritual spaces in multipurpose rooms, potentially useful liturgies, and certificate templates. Appendix II provides the ceremonies' program format, which the readers can adapt with items specific to each ceremony to tailor them for their community. Higher education is dynamically evolving, and this chapter hopes to be an open gate for the chaplains serving such communities to probe the possibilities of providing traditional ceremonies for their *sangha*.

Buddhist Ceremonies and Higher Education

Ceremonies from faith-wisdom traditions are familiar offerings at many higher education institutions. For example, the Catholic Church operates at some residential campuses as stand-alone parishes, and organizations such as Hillel International support the religious needs and rituals of their communities at many universities. Following their suit, the expectations and demands for Buddhist chaplains at universities to offer ceremonies are ripe, and it is crucial to craft ceremonies meaningful to specific communities as Buddhism gradually integrates into the fabric of Western society.

Ceremonies are carriers of our vows, dedications, reverence, and much more that are challenging to fully articulate or transmit through other means. Most members of higher education are on a path to conventional, social, and intellectual maturity, and Buddhism offers all practitioners vehicles to radical spiritual maturity. The traditional ceremonies warmly connect the entire community, bridging members from the student *sangha* with sages and ancestors from Buddhist cultural and spiritual history.

Such connections are significant and needed by the postsecondary community in this day and age. At many universities, the students come from all over the country or world to intentionally challenge and expand from their home cultural and intellectual traditions. After their program, they will often go somewhere else. While all of this is a necessary component of education and development, it can create an unarticulated sense of displacement, which is also present in the institution at large, where professors and staff members often also have migrated from place to place in their own academic pursuits. The connecting and grounding qualities of ceremonies can create possibilities to address and transform this into healing openness. The Buddhist ceremonial repertoire contains a plethora of offerings to mark significant occasions and daily sacredness. Selecting meaningful ceremonies for the community and adapting them to be inclusive of the varieties of Buddhist culture present at a university is vital. With all the above in mind, I carefully translated the respective liturgies, adapted the ritual activities, and curated imageries and altar items to respect the community's cultural diversity while remaining authentic to the Buddhist heritage for the ceremonies in this chapter. Before explicating each in the subsequent section, let us explore some strategies that address the concerns and challenges specific to higher education.

The individual attitude toward ceremonies can vary within the same community. While some are drawn to Buddhism or their teachers because of the elegance of ceremonies, some find ambivalence and trepidation toward them. Each individual has a set of Dharma gates that is meaningful and transformational, and any ritual can be a potent practice for some but not others. What comes up while working on the ceremonies are also practice opportunities and Dharma gates for the officiators. It is an important service for the chaplains to face our own nuanced attitude toward them and hold these Dharma gates open for those in need.

A typical attitude toward traditional ceremonies is being overwhelmed. It could be hard to imagine how widespread this attitude is, so let me illustrate with an anecdote. I spent some time at the Dajue Chinese Temple in Bodhgaya, India, and befriended the monks stationed there. One breakfast, the conversation topic turned to the first time they entered the main ceremony hall. As the monks recalled their early days, both bursted out in laughter and self-deprecating humor about their awkwardness and anxiety. If the ethnically Chinese bhikshus stationed in Bodhgaya feel this way, it does not surprise me that anyone with less cultural and institutional heritage in Buddhism might find the traditional ceremonies intimidating.

As officiants, it is important to address this trepidation within ourselves and for the participants and the witnesses. The Chinese monks in Bodhgaya eventually overcame their discomfort by living in monasteries 24/7 and participating in traditional ceremonies daily. Although some university chaplains have experienced that as a part of their training, it's worthwhile exploring some techniques to overcome these feelings for those of us who did not.

A part of the function of all chaplains at Stanford University is to serve in multifaith events in the historical Leland Stanford Junior Memorial Church. Our head dean, Reverend Doctor Tiffany Steinwert, often says, "Remember, we are the only ones with the detailed script. To the participants sitting out there, whatever happened is what is supposed to happen."

The key is to carry on with composure and embody dignity. This reminder helps tremendously in soothing the group's nerves as we form the procession to enter the historical chancel, with the antique altar and decorated by neo-classical art.

While some facilitators find solace in enacting every move in their ceremony as a dance, for those not at ease with performing art, a solid foundation in mindfulness of movement and breathing is an excellent aid. For the chaplains versed in Tantra, their lineage's rich visualization and embodiment practices can serve well as they officiate. In a nutshell, dialing down the afflictions of "I-me-mine," tuning into the participants' collective emotional ambiance during the ritual, and intuitively guiding it along is an excellent way to overcome intimidation.

On the community's side, many can find the multiplicity of iconography, symbol-laden gestures, and the perceived particularities at traditional Buddhist ceremonies overwhelming.

As Buddhist professionals, we inherit a visual tradition from cultures that believe "the gods rejoice in multiplicity" (Wolff, 2021). Centering the setup around one representation of an awakened one and having decorative elements to represent the rest can keep the ceremonies' visual elements accessible to the community and manageable for the officiants. Appendix I details the room and altar setup.

Let us outline some adaptations here. One crucial adjustment pertains to full prostration, the context of which is much more casual in traditional Buddhist cultures than in the West. In the social and cultural environment from which many Buddhist ceremonies originate, the gesture is a way to show respect to elders, teachers, and government ministers. In Western culture, full prostrations often represent a relationship with the highest divine. The membership diversity in postsecondary Buddhist communities also add complexity: while some Asian students might find the ceremony incomplete without full prostration, the gesture can be prohibitive to those with disability or from Abrahamic cultural traditions. We can approach it by respectfully connecting with each participant to explain the traditional Buddhist social context and reassure them that the standing bow is an excellent alternative to embody the same values. During the event, the officiant sets up stations for full prostration and educates the community about these nuanced cultural differences. The same level of attention and care is applied to the figurative images of the Buddha, and we offer a calligraphical representation as an authentic alternative if any participants were to have issues with anthropomorphized imagery.

Another way to help the participants with ambivalence and intimidation is to invite them to set up the room together. During the process, the officiant can patiently explain the symbolism of each element as an educator. Providing a rehearsal to prepare the participants for the ceremonies' embodied practices, such as prostrations, offerings, and so on, can also go a long way. It is often helpful for both participants and witnesses if the head officiant takes it slow at the beginning and explains the symbolism and significance of the upcoming segments in plain English.

The most important preparation is to assure the participants, witnesses, and ourselves that the Buddhas and Bodhisattvas do not judge ceremonial performances or assign grades. Setting an intention of wholehearted respect and mindfulness while supporting each other as a caring community can help everybody practice with whatever comes up during the ceremonies as Dharma gates.

Let us now dive into each ceremony, and the readers can add the content of the event's Ceremony-Specific Manual section to the general program format in Appendix II with necessary adaptations to create meaningful rituals for their community.

The Ceremonies

Buddha Bathing

Buddha Bathing, also known as Vesak, celebrates the birthday of the historical Buddha. It is a lighthearted ceremony on the eighth day of the fourth month and an excellent time for the community to come together and connect in festivity. The Stanford Buddhist Chaplain's Office initiated the annual Buddha Bathing ceremony inspired by the Christmas celebration in the university's historical Chapel. The Buddhist community also has a need to come together, cultivate a sense of belonging, and connect with the global tradition. An international student from Thailand once remarked that this ceremony created a ritual for remembering home, and having it on campus was significant to his well-being. Many more like him attend Vesak as a touch point with the community, and the offering effectively creates a meaningful connection between some cultural Buddhist members and our *sangha* of regular practitioners.

Like all Buddhist ceremonies, Buddha baths plants and nourishes the seeds of *anuttarā samyak-saṃbodhi* [Pāli: *anuttarā sammā saṃbodhi*] (Buswell & Lopez, 2013) and clear our afflictions. It invites the participants to participate and embody inner teachings that are hard to put into words. In the Zen tradition, the baby Buddha symbolizes the beginner's mind and enlightened heart in every sentient being. Pouring water over the statue of the infant Buddha three times symbolizes the cleansing of our body, speech, and mind to clear away the three poisons and let our innate enlightenment shine through. The teaching is that "it's easy to wash away physical dirt but takes more effort to cleanse one's afflictions."

Preparing for Stanford's version of the ceremony, we invite the participants to bring flowers as offerings to decorate the altar together and add fragrance to the water-filled container where the Baby Buddha stands. The community also brings dessert offerings, which will then be shared at the reception after the event.

Refuge in Triple Gem

Refuge in Triple Gem is a non-sectarian ceremony for participants to formally embark on their Buddhist path. It is tremendously rich in creating and strengthening the sense of community and the individual's connection with the global and historical tradition. The Refuge Ceremony is meant to formally affirm the participants' existing practices and dedication to Buddhism and open up new possibilities. It does not turn anyone away from their cultural-ethnic heritage or related spirituality, nor is it for establishing a teacher-disciple relationship with the officiator.

Stanford University is home to a long-running Buddhist community, where a sense of belonging needs to be continually cultivated. By recognizing the *sangha* as one of the three pillars of Buddhism, Refuge in Triple Gem brings up the conversation that we can trust each other and give to each other, even though we are different and most members are in a transient state of life. The ceremony also encourages the members to overcome shyness and become more integrated into the collective.

A student leader initially requested this ceremony for himself, and the Buddhist Chaplain's Office expanded it to a community-wide regular offering. In recent years, an increased yearning to be more "real" as Buddhists has become noticeable from all levels of the campus Buddhist community, including the students, the staff, and the faculty. Real is a loaded term. After many listening sessions, I recognize what the community means is to be more grounded and connected to the traditions and forms we inherit from classical Buddhism. There is also a sense of displacement for the students due to being drawn from all over the world and then shortly going somewhere else, facing an uncertain future. As a result, many want a metaphorical place of belonging that they can take with them wherever they go and draw strength and resilience from it. The Stanford community has members who have been practicing and identifying as Buddhists for years, going from *sangha* to *sangha* without a strong identification with any, partly due to their locational impermanence. A non-denominational Refuge in Triple Gem independent of a Dharma center can serve to formally recognize them as sincere and valued practitioners. In addition to addressing these complex needs, the Refuge in Triple Gem is an excellent vehicle to uplift our campus Buddhist community and assist its members in creating meaningful spiritual homes and way-markers along their Buddhist path.

Education is at the heart of preparing for The Refuge in Triple Gem, and we initiated it with an invitation to the whole community, addressing the sentiments outlined above in broad strokes and welcoming language. Although we presented group studies and one-on-one discussions as equally valuable ways to explore the topic, most participants chose private meeting sessions. Let us dive into the Dharma-interview-style conversations now.

Dharma Interview to Prepare for Refuge in Triple Gem

This section will outline some possible topics to help the chaplains prepare for the educational conversations elucidating Refuge in Triple Gem for their community members. The chaplains can also adapt the content to create group studies if that format resonates with their community.

The meetings typically start with a deep dive into what is the Triple Gem and what is Refuge in them. Like many Buddhist concepts, the Buddha, Dharma, and *Sangha* have manifolds of manifestation and embodiment. Table 1 on the next page provides a pan-denominational view of the outer, inner, and innermost meanings of these three pillars of Buddhism.

By taking Refuge in Triple Gem, the participants formally establish a spiritual home and sanctuary where they can trust to be accepted, loved, and cared for. The outer refuge takes the form of a formal ceremony, regular personal rituals, and the refuge liturgy. The inner refuge is to establish proper śraddhā [Pāli: saddhā]. This first of the five spiritual faculties means faith, belief, and confidence. A meaningful discussion about the nuances of faith in Buddhism usually ensues from here, and it is crucial that the chaplains guiding the conversation have done self-work regarding faith since it could be a loaded practice point depending on the spiritual tradition of their heritage. In Buddhism, the most important factor of proper śraddhā is the confidence that we, like each and every sentient being, have the potential to awaken like the Buddha and transcend all suffering. It is also essential that this belief and dedication to inner growth, self-care, and community care is based on reason and evidence. Śraddhā needs continuous cultivation, typically has its initial formalization at the Refuge in Triple Gem ceremony, and matures at the stream-entry stage (Shengyan, 2015).

Table 1: Manifolds of Triple Gem (discuss and explore outer & inner)

	Buddha	Dharma	Sangha
Outer	• Historical Sakyamuni Buddha.	• Sakyamuni Buddha's teachings and works of subsequent generations of teachers who make these teachings accessible. • Four Dharma Seals.	• The generations of enlightened teachers and Buddhist ancestors. • The Buddhist community: community here and globally.
Inner	• Your inner Buddha. • Awakened nature shared with all sentient beings.	• Teachings and practices that can help you transcend your suffering and attain enlightenment.	• Your teachers, dharma friends, and dharma helpers. • All beings dedicated to Awakening.
Innermost	• Primordial Awakened one, unborn-undying, nondeveloping.	• Boundless and timeless freedom. • Effortless embodiment of full Awakening.	• Inseparable connections we share with the entire ecosystem and universe.

Some key clarifications are that:
1. Refuge in the Triple Gem is non-sectarian. The participants take refuge in the global Buddha, Dharma, and Sangha and their manifolds, not any individual teacher, facilitator, or denomination.
2. The ceremony is non-binding, as the participants will not incur divine wrath if they explore atheism or other religions after part-taking (*Guiyi de Yiyi – Weiheyao Guiyisanbao*, 2018).
3. Refuge in the Triple Gem is an open gate: studying and practicing Buddhism without the ceremony is permissible. In the language of higher education, being a Buddhist without taking Refuge is like being an auditor in a class, whose motivation to study and learning outcome often isn't the same as that of an enrolled student.

Besides "formal matriculation," the Refuge in Triple Gem Ceremony also has additional benefits. It establishes an official connection between the participants and the global Buddhist community and embarks them on the Buddhist path. The ritual of taking refuge can be a beacon as we navigate the challenges on our spiritual path (*Sangui Wujie de Renjian Yiyi 8*, 2014), and as Jack Kornfield explains in *Finding Refuge*, it "can transform our consciousness (2015)." In short, by ceremonially taking Refuge in Triple Gem, the participants can sow seeds of awakening for their entire future as they traverse the *saṃsāric* cycles. It is also a prerequisite to taking Five Precepts. For those open-minded about traditional worldviews, it can also be engaging to mention that the Classical Buddhist texts describe how those who have formally taken Refuge in Triple Gem will not fall into the three lower realms (Khyentse, 2020) and that 36 devas vow to bestow heavenly protection on them (*Guiyi de Yiyi – Guiyisanbao de Yiyi*, 2022).

If the participants' interest continues, this can be a critical point to engage them in some open-ended discussions. A few seed questions can be: what aspect of the Refuge particularly engages you? What challenges in your life and practice could formal Refuge help you address? What actionable ways and personal rituals can you perform to strengthen your refuge to the Outer and Inner Triple Gem? Besides a promise to avoid superstitions, the vow aspect of the Refuge Ceremony is to treat Buddha, Dharma, and Sangha with respect. Asking the students how they plan to bring it to life can be another meaningful discussion question. After the discussion about Refuge, the follow-up steps are to help the participants prepare for the ceremony, where they will have input in finalizing their Dharma names and can invite witnesses. The convention we follow at Stanford is for the participant to provide the officiant with some Buddhist imagery or concept that resonates with them to incorporate into their Dharma names. Since the discussion of faith and faith-switching can be delicate in some social and familial contexts, the chaplains should offer continued support as the participants prepare for their Refuge in Triple Gem while working on the ceremony day, as detailed in Appendix II.

Five Precepts

The Five Precepts (five *śīla*, Pali: five *sīla*) are foundational moral guidelines in Buddhism, and their formal ceremony is administered throughout the Buddhist world. The following version, adapted from Dharma Rain Zen Center, presents the Five Precepts in the traditional abstaining formulation and a positive presentation.

- Do Not Kill – Cultivate and Encourage Life.
- Do Not Steal – Honor the Gift Not Yet Given.
- Do Not Misuse Sexuality – Remain Faithful in Relationships.
- Do Not Speak Dishonestly – Communicate Truthfully.
- Do Not Become Intoxicated – Polish Clarity, Dispel Delusion.

Many Western *sanghas* present the precept ceremony for organizational purposes usually absent in a secular setting, such as establishing a commitment to the lineage and institutional spiritual leadership conferral. However, the scope of the classical five precept teachings is broader and can benefit all Buddhists, especially youths developing into their full adulthood in today's world. Following the *Brahmajāla Sūtra* (Kumārajīva, 406), the Chinese and Korean Mahāyāna tradition mandates qualified preceptors to teach and offer the Five Precepts to anyone asking for them and prohibits the preceptors from interpreting the ceremony as establishing any form of bondage.

Studying and practicing morality, starting with the five foundational precepts, can open the Dharma gates to Right Speech, Right Conduct, and Right Livelihood, integral aspects of the Eight-Fold Path with immense potency when practitioners begin to establish their lifestyles and careers. In many traditional Buddhist countries, where *śīla* is well established, the Five Precepts are intended for anyone interested in having the Dharma encounter and transforming their day-to-day complexity into gates of growth. These moral guidelines taught by Shakyamuni Buddha can help the students discover practice opportunities in their daily routines and transform their unconscious habits into insights.

The many possibilities in the Five Precepts and meaningfully bringing them into daily life are nuanced. For example, the bhikshus from Mainland China disagree with those from Taiwan on specific culinary details only relevant to the diet of Mandarin-speaking people. The precepts, even the monastic ones detailed by Vinaya, have changed little since the time of the historical Buddha. However, how communities embrace them as living practices has evolved, sometimes through downplaying or highlighting specific details in the canon (Groner, 2018). Each traditional Buddhist society has a version that has been debated and worked out for its particular demographics, and the process varies greatly. Some traditions have a *śīla* study and research as an independent career track for monastics (Popkwang, 2010), while others may follow the procedure outlined in the Vinaya (Prebish, 2018) or defer to the nation's justice system (Interview with Shi Chanyu, 2023). The living process is dynamic in today's world and still in its infancy in the West, where morality and ethics are currently undergoing unprecedented changes. To address these challenges and make the Five Precepts meaningful to here and now, the chaplain's office conducted discussion groups and invited participants to explore these five moral guidelines in their daily lives.

Following the model in traditional Buddhist countries, we do not have retreat hours or group meditation as a prerequisite for precept studies. Meanwhile, the facilitators of Five Precept studies and ceremonies must have received at least the next level of precepts for over five years. For instance, some of these next-level precepts are the Eight Precept in Theravada Buddhism or the Ten Precepts in Mahayāna Buddhism. The demographics of those attracted to *śīla* often differ from the members who frequent meditation. The precept studies groups we have conducted attracted members from traditional Buddhist cultures and law school at a higher proportion than other activities.

The subsequent section centers on conducting precept discussion groups and encouraging participants to bring these moral guidelines and reflections into their daily activities. The students can participate in a three-meeting or five-meeting discussion group designed to make the *śīla* practice available to those with different levels of academic demands. This chapter details the five-meeting discussion group, and the readers can adapt it for their *sangha*. Generally, each meeting starts with a short meditation and progresses to checking in with the participants. Then, the facilitator can present the session's content and invite the participants to discuss it with mindful listening and whole-hearted speaking. The meetings conclude with reading the list of Five Precepts and optionally a one to two-sentence expose of each precept following the facilitators' particularity.

The facilitators can start the first session with open questions such as "What draws you to explore the precepts?" and "How do you hope it might change your practice and day-to-day interactions?" If authentic to the precept teachers, it can inspire the students to share personal anecdotes about the facilitators' relationship with one or a few precepts. It can also help to touch on how precepts and commandments differ in a lighthearted manner and stop there since the full exploration of this comparison fuels many academics' careers. During the first meeting, it is critical to clarify that, as Charlotte Joko Beck puts it, "precepts aren't simply 'Thou Shall Not' rules, which can be harmful. It is instead about choice, responsibility, and being awake to the motivation and consequences of our actions (Baker, 2022)." Precepts are moral guidelines for ourselves, as "signs above the door that encourage us to enter and explore the blind spots in our thoughts, feelings, and actions (Rizzetto, 2012)." These inner dimensions of the precepts made ever-deepening insights possible, so there is little wonder why the pan-denominational teachings present *śīla* as the cornerstone of cultivating concentration, wisdom, and enlightenment.

The second meeting dives into the nuances of practicing with the precept. The Chinese and Tibetan traditions present four states in the practitioners' relationship with each precept:
1. Observing is where one acts and lives according to the precept.
2. Concealing is where the practitioner acts against the precept due to misunderstanding or circumstantially acceptable reasons.
3. Opening is where one acts against the precept for the greater good.
4. Violating is when the practitioner acts against the precept for reasons other than 2 or 3.

For example, when working with the No-Stealing precept, if someone takes an item, mistaking it as a gift or his/her own, or because the item is grouped with waste items, it is considered a concealing of the precept and not violating it. The same goes for temporarily borrowing something reusable, like scissors, and then bringing it back before the owner needs it. An illustration of the opening state is if the practitioner steals the weapons to prevent a fight from turning lethal. We live in an age of rapid lifestyle and worldview changes, so it is skillful for educators to elucidate these high-level principles of precept practice and encourage the students to create and analyze case studies based on their daily lives.

Kṣamā [Pāli: khamā] is the topic of exploration in the group's third meeting. We all make mistakes amidst the complexity of real life, and this meeting addresses the teachings about that fact. We practice Buddhism to cultivate our innate wisdom, unleash our fullest potential, and transcend all suffering. Falling into denial or becoming bound by endless guilt is not beneficial to this intention and should not be an outcome of the precept practice. As the Kwan Um School of Zen says, "Every human being makes mistakes. From a Zen point of view, the question is how clearly we see our mistakes and how we can correct them (Kwang & Arnold, 2011)." The Middle Way is to transform our mistakes into growth opportunities by seeing our mistakes, take responsibilities, and avoid them moving forward. According to the students' feedback, the teaching and ritual of Buddhist kṣamā is so powerful and relevant that this chapter structures it as a stand-alone ceremony in the next section. Those who received precepts should add śīla reading to their kṣamā ceremony.

Each precept item is also worthy of exploration, and the participants will explore one precept item per session in the five-meeting format. The first session is an excellent time to explore the precept on No Killing – Cultivate and Encourage Life. Many conversations about this precept go into vegetarianism, but topics such as abortion, war, and genocide can also surface. It would be wise to prepare for the full range of possibilities according to their community and tradition and not shy away from the uncertainties and side-step richness open discussions can present. Instead, they can guide the group to deepen their reflection on "Do Not Kill" with suggested readings and bring mindfulness about this precept into their daily life until the subsequent meeting. Using no-stealing as an example of the four states of precept practice segues into exploring the second precept. Since the discussion of sexuality and related conduct can be highly personal, our office structures it at the end of the rich discussion on kṣamā and offers one-on-one conversations by request to respect the participants' privacy. The fourth and fifth precepts on speech and intoxication can quickly get complex with our updated understanding of substances, addiction, and neuroscience, compounded by new technologies such as instant messaging, social media, and psychedelics. We devote the entire fourth and fifth meeting to the case study and discussions of these precepts.

Śīla and Right Conduct are at the foundation of any Buddhist path. Each Buddhist denomination has its wealth of teachings on the topic in addition to the canonical, paracanonical, and non-canonical vinaya (Cozort, et al., 2018). *Vinaya Piṭaka* is the undisputable source of this topic, and each denomination also has contemporary resources the chaplains can draw on to structure study groups authentic to them. The particularity of Stanford's Buddhist Chaplain's office is Zen, and we lean heavily on Nancy Mujo Baker's *Opening to Oneness* (2022) and Diane Eshin Rizzetto's *Waking Up to What You Do* (2012) to support the precept studies here. For chaplains who want to explore precept teachings in other traditions, *The Noble Eightfold Path* by Bhikkhu Bodhi (2000) and *Treasury of Precious Qualities* by Kangyur Rinpoche (2001) are excellent resources in the Theravada and Tibetan traditions.

Kṣamā (Atonement)

Atonement is a translation of *kṣamā* (pronounced *kshamaa*), which some also render as repentance or confession in English (Muller, 2012). However, all three renderings carry Christian connotations that make them inadequate in summarizing the practice and ceremony rooted in a value system foundational to many lifetimes-long practices in classical Buddhism, the supporting worldview of which is outside of this chapter's scope. Nevertheless, the Kṣamā Ceremony and its teachings can be powerful for transforming many generational and social justice issues currently miring the college community.

Even without a deep dive into the karmic cycles and reincarnation, kṣamā is centered around responsibly facing difficult past and challenging present circumstances, internal and external, and transforming them for wisdom and healing. For example, we offered an introduction and group practice of kṣamā as a part of Stanford Associated Religion's inaugural Day of Prayer event in "in light of the current time of global violence, death, and grief (Stanford Report, 2023)." Many college-age individuals are at a loss regarding paramount challenges such as climate change, the country's colonial and human-owning past and its contemporary consequences, and violent global conflicts. Many young people courageously take on these issues personally and emotionally, often coming from a position informed by guilt, shame, anger, and overwhelm. Holding these, in addition to academic, professional, family, and personal challenges, can take a significant toll. These unprocessed sentiments, among other issues, can make an individual or group channel it in destructive ways and add to the volatility of youth communities. As college-serving professionals, we must uplift the young people we work with and help them untether their creative and healing potentials from these emotional sinks for humanity's brighter and more sustainable future.

Bearing the mark of Buddha Dharma, kṣamā is about transforming these circumstances and the afflictions that arise alongside or even cause them, allowing everyone involved to see and respond with wholesome intentions and wisdom. Many Western sanghas already offer kṣamā. Zen centers from the Japanese lineages have the four-line kṣamā excerpt from Avataṃsaka Sūtra (Śikṣānanda, 699) in their regular liturgies. Many communities embrace group ceremonies or retreats as a part of their crisis resolution process. The power of kṣamā and the resilience and healing that comes from it can be leveraged for young adults.

This chapter presents a version of the Kṣamā Ceremony crafted with that intention and audience in mind. Respecting the private and challenging nature of guilt, family history, and personal history, our initial attempt was to offer kṣamā as a program for individual or small group practice. After group studies of the ceremony program and its implications, the students agreed that it will be meaningful practice and can have tremendous potential for their communities, even the non-spiritual members.

Conclusion

Rituals like celebrating Buddha's birthday, taking refuge, and other life ceremonies are essential to sangha growth and community building. This chapter delves into higher-level considerations and specifics of making these ceremonies available to higher education. Expanding the author's work at Stanford University, it hopes to offer a toolset that can benefit all the Buddhist chaplains from cultural and lineage backgrounds as diverse as the traditions currently present in the English-speaking world. The demographics and culture at postsecondary institutions are highly dynamic. Therefore, the content in this chapter calls for adaptation and frequent updates to be practical and relevant for each college. Planning and executing programs and rituals that connect with the multitude of Asian heritage in higher education while remaining welcoming and accessible to those culturally new to Buddhism can be challenging. The chapter outlines some initial attempts to provide ceremonial services and related teachings to a college sangha and hopes to provide a conversation starter for university Buddhist chaplains to continue the efforts started here.

Appendix I: General Altar and Room Setup

This section details how to set up a portable altar to facilitate the ceremonies in a multipurpose room available at secular institutions.

Item List
- Representation of a Buddha (calligraphical or figurative, consecrated). Images on a scroll like thangkas can be convenient to carry and save tabletop space, but they might need a portable easel if the room doesn't provide hanging options.
- A table to serve as the altar.
- Any sutra to represent the *Dharmakāya Śarīrā*.
- Specific for Precept: a mirror to represent clear discernment.
- Altar decoration: 2 flower arrangements, 2 vases, 2 plates of fruits, 7 candles, tablecloth, portable speaker (optional).
- Ceremonial items: incense and holder, bell, cups, glass water vessel, certificates.

Altar Setup
- <u>Back</u>: Representation of a Buddha.
- <u>Under</u>: tablecloth underneath.
- <u>Middle</u>:
  - Sutra, optionally supported by a book stand on each side.
  - For the Precept Ceremony: the mirror.
  - 7 candles.
- <u>In front</u>:
  - 2 plates of fruits flanking the sides.
  - Incense, flanked by flowers in vases.
  - Water cups.

Room Setup
- Altar at the back.
  - For Buddha bathing, station with a consecrated baby Buddha in the basin 3 feet in front of the altar. Optionally, line with a towel and an additional tablecloth.
- Participants' zabuton/zafu seats are symmetrically arranged.
- Officiator location:
  - Zabuton/zafu seat centered in the middle of the participants' seating.
  - Standing by the water station if providing water offerings or certificates.
  - Bell station to the side, away from the audience's view.
- Witnesses and the community sit in chairs with a walkway in the middle.
- Portable speaker on the side and play light Buddhist music (optional).

Appendix II: Ceremony Programs

Opening Rituals
1. Prepare the Altar.
2. Doors open to the broader audience.
3. Welcome Speech: outline the rituals and explain their symbolism
4. Opening Bell 3 times.
5. Invocation of The Three Precious Ones from 10 Directions (facilitator, solo)
6. Participants present offerings such as candles, incense, and water.
7. Asking Buddhas, Bodhisattvas, and indigenous deities to be our guides and protectors. (Together)

Ceremony-Specific Rituals

Buddha Bathing
It is essential to explain the significance and symbolism of each ritual activity during the welcome speech of this multifaith ceremony.
1. Participants form a line. The officiant is at the head of the line to demonstrate and then moves to the side to ring the bell after each person has poured the water 3 times.
2. Participants take flower petals with their right hand and put them in the water basin.
3. Participants use their right hand to pour water over the baby Buddha 3 times while paraphrasing the symbolism of their action in their own words, out loud or in silence.
4. Participants return to their seats.

Refuge in Triple Gem
There will be non-Buddhist witnesses at this ceremony, so paying particular attention to explaining the significance and symbolism of each ritual activity during the welcome speech will serve well.
1. Prostrations, allowing adaptations.
2. Participants and the officiant chant Homage to Triple Gem facing the altar.
3. Participants line up, facing the witnesses. The facilitator hands participants refuge certificates, "___ with dharma name ___ (meaning), welcome to the global Buddhist family."

Five Precepts
A ceremony for the students to formally take the Five Precepts is offered at the end of the five or three-session exploration period if they commit to living accordingly for the rest of their lives. In addition to generic ritual items, the precept altar features a mirror representing clear seeing. To keep the whole program coherent, the facilitators of the study groups (precept teachers) will ideally be the officiants in this ceremony if their traditions grant them authorization. If it is aligned with their tradition, the precept teachers can also hand out the precept robes to the participants and teach them how to put them on before the ceremony.
1. Homage to The Triple Gem Together
2. Group Read the Verse of *Kṣamā* together, all facing the altar.
3. Receiving Precepts.
   o The precept teacher reads each precept out loud, and the group has the following exchange at the end of each precept.
   <u>Precept teacher</u>:
   Can you keep this precept or not?
   <u>Precept Receivers</u>:
   Yes, I can.
4. (Optional) Receiving the Five Precept Robes.

The precept teacher moves to the standing round podium, facing the room.

We go for guidance from the Holy One, the Buddha, who delivers freedom from unwholesome states to all sentient beings.

We inspire to bring all sentient beings into the bliss of the peaceful abiding beyond arising.

We who still suffer and are not yet freed from our desires, aversions, and ignorance.
May we cast off these three poisons and enter into peaceful abiding beyond arising,
And by doing so, fulfill our greatest inspiration.

Each precept receiver comes forward one by one, receives their five-precept robe, and returns to their seats.

<u>Precept teacher:</u>
Great are you who understand the impermanence of this world.

You have renounced the conventional realms of instinctual desires and their fulfillment.
You are entering into nirvana, an event hard to conceive of and rare in this world.

How exalted, the robe of liberation, a symbol of embodying the highest good.

We now receive it, and may we receive it perpetually,
Going forward, life after life.

5. Prostrations, allowing adaptation. Precept receivers stand up, wear their five precept robes, and do nine prostrations at their seats. The precept teacher rings the bell once after each set of three prostrations.
6. Receive the Precept Certificates
   o After the last of the ninth prostration, the precept receivers remain standing, walk to the precept teacher in a single

file, receive their precept certificates, return to their seats, sit down, and wait for the others to receive theirs.

Kṣamā (Atonement)
1. Homage to The Triple Gem
2. Begin *Kṣamā*:

Recite the Verse of Kṣamā *(3 times)*

Place your palms together and recite the following with utmost sincerity:

I, _____, now being mindful of my actions, speech, and thoughts, I commit myself to observe this Day of Reflection with the following practices:

I, _____, for the coming day(s), commit to not-knowing by giving up fixed ideas about myself and the universe. I commit to mindfully listening to the joy and suffering of the universe, including myself. I commit to compassionately taking the actions of no harm that arise from not-knowing and mindful listening.

Personal Retreat
1. Write down the issue(s) instigating the *kṣamā* retreat and place it on the altar.
2. Alternate prostration/standing bow practices (3, 9, or 108 times, depending on physical fitness) and sitting/walking meditation with appropriate breaks between sessions.
3. Write down your reflections on the paper(s) with the issue(s) written and burn it at a fire-safe place.
4. 4Chant the Vajrasattva 100 Syllable Mantra (optional).
5. Prostration/standing bow practice (3, 9, or 108 times, depending on physical fitness).

Group Retreat
Set up a circle of chairs/meditation seats behind the mat in front of the altar.

1. The person(s) making the apology approach(es) the altar (one after another) and prostrate(s)/bow(s) three times.
2. The group conducts a council regarding the issue(s) instigating the *kṣamā* retreat.
3. The group alternate prostration/ standing bow practices (3, 9, or 108 times, depending on the group's average physical fitness) and sitting/walking meditation with appropriate breaks between sessions.
4. The group conducts another council reflecting on the day of *kṣamā* and the issue(s) instigating the retreat.
5. Chant the Vajrasattva 100 Syllable Mantra (optional).
6. The person(s) doing the apology approach(es) the altar and prostrate(s)/ bow(s) three times.

Closing Rituals
1. Four Great Vows together.
2. Dedication of Wholesome Deeds.
3. Short closing remarks and invite participants to a reception.

Appendix III: Kṣamā Liturgies

The classical liturgies for *Kṣamā* may not be widely available, so the author has translated and adapted the Verse of *Kṣamā* following from the *Avataṃsaka Sūtra* (Śikṣānanda, 699) for the Five Precept and *Kṣamā* ceremonies and have a transliteration of the Vajrasattva 100 Syllable Mantra here. Depending on the context, the practitioners can change the pronouns to reflect a group, a nation, a race, or all sentient beings.

Verse of Kṣamā
All twisted karma ever committed
  since time immemorial,
Because of beginningless desires,
  aversion, and ignorance,
Arising from body, mouth, and
  thoughts,

I now practice *kṣamā* for it all.
All transgressions arise from the mind and heart,
And I practice *kṣamā* through my mind and heart.
The afflictions cease,
When the *śunyata* of the *citta* is attained.
Only that is the real *kṣamā*.
I vow to be released from the transgressions
By attaining this twin Emptiness.

Vajrasattva 100 Syllable Mantra

oṃ
vajrasattva samayam anupālaya
vajrasattva tvenopatiṣṭha
dṛḍho me bhava
sutoṣyo me bhava
supoṣyo me bhava
anurakto me bhava
sarvasiddhiṃ me prayaccha
sarvakarmasu ca me
cittaṃ śreyaḥ kuru
hūṃ
ha ha ha ha
hoḥ
bhagavan sarvatathāgatavajra
mā me muñca
vajrī bhava
mahāsamayasattva
āḥ

Om
  [the supreme expression of praise]
Vajrasattva, keep your samaya.
Vajrasattva, remain near me.
Be steadfast in your care of me.
Grant me unqualified contentment.
Enhance everything that is noble within me.
Look after me.
Grant me all accomplishments,
And in everything I do
Ensure my mind is virtuous.
Hum
  [Vajrasattva's wisdom mind]
Ha Ha Ha Ha
  [the four immeasurables, the four empowerments, the four joys, and the four *kāyās*]
Hoh
  [What joy!]
Blessed One, who embodies all the *tathāgatas*, Vajra(sattva),
Never abandon me!
Grant me the realization of vajra nature!
Great samayasattva,
I am one with you.

Bibliography

Baker, N.M. (2022). *Opening to Oneness: A Practical and Philosophical Guide to the Zen Precepts*. Shambhala.

Bluck, R. (2006). *British Buddhism: Teachings, Practice and Development*. Routledge.

Bodhi, Bhikkhu. (2000). *The Noble Eightfold Path: Way to the End of Suffering*. PBS Pariyatti Editions.

Buswell, R. E. & Lopez, D. S. (2013). *The Princeton Dictionary of Buddhism*. Princeton University Press.

Cozort, Daniel, & Shields, J. M. (2018). *The Oxford Handbook of Buddhist Ethics*, Oxford Handbooks.

Dharma Drum Mountain. (2018). *Guiyi de Yiyi – Weiheyao Guiyisanbao*. Dharma Drum Mountain – SF. https://www.ddmbasf.org/zh-hans/%E4%B8%BA%E4%BD%95%E8%A6%81%E7%9A%88%E4%BE%9D%E4%B8%89%E5%AE%9D

Dharma Drum Mountain. (2018). *Guiyi de Yiyi –Guiyisanbao de Liyi*. Dharma Drum Mountain – SF. https://www.ddmbasf.org/zh-hans/%E7%9A%88%E4%BE%9D%E4%B8%89%E5%AE%9D%E7%9A%84%E5%88%A9%E7%9B%8A

Digital Dictionary of Buddhism. (n.d.). Chanhui. In buddhism-dict.net Dictionary. Retrieved November 1, 2023, from http://www.buddhism-dict.net/cgi-bin/xpr-ddb.pl?q=%E6%87%BA%E6%82%94

Foguang Shan (2014, October 14). *Sanguiwujie de Renjianyiyi* (8). Foguang Shan Taipei. https://www.fgs.org.tw/fgs_download/D40200/2014100010.PDF

Groner, P. (2018). 2. The Bodhisattva Precepts. In *The Oxford Handbook of Buddhist Ethics* (p. 29-49). Oxford: Oxford University Press.

Khyentse, D.J. (2020). *Living is Dying: How to Prepare for Death, Dying and Beyond*. Shambhala.

Kornfield, J. (2015, May 11). Finding Refuge Part Two. *Jack Kornfield Blog*. https://jackkornfield.com/finding-refuge-part-two/

Kumārajīva. (406). *Brahmajāla Sūtra*. CBETA T1484.

Kwang, H. & Arnold, A. (2011). *Dharma Mirror: Manual of Practice Forms*. Kwan Um School of Zen.

Longchen Yeshe Dorje, Kangyur Rinpoche (2001). *Treasury of Precious Qualities: A Commentary on The Root Text of Jigme Lingpa Entitled The Quintessence of the Three Paths* (Trans. Padmakara Translation Group). Shambhala.

Matthews, B. (2006). *Buddhism in Canada*. Routledge.

Popkwang Sunim, (2010). *Korean Buddhism*. Bulkwang Publishing.

Prebish, C.S. (2018). 5. The Vinaya. In *The Oxford Handbook of Buddhist Ethics* (p. 96 – 115). Oxford: Oxford University Press.

Rizzetto, D. E. (2012). *Waking Up to What You Do: A Zen Practice for Meeting Every Situation with Intelligence and Compassion*. Shambhala.

Rocha, C. & Barker, M. (2011). *Buddhism in Australia: Traditions in Change*. Routledge.

Seager, R.H. (2012). *Buddhism in America: Revised and Expanded Edition*. Columbia University Press.

Shi Shengyan (2015). *Zhengxin de Fojiao* (Traditional Chinese Edition). Fagu Wenhua.

Śikṣānanda. (699). *Avataṃsaka Sūtra*. CEBETA T10n0279.

Stanford Report (2023), *Stanford's multifaith community observes a Day of Prayer*. https://news.stanford.edu/report/2023/11/29/stanfords-multifaith-community-will-observe-day-prayer-week/

Wolff, C. (2021). *Beyond: How Humankind Thinks about Heaven*. Riverhead Books.

Part III
University Systems

Part III: University Systems
Introduction

Within Hua Yen Buddhism, the powerful image of Indra's Net is used as a way to develop Nagarjuna's teaching on emptiness.

> This illustrates how the many things interpenetrate like the realm of Indra's Net of jewels…. The pure body illustrates how all things simultaneously enter each other…. This imperial net is made all of jewels: because the jewels are clear, they reflect each other's images, appearing in each other's reflections upon reflections, ad infinitum, all appearing at once in one jewel, and in each one it is so…. Because in one jewel there are all the other jewels….[1]

Within the net of beads that comprises university systems, the Buddhist chaplain can provide essential spiritual care by lifting up the systemic interdependence of the campus community. This is a healing intervention, given the different silos (departmental, geographic, employment status) which contribute to academic stratification. Working intentionally to build relationships across campus communities, reflecting back the innate clarity and wholeness within the system, is a path to restoring that hidden wholeness.

Roshi Zoketsu Norm Fischer expands the web of life through a Baccalaureate speech delivered at Stanford University in which he transgresses conventional expectations of this genre. "Today you fall out of heaven," Fischer reminds students, "It is not going to be so easy to survive your promising life." Success may take more from us than is expected, despair or discouragement will visit. There will be questions for which years of study have not prepared an answer. (To provide students with an existential question on this day of celebration is grandmotherly kindness, by Zen standards.) So then, if graduation is not, in the final analysis, a resolution of the mystery of life, what can we do – When we face the unfathomable, "the only thing that makes sense and that is completely real is love." To commit oneself to love, it is helpful to find a spiritual practice. Spiritual practice is not goal-oriented, it does not help us to actualize our best version of ourselves. It reconnects us with the source, serving as a thread of meaning that reaches before and beyond the self, through which we can discern the way through the mystery.

Matthew Weiner has created a secular ceremony that identifies and celebrates the invisible work that weaves connections of wholeness across the university campus, through a program called "Hidden Chaplains." When entering the dining hall one day, he noticed that the dining hall clerk knew each student and made contact with them in kind and meaningful ways. These moments of connection were experienced by students as transformative. Weiner shares a story of the Dalai Lama's visit to Princeton, in which the community is brought to reflect upon its shared humanity. Through that process of self-reflection, the blessing of compassion which has always been pouring forth is illuminated, newly revealed. In that sense, this process of identifying Hidden Chaplains is a contemplative intervention:

---
1 Cleary, 2000, pp. 58-59.

the search itself sparks gratitude, vulnerability, openness and awareness of interconnection.

Henry C.H. Shiu supports a wider vision of interdependence through careful consideration of the chaplain's function within Canadian university systems, which have been influenced by shifts in immigration policy and the increase in student services. As Shiu notes, "the modern university chaplain's role is multifaceted, extending beyond traditional religious counseling to encompass broader spiritual, ethical and community-oriented functions." The challenges facing contemporary Canadian Buddhist chaplains include the use of Christian-centric terminology when serving a religiously diverse community, the need for a campus chaplaincy association, the need for fully-resourced positions, and the need for chaplains to advocate for their relevancy in an increasingly secular world.

Jonathan Makransky reminds us not to leave ourselves outside of the circle of care. Even as we see that the self is not solid, but continually changing, and contingent upon non-self elements, the needs of this (provisional) self for nourishment and care are absolutely real. As chaplains hold space in transformative times, and traverse complex campus systems, the meeting of self-care needs is the path to the radical interconnectedness of systemic care.

As we bring intentionality to the mutuality with which we in the West enter the path of Dharma, awareness of the social-cultural patterns of relationship is essential. Kusa Mayerhofer writes of the need we have to engage in mindfulness training through examination of the samskara of cultural identity, so as to relate with respect, gratitude and mindfulness to Asian heritage Buddhism and heritage Buddhists.

One aspect of this systemic servant-leadership of chaplaincy is the multifaith work through which we recognize the wisdom found within other spiritual traditions and work together to support the spiritual life of the campus as a whole. By so doing, as Victor Kazanjian notes, we are preparing students to live equitably in a pluralistic society, with the skills to navigate conversations of difference. As we find ways as a campus community to resolve religious conflict, these skills in conflict resolution will then make it possible to live sustainably within our increasingly interconnected – and interdependent – world. Dean Kazanjian's work cleared a path for all of us who are integrating spirituality into higher education. There are certain key principles that Kazanjian identified, to guide these processes of multifaith work in higher education. First, it is our job to reflect on the way that religion and spirituality enhance education: no one else on campus bears that responsibility. Second, we need to move beyond mere tolerance of religious difference to active appreciation of, and engagement with, religious diversity. Third, culture change takes time and will not make everyone happy. Finally, the increase in multifaith activity means that more resources must be made available, so that communities are not required to compete for access to funding, space or other necessities.

Nathan Michon provides us with skillful means for strengthening the campus community's wellbeing through nonviolent conflict resolution that is anchored in right speech, deep listening, explorations of values and circle process. During these transformative times, it is not possible to avoid experiencing conflict. However, as Michon notes, by exploring points of stress and suffering, and releasing these factors, we broaden our overall awareness of the community as a web of interdependence. He offers us these guiding words, "May all beings in conflict find the ways to use that energy to unbind the violence within and around them, and may we listen to these stories in ways that assist them in that process."

13
How to Survive Your Promising Life: A Baccalaureate Address

Zoketsu Norman Fisher

Stanford University, June 14, 2014

Good morning, everyone. I am honored to be here this morning with all of you. It is, literally, awesome to see – a sea, an actual sea, of waving faces. I have no idea why I am here, but I feel quite lucky to have the chance to reflect, to muse, to ponder with you at this important moment in your lives. A moment is a moment.

It is a long while since I have been a university student. I enjoyed that time in my life immensely. It was full and it was exciting, a time almost completely devoted to study and exploration of life's big questions, with a little fun thrown in, and powerful friendships, and, yes, a certain amount of misery and angst. College is a privilege, but it is not necessarily the easiest time of life. As with all other times of life – but perhaps even more so – there are highs and there are lows. I hope today you are feeling the high.

But time passes and you forget. These days when I go to university campuses, which I do from time to time, I feel as if I were in heaven. I imagine that heaven must be exactly like a university campus – everyone young and healthy, spending their time in social and intellectual pursuits, flowers in season, the trees well trimmed, the lawns manicured, the buildings more or less matching and clean. A university is by definition a place of promise – and students are promising individuals – you perhaps more than most because Stanford is more than just another university; it is a great and storied university that, these days, seems to be at the center of the universe. Because of what you have received – not only from Stanford, but also from your families and friends, who have given you a lot of love and support – you now have the skills and the connections – and the obligation – to do great things. And this means not only great things for yourselves: You are expected to do great things for others, and for the world. We all have high hopes for you, probably higher hopes than you have for yourselves. Let's be honest – as much as we discuss and practice wise punditry, we older people don't really know what the world will require in the coming times – and we are a bit bewildered, and unsure, though we hate to admit it. To grow old is to gradually cease to understand the times in which you live. So we are placing our trust and our hope in you. No pressure, of course. But the promise of the future really is yours.

And yet the truth is, it is not going to be so easy to survive your promising life. For one thing, there are a lot of promising young people out there – not only here at Stanford, or here in California, here in the United States, but also in Europe, in China, in Latin America, all over Asia, and in India, and Africa – some of you in fact *are* those people – bright, energetic, and mobile. With so much competition, and so much anxiety about that competition, it is possible that success, if it comes, will not come easily. It is also of course possible that success will not come – or that it will come, abundantly, but that you will not find it as meaningful as you had expected. It is also possible that success comes, and you do find it meaningful and satisfying – but only at first, when it is still bright and shiny. And that later, the state and pace and social implications of the successful and ambitious life you will have lived will wear you down, and you'll find yourself tired and bewildered.

It's also possible that as time stretches on your personal relationships will not work out as you had hoped, your sense of yourself will not hold up to scrutiny, that there will be disappointments and setbacks, acknowledged and unacknowledged – in short, it is possible, even likely, that there is some pain awaiting you as you go forth from this bright day – ruptured love affairs, betrayals, losses, disillusionments – seriously shaky moments. It's possible too that, as you move through the decades, it will become increasingly difficult for you to maintain the idealism and the hopefulness you have today. It's possible that one day you will find yourself wondering what you have been doing all these years, and who you have become. It's possible the life you wanted and have built will not be as you'd expected it to be. It's possible that the world you wanted and hoped to improve will not improve.

Anyway, you will keep busy, you will have things to do. And you will try not to notice such feelings. You will try to deny any despair or disappointment or discouragement or boredom you may be feeling two, five, ten, fifteen, or twenty years from today. And probably you will be able – more or less – to do that. But only more or less.

I am sorry to say all these things to you on such a wonderful day and in such a beautiful place as this.

I realize that baccalaureate speeches are supposed to be bright, uplifting, and encouraging. The folks at Stanford who invited me to speak today sent me links to previous baccalaureate talks so I would know how they usually go. The speeches I looked at were wonderful – they were serious about challenges ahead – but they were always positive. So, yes, I too intend to say something bright and encouraging. But I thought I would be more convincing if I were also realistic. And it is realistic to say that your lives from now on are likely not going to be entirely smooth sailing. The skills you'll need to survive may be more than or other than the skills you have been focusing on so far in your life. The truth is, it takes a great deal of fortitude and moral strength to sustain a worthwhile, happy, and virtuous human life over time in the world as it actually is.

OK, here is the uplifting part:

Your life isn't and has never been about you. It isn't and has never been about what you accomplish, how successful you are or are not, how much money you make, what sort of position you ascend to, or even about your family, your associations, your various communities, or how much good you do for others or the world at large. Your life, like mine, and like everyone else's, has always been about one thing: love.

Who are you, really? Where did you come from? Why were you born? When this short human journey is over, where are you going? Why – and how – does any of this exist? What is the purpose and the point of it all?

Not even your Nobel Prize-winning professors know the answers to these questions, the inevitable, unavoidable, human questions. None of us knows the answers. All we know is that we are here for a while before we are gone, and that we are here together. The only thing that makes sense and that is completely real is love. Love is the only answer. This is no mystery – everyone knows this. Whether your destiny is to have a large loving family or to have no partner and no family – love is available to you wherever you look. And when you dedicate yourself to love, to trying your best to be kind and to benefit everyone you meet – not just the people on your side, not just the people you like and approve of, but everyone, every human and nonhuman being – then you will be OK and your life – whatever it brings, even if it brings a lot of difficulty and tragedy – as so many lives do – as even the lives of very privileged and promising people sometimes do – your life will be a beautiful life. As I promised, this is uplifting – or at least I hope you find it uplifting.

But there's more. *How* do you love? *How* do you make love real in your life? This doesn't happen by itself. It takes attention, it takes commitment, continuity, effort. It won't come automatically, it won't come from wishing or from believing or assuming. You are going to have to figure out how to not get distracted by your personal problems, by your success or your lack of success, by your needs, your desires, your suffering, your various interests, and keep your eye on the ball of love even as, inevitably, you juggle all the rest of it.

To find and develop love you have to firmly commit yourself to love. And you have to have a way, a path, a practice, for cultivating love throughout your lifetime, come what may. Love isn't a just feeling. It is an overarching attitude and spirit. It's a way of life. It's a daily activity.

In my life I have cultivated love through a path of spiritual practice, a life of meditation and study and reflection. I think you also will need a path of spiritual practice. You also will need some kind of religious life if you are going to survive this difficult human journey with your heart intact and your love generous and bright.

A spiritual or a religious life doesn't need to look like what we have so far thought of as a spiritual life. The world now is too various and connected for the old paths to work. Not that the old paths are outmoded – they are as useful today as they ever were, perhaps more so. But they need to be re-formatted, re-configured, for our lives as they are now. And above all, they need to be open and tolerant, transparent and porous rather than opaque, and expansive rather than exclusive. A spiritual life can and should be much more lively and various and interesting than we have previously imagined. To investigate at the deepest possible level the human heart and the purposes of a human life that is essentially connected at all points to and with others and the planet Earth can be – and should be, maybe must be – deeply engaging and satisfying. There are a million ways to approach it. But the main thing is, I think, that you need some commitment, some discipline – and you need a regular practice, something you actually do.

The most important characteristic – the defining characteristic, I would say – of a spiritual practice is that it is useless. That is, it is an activity that has no other practical purpose than to connect you to your heart and to your highest and most mysterious purpose – a purpose that is literally unknown, because it references the unanswerable questions I mentioned a moment ago. We do so many things for so many good reasons – for our physical or psychological or emotional health, for our family life or economic life, for the world. But a spiritual practice is useless – it doesn't address any of those concerns. It is a practice that we do to touch our lives beyond all concerns – reaching beyond our lives to their source.

For me that practice is and has been for a long time sitting in silence. That's a good one; maybe it will also be good for you. I certainly recommend it to everyone – regardless of your religious affiliation or lack of one. But there are many others. Prayer, for one. Whether or not you believe in God you can pray. You can contemplate spiritual texts or art, poetry, or sacred music. You can walk quietly on the Earth. You can gaze at the landscape or the sea or sky. And there are many other such useless practices you can devise or invent.

You could practice gratitude – when you wake up every morning, as soon as you put your feet on the floor from bed, sitting on the side of the bed you can close your eyes, be quiet for a minute, and say the word "grateful" to yourself silently, and just sit there for a moment or two and see what happens. You could practice that right now….

Or you could practice giving – always making the effort to intentionally say a word or offer a smile or material or emotional gifts that confer blessings on another person.

Or you could practice kind speech – on all occasions, even difficult ones, committing yourself to speaking as much as you can in kindness and with inclusion of others and their needs, their hopes and dreams. Not just speaking from your own side.

Or you could practice beneficial action, committing yourself to intentionally acting with a spirit of benefiting others, of being of some use to others, in whatever way you can, even stupid ways that seem not to be useful or beneficial but could be if you intend them to be. For instance, you can practice benefiting others by wiping sink counters in public restrooms, or in your own kitchen. Wiping counters with a spirit of beneficial action – with that thought in your mind intentionally – can be a daily spiritual discipline. Or you can cook a meal with love for others, with a spirit of benefiting others. Even if the meal is for yourself, you can benefit yourself with the good food, that you paid close attention to when you prepared it, because one's self, truly and kindly understood, is also another.

Or you could practice identity action – recognizing that when you do anything, whatever it is, you are not, and cannot, do it alone, by your own power. Inevitably whatever you do involves others and the whole world, this Earth we live on, its life-giving sunlight and plants and animals. So that every action we ever take involves others and a world of support. You could notice that whenever you do anything.

Or you could practice compassion – going toward, rather than turning away from, the suffering of others – and your own suffering too. We all want to avoid pain, to make it disappear. But when it's impossible to make the pain disappear you can go toward it rather than running away – you can become softened by it.

I could go on and on. Spiritual practices are unlimited – and they are imaginative. And – especially – full of love. They come from love, they encourage love, and they produce love. When you do them over time you find that you are living in a world full of love. And for your life and for our lives collectively in the times to come we are going to need love – lots of love. In good times, love is lovely. Nothing can be better. And in hard times, love is necessary. It turns tragedy into opportunity – something difficult and unwanted becomes a chance to drive love deeper, to make it wiser, fuller, more glorious, and more resilient.

A while ago my friend Fenton Johnson, who is a wonderful novelist and writer and professor of literature, and a lifelong spiritual practitioner – and who is sitting in the audience today! – sent me an email about this talk. He wrote, "If I were giving such an address I'd talk about the mystery of life, how one can and should lay great plans, but how life has its own ebb and flow, and our first duty is to be present to that ebb and flow, to realize that failure and success are social conceptions that can be useful but that in their conventional definitions have little to do with what really matters, which is the study and practice of virtue." As Timothy Kelly, who was abbot of Gethsemani Monastery, Thomas Merton's monastery in Kentucky, said, "How one lives one's life is the only true measure of the validity of one's search."

The Beat poet Philip Whalen was my dear friend and teacher. Like me, he was also a Zen Buddhist priest. As a poet and a spiritual practitioner, he couldn't do anything other than search. His genius was that he could express the seriousness of his search while maintaining not only his sense of humor and play – but also a clear and sane knowledge that the whole thing is actually as ridiculous as it is tragic. Here is a poem of his, written in the 1960s:

TO HENRIK IBSEN

> This world is not
> The world I want
> Is Heaven
> & I see
> There's more of them
> *

I've seen most of this world is ocean
 I know if I had all I wanted from it
 There'd still not be enough
 Someone would be lonely hungry
    toothache
 All this world with a red ribbon on it
 Not enough
 Nor several hells heavens planets
 Universal non-skid perfection
    systems
Where's my eternity papers?
 Get me the great Boyg on the phone.
 Connect me with the Button Moulder
    right away.

So please do seriously think about it – but not without some joy and some lightness. Today you are closing the door on one life and opening the door to another. Today you fall out of heaven. Where will you land? What will you do there? What is really worthwhile and what is just distraction – however much people tell you it is not? You are the only one who can ask and answer these questions.

So I am saluting you this morning – you and the wonderful life of promise you have lived up to this moment, and the new life of challenge and difficulty and passion that you are entering. Cheers and congratulations.

14

Hidden Chaplains: A project for Buddhist seeing and reflection

Matthew Weiner

Introduction

Hidden Chaplains is a project based at Princeton University that invites students to identify those people on campus who change their day in small but meaningful ways through routine interaction. Importantly they are not their fellow students or professors or senior administrators or even professional counselors, but rather the dining hall worker, secretary, or facilities staff who smile at them, ask them about their day, know their name, engage in small talk for a moment. Students "nominate" a hidden chaplain by reflecting on their interaction and its meaning. All nominees are invited to a dinner with the student nominators, and in turn are invited to bring their own hidden chaplain, with the notion that they too have people who change their day in a similar way.

Hidden Chaplains was not explicitly organized as a Buddhist program, and I am not a traditional Buddhist chaplain, and yet the program can serve as such: both as a creative way for Buddhist student communities to explore specific ideas and practices, and as a means for engaging the wider religiously plural and secular community as Buddhists.

With this in mind, the present chapter will be organized into four parts. *Part one* will describe how *Hidden Chaplains* was was developed and carried out, with the hope that Buddhist chaplains might implement the logistics and ideas for themselves. *Part two* will provide the larger context of the project and the Buddhist thinking in which it was implicitly situated, which speaks to Buddhist pedagogy, principles, and practice. *Part three* will offer examples of how the project might serve for deeper Buddhist practice for Buddhist student groups, drawing creatively upon Buddhist concepts. *Part four* will explore how *Hidden Chaplains* provides a way to engage in Public Buddhism, and how doing so relates to other forms of service, social justice, DEI, and mental health initiatives.

1. Background Story

I am a chaplain at Princeton University. One day I was swiping in at the Whitman College Dining Hall for lunch when I started talking with the clerk who oversees student entrance. As we talked, I noticed that the clerk interacted with every student who came through: they greeted each other by name and had small and often personal exchanges. What was taking place struck me as both ordinary and remarkable. I also realized that the clerk was in many ways doing my job.

The next day I shared the story with Kyle Berlin, an undergraduate senior whom I met with regularly in the mornings along with my three-year old son Louis. In those days I spent an hour each morning before work technically began with Louis who in this phase of his life was especially interested in the new roof being put on our building and in those doing the work. So these early morning chaplaincy sessions often revolved around interaction with roofers, questions about various pieces of equipment, learning their names, and the particular tasks taking place that day.

When I told Kyle the story of my dining hall encounter, he smiled and said, "That's

Catalina," and then named a few others who did the same thing for him in other parts of campus – the secretary of his academic department for example. As we reflected on my encounter with Catalina, we realized that most every student at Princeton had a person or two who served this informal, almost hidden, and yet precious role in their lives.

After our conversation, we gathered a group of students who could help us explore the matter further. They called themselves the Informal Committee to Investigate Hidden Chaplains, and established the above format that would include both a venue for public acknowledgement and celebration, as well as the opportunity for serious reflection. With little effort, students nominated hidden chaplains – and they came to our dinner, dressed up, with their loved ones. It was something we had not anticipated. Students shared openly about how their hidden chaplain had made them feel at home and assured them that someone cared, and chaplains shared back: how they hardly noticed what they did, or conversely how their lives were given meaning by their opportunity to be kind to those who passed by.

Such relationships, however particular in each telling, were nearly a universal part of any student's experience. Students smile and often say the name of their hidden chaplain upon being asked if they have one. While their encounters were so very small, informal, and hardly noticed, they were, upon spontaneous recognition, deeply meaningful. It was something that they rarely, if ever, talked about. The overarching themes gathered by the informal committee included the following: Why did staff apparently commit regularly and throughout their days to a practice that was not part of their job description? What did these encounters say about the nature of informal interactions, kindness, and the experience of students and workers on campus?

2. Seeing and Engaging Compassion

This is how *Hidden Chaplains* was developed. In this section I provide as a kind of "how to" story: how I met Kyle, my student conversation partner, and how our shared thinking might teach something about the nature of compassion in a way related to Buddhist ways of attending.

Three years before Kyle and I met to reflect on Catalina, our office had hosted His Holiness the Dalai Lama at Princeton. We had selected one hundred and fifty students who engaged in service to meet with him. We guided them not to 'try to sound smart,' but to ask a question from their heart. We explained that His Holiness was very smart and knew a lot of smart people and was not so impressed by intelligence but was instead drawn to sincerity. When the Q/A period came, I handed the microphone to a student I did not know, and his question hit the mark. Your Holiness, how do we get people to care, when so many of us are caught up in ego and selfishness?

The student was Kyle, and in this encounter he was a freshman. His Holiness' answer came after a long sigh. I have been asking myself this question for over seventy years, he said. And I do not know. Was it a way of sharing Kyle's dismay, that two highly intelligent beings, aware that all their smarts were useless in this arena? I have tried argument and I have tried rules, His Holiness continued, and they do not work. I think all you can do is to have kindness in your heart, to work to have kindness, and to hope that such kindness sparks it in others.

When Kyle and I came upon hidden chaplains, we reflected back on this question about the compassionate university and our interaction with the Dalai Lama. We were struck by what we found. His Holiness had laid out two failed strategies for developing compassion, first in logistical argument and then in rules, that might work well for creating other moral structures (say justice). He landed on a third strategy of developing one's own compassion.

The first and second strategies might be called forms of utilitarian and consequentialist ethics, and the third a form of virtue ethics (developing particular virtues for character development).

But our project appears to be something else altogether. We had, by accident, noticed that compassion was taking place and *we had noticed the response to noticing*. Then, almost by accident, we designed a strategy that triggered those involved in these micro actions to see and appreciate them. The world is cluttered with anger and greed, or your day is boring; a question is asked ("Who is your Hidden Chaplain?"), and you smile. You remember that you encounter kindness by virtual strangers, and it is something that has always been there. Compassion is revealed as it unfurls. It permeates the world, as we notice and share in reflection. And from all this, we learn more, and in ways we cannot predict.

This strategy of seeing, designed in reflective response to noticing an encounter and how something emerges from it, does not make me compassionate. Nor does it ask or argue for others to be compassionate, nor does it make programmatic or policy decisions about compassion for the institutions we work for based on committee work or statistical findings. Instead, it simply draws attention to the compassion that is already unfolding. This creates the opportunity for reflection, which seems often to trigger appreciation, gratitude, vulnerability, and openness to the experience of encounter.

3. As Buddhist Contemplative Practice

Hidden Chaplains can be understood as a service, gratitude, or community building project (in somewhat standard Higher Education Institution accounts) but the focus of this chapter is on its contemplative nature. With this in mind, the suggested approach to *Hidden Chaplains* as a Buddhist contemplative project is simply to help students organize it, and then reflect upon it, asking what was noticed or learned in a general sense, and to do so as humans and Buddhists, and to see what emerges. This allows the Buddhist chaplain and their students to figure out the value and meaning for themselves, following the Buddhist principle of practice for self-understanding and liberation among friends. What any given Buddhist chaplain and their students will uncover has yet to be found: it will always be as unpredictable and as valuable as the next group, or what this particular author-chaplain has to offer below. This is because it is in the practice itself that the real work and community building happens. By reflecting on the unique context, that includes the hidden chaplains and the encounters students have with them, the learning experiences that we require will amplify and deepen.

An alternative approach is to lay out concepts ahead of time or to have them at the ready as students happen upon them. This way what they are learning about can easily relate to important Buddhist ideas, often in ways that are different from how they directly appear in scripture, tradition, or the study of Buddhism per se. What follows are just a few of the ways that emerged in our own reflections intended both for students who are keenly interested in Buddhism and for the general college student. They are sketches of what might be considered the opposite of declarative statements on the topic.

Alternative Metta *Practices*

When it comes to the idea of hidden chaplains, an obvious connection to Buddhist principles is that of the *brahmaviharas* (divine abodes) and in particular to metta (loving kindness). The better translation of metta as friendliness is well suited for the oreintation that tends to accompany hidden chaplains. The connections here are at once obvious, and worth exploring more deeply. For example, the divine abodes tend to be understood in terms of meditative practices that we take on for ourselves and others, and thus the term *mettabhavana* (mental cultivation of *metta*) for how *metta* is practiced. But in this case we are instead very specifically sensitizing ourselves to someone else's *metta*. This strategy has some connection to the larger tradition because it is understood that one can feel or tune into another's *mettabhavana*; and in some schools of thought the compassionate nature of the universe. When the Buddha or other *arhants* practice *mettabhavana* it becomes something tangible for us to attend to. What is taking place with the encounter of hidden chaplains is related to but distinct from this. To begin with it is not necessarily the 'great metta' of a recognized deep spiritual practitioner, and it may very well not be kindness that was directed or intended in a particular way. It is, rather, the spontaneous and fleeting kindness of an ordinary person that a student notices.

But also, the student is invited to notice kindness and reflect upon it, as opposed to carefully develop this kindness themselves. The process might thus be called a kind of *mettasati* (awareness of *metta*) and *mettanupassana* (contemplation on *metta*); and as such it can be extended to other divine abodes such as *karunanupassana* and *muditanupassana* (the contemplation of compassion and sympathetic joy). Traditionally such practices of *sati* (awareness/sensitivity) and *anupassana* (contemplation) are designated for investigating specific aspects of the individual practitioner (such as body, feeling-tones, mind) or phenomenon (*anicca, dukkha, anatta*). Here, however, attention is simply directed to see or sensitize oneself to kindness in the world, which will lead naturally to reflection upon it. Likewise, the invitation is done by asking a question, as opposed to an instruction or command ("Who is your Hidden Chaplain?"). The idea here is that spontaneous seeing, free from identity-based calculation, can take place. What seeing with less intention and identity-creation has to do with deeper Buddhist practice is itself an issue well worth exploring.

Whether taken discretely or collectively, considering these ideas together is surely one way to participate in the *brahmaviharas*, (or perhaps this too could be a question for students). True, it does not follow traditional meditation methods. But such an exercise might point to the reality that these are in fact realms or dwelling places as they are called (*viharas*) as opposed to a narrower understanding of them as identity-based virtues for us to develop. And this further insight can come from the exercise at hand which forefronts a reciprocal relationship. If I notice kindness wherever I see or feel it through the day, without judgment or calculation about intentions or power structure, I suddenly find myself participating in a realm infused by kindness that is not controlled by anyone, and one that I help shape by my sensitivity to it.

Bodhisattva Relationships

Traditionally we think of the Bodhisattva ideal (both as a vow that a regular courageous human takes on, and as celestial beings to be venerated) as propelled by the particular intention to save all beings from suffering. Intention shapes the mind for nothing less than heroic act of releasing all beings from suffering. The designation of hidden chaplains is quite different from a Bodhisattva in terms of status, practice, and intention. Their kindness tends to be experienced as informal, occasional, uncalculated, and momentary, and there is no reason to think their concerns are sotereologically salvific. Drawing this comparison assumes a distinction of measure, and yet it tells us something important about the nature of hidden chaplains and about the nature of compassion itself outside of religious and heroic ideals.

Put another way, if the Bodhisattva is a manifestation of the compassionate nature of the universe, then the endless specks of kindness we experience in a multitude of ways are as well. What draws us especially to this kind of manifestation is its normalcy, its lack of apparent sacredness, its effervescent quality.

Supports and Gratitude

When seeking Buddhist models of kindness, our instinct is to look to the great model of the Bodhisattva, but within Buddhist narrative literature it might be the hardly noticed individuals whom over lifetimes feed and care for the Buddha that are most closely affiliated with the compassionate sensibilities of a hidden chaplain. According to tradition, the Buddha walked through endless lifetimes to find ultimate peace, and as he did so he was fed by countless beings whose identities will forever be lost to us; beings who fed someone in need of food, most often without recognition outside of the one being fed. An important exception to this anonymity is of course Sujata, the farmer's wife who offers the future Buddha a glass of milk at the moment of his death-starvation, a gesture that leads to his enlightenment. The Buddha to be needs the help of others, regardless of his remarkable qualities. But also, we are witness to a regular act of kindness by someone, and though the scripture says her intention is to receive a blessing, we can also understand it as a regular human helping another, and in so doing she helps the whole world. This moment is central to the Buddha's story, but here it reminds us of all the all but endless beings who fed him along the way. They were all involved intimately and selflessly in the Buddha's liberation which then in turn helps us all. Endless hidden chaplains.

Friendship

The idea of hidden chaplains is related to notions of *kalyanamitta* (spiritual friendship), in the sense that it is takes place outside of one's own practice and agency. I cannot choose to make a friend. Instead, friendship happens to me or with me. I find myself naturally liking someone and wanting to be their friend: when the feeling is mutual, friendship is there. In a similar way, I do not choose to find a hidden chaplain, rather when the question is asked, the hidden chaplain is *revealed to have been there*. Something has happened outside of my full awareness, intention, or understanding. Likewise, the hidden chaplain does not know they are a hidden chaplain until provoked to notice by being nominated by a student.

Friendship is central to the Buddhist path, and we can learn something else from the model of *Hidden Chaplains*, because they are not central to us. What do we learn by decentering instead of centering, as a strategy for seeing? Indeed, this manifestation of kindness and support at least appears to be incidental in ways that may elude the standard matrices that accompany issues of control and identity.

Let's say that hidden chaplains are not friends: they are more circumstantial and ephemeral, they need not be privy to our private stories or grief, their relation to us is defined in a particular work-a-day way. Drawing this contrast between personal friend and hidden chaplains within the affinity that already exists is another way to deepen Buddhist practice.

4. Public Buddhism as Public Religion

Hidden Chaplains can be created and explored within a Buddhist student group as we suggest above, and it can be planned simultaneously or exclusively for the general public by a Buddhist student group. In this case it would become a form of public religion or what we might call public dhammology. There are two easy ways to think about this.

First one could think within Buddhist terminology and see the hidden chaplains project as a vehicle for *upaya* (skillful means by which to teach the *dhamma*). Public religion is traditionally understood as an aspect of one's religion that is made understandable for the public. Often the particularity of the religious tradition's ideas are present but in the background or else articulated in more secular terms for the purposes of accessing a wider audience. Perhaps the most known example of public religion in the United States are the Catholic Social Teachings, in which the Catholic Church, through encyclicals and Catholic Charities, explains itself and serves the wider public in very secular terms, and yet the justification behind the scenes is explicitly based in traditional Catholic Moral Theology. Another example are books by His Holiness the Dalai Lama, and conversations such as the one he had with us, that argue for compassion without making explicit references to Buddhist philosophical ideas around the nature of the universe. In this way hidden chaplains can be both implicitly Buddhist (as they might be implicitly Catholic for example) for the larger public and explicitly Buddhist for those Buddhist chaplains seeking a program through which to explore Buddhist ideas.

A second way to include the wider public is to be explicit, instead of invisible, about one's Buddhist perspective by convening an interfaith dialogue around the question of hidden chaplains. How does kindness manifest itself in small but meaningful ways from the perspective of different faith traditions? One way to explore this came about from another part of the story. When this program was covered in *The New Yorker*, Keith, one of the *Hidden Chaplains*, clarified that he thought angels were helping all around us, we just ordinarily could not see them. Keith is a Christian, and the student who nominated him is Muslim who also believes angels and Jinns are often helping us in ways we mostly cannot see. Every religious tradition maintains that mysterious compassionate beings help us in ways that we can rarely see and never fully understand. The guidance we receive from non-material spheres, ephemeral or embodied, is a potent focus and could be a prompt for an interfaith conversation as a way to further explore our religiously diverse perspectives about kindness. In any case, *Hidden Chaplains* taken up by religiously diverse chaplains would greatly deepen our shared sense of the theological histories of how compassion is seen and experienced, and would be a boon to our public understanding.

A third way is to see the project in engaged Buddhist terms. Though students have responded with spontaneous appreciation to *Hidden Chaplains* and the program was an overwhelming success, there was also some low key suspicion from those most concerned with social justice. Is compassion and appreciation enough? There is structural injustice in institutions born of capitalism, one version of the critique goes. Does appreciation, formally recognized by a wealthy employer, merely reinforce the structural inequality? Instead of being kind, which involves a certain condescension (so the argument goes), why not fight for better wages for those who serve you?

These questions were asked or implied and they are a good opportunity to reflect on the nature of justice work within an institution and what engaged Buddhism has to say about it. More broadly what does it mean to be a chaplain in the face of activism that we may or may not personally align ourselves with? Along-side the embodied qualities of chaplaincy and friendship, and the social moral value of encounter, we might work toward developing a Buddhist version of this question for ourselves, as Buddhist chaplains who help Buddhist student groups. While *Hidden Chaplains* is not an engaged Buddhist program in a standard way, it does very quietly create new relationships across class lines. It is also a project about seeing and the response to seeing. Maha Ghosananda, the Buddhist Patriarch who led peace walks in post-war Cambodia famously encouraged Cambodians to listen carefully for the peace that was growing. For Ghosananda, this listening was the crucial first step in engaged Buddhist work. As Charles Hallisey has noted, when it comes to contemporary institutions of higher education, perhaps it is more in helping us "to see" better than in giving guidance about how "to act" one way or another that Buddhist ethics can be at its most efficacious.

Conclusion

The hope of this chapter is that describing and reflecting on hidden chaplains can in some tiny way help others practice and forge their college-based Buddhist ministry. Asking new questions as a way to conclude might help move this along. Here are three that come to mind.

What does Buddhist chaplaincy look like in a secular university context that is religiously diverse and likely has an eclectic Buddhist population? Does the answer change when we recognize that, from the perspective of the institution, issues of belonging and mental health are at the forefront? One dramatically successful answer has been the mindfulness movement. A regular and important critique of secularized mindfulness is that while it emerges from Buddhist meditative practices, it misses important and complementary aspects of Buddhism. Reconfiguring mindfulness practice to address another aspect of Buddhist ethics altogether, such as the nature of kindness and gratitude, is a strategy worth exploring.

More broadly what is the face of chaplaincy in the paradox of a religiously diverse student population housed in a secular institution? Institutions by nature focus on measurable outcomes, but chaplaincy is about the invisible work, as Rabbi David Leipziger Teva has said. It is by nature *appameyya*, not measurable. The standard American model of college chaplaincy centralizes availability and listening with an open heart, and providing religious education for students of that particular faith. This story suggests that a chaplain's responsibility is also to listen and direct attention to the kindness that is around them in ways not performative or scripted and in ways not unrelated to caring about justice in the world. In this way *Hidden Chaplains* provides an example of an alternative mode of chaplaincy – one that emphasizes the value of learning with students by attending and responding to their lived experience. This brings to mind what the Russian Philosopher Mikhail Bakhtin considers central to dialogical ethics: response as a necessary and integral aspect of listening from a unique human perspective. In this case the response manifests itself programmatically, with pastoral care coming through the work and reflection itself.

Finally, what would a compassionate American university look like and what can Buddhist chaplaincy within universities do to help us to begin to see answers this question? This will always be just a fanciful and experimental question, but it might help draw connections between the intimate spiritual practice we engage in as a small minority religious community and the institutions that we shape as we are shaped by them. A small project like *Hidden Chaplains* can help us think creatively about the relationship between diverse actors within institutions and where compassion emerges.

In my own contemplative investigations, such responses seem to spring from the mirth we experience upon first realizing that kindness swirls all around us, and that it does so despite the law of suffering and stress that we all also live under, according to Buddhist tradition. Kindness is an endless and endlessly fascinating human impulse, drawing us ever more intimately and caringly along the way.

15
Canadian Chaplaincy: A closer look at the distinctive role of Buddhist chaplains

Dr. Henry C.H. Shiu

I. Development of University Chaplaincy in Canada

In the aftermath of the Second World War, Queen's University initiated a tradition of annual fundraising campaigns to aid students whose education had been disrupted by the conflict. This initiative was led by The International Student Service (ISS) under the guidance of its then Chairman, Roy Patterson. In 1945, during a meeting of the Executive Committee, Patterson delineated the upcoming year's plan, which included the appointment of Major Rev. John Ronald Leng as the veteran's advisor at the University (*Queen's Journal*, 5). Rev. Leng, an alumnus of Queen's University who earned a Bachelor of Arts degree in 1935 and a Bachelor of Divinity degree in 1938 (*The Queen's Review*, 185), was a minister in the United Church of Canada and had served as a Canadian military chaplain during the war. His role, formally titled Advisor to Ex-Service Personnel, was principally to provide advice and counselling to veteran students.

Two years later, in 1947, a transition occurred with the appointment of Rev. Dr. A. Marshall Laverty, as the successor to Rev. Leng. Laverty's position was renamed "University Chaplain," a title he held for an impressive tenure of 36 years, until 1983. This marked the inception of university chaplaincy in Canadian universities, a pioneering development in higher education. Rev. Laverty, like his predecessor Rev. Leng, was a minister in the United Church of Canada and had enlisted as a military chaplain in 1942. The contributions of this first Canadian university chaplain were subsequently recognized when he was made a member of the Order of Canada in 1985.

The appointment of Rev. Laverty by Queen's University is not only a testament to the evolution of university chaplaincy in Canada during the 1940s but also reflects the shifting spiritual needs of Canadian students in the post-war era. Dr. Robert Charles Wallace, who served as the 11th Principal of Queen's University from 1936 to 1951, played a crucial role during one of the university's most tumultuous periods, which spanned the Great Depression and the Second World War. In 1946, Principal Wallace persuaded the university trustees to institutionalize the role of a chaplain as a permanent staff position (McDowall 2016, 342), a decision likely influenced by the support and services provided by Rev. Leng,

Queen's University, originally established as "Queen's College at Kingston" in 1841 with the objective of training clergy for the Presbyterian denomination in Canada (Morrow 2022), underwent significant transformations over the years. Its affiliation with the Presbyterian Church ceased in 1912 following the Canadian government's decision to withdraw financial support for religious higher education. This led to a change in the institution's name to Queen's University at Kingston and the establishment of a separate Queen's Theological College, which continues to provide theological education. This arrangement persisted until the theological college's centenary in 2012, after which admissions were suspended and the program was ultimately merged with the Department of Religious Studies in 2015.

The evolution of the university chaplaincy at Queen's University can be considered a microcosm of the broader shifts in Canadian society, particularly in terms of secularization and the growing religious diversity among the student population. This diversity was not limited to the traditionally dominant Presbyterian values but included a significant representation of Catholics, Jews, and other faiths. Principal Wallace, understanding the varied spiritual needs of his students – particularly in the postwar context with approximately 1,900 veterans on campus and the sombre reality that over 60 did not return from the war – envisioned the chaplaincy as a role transcending religious guidance to become "a friend and counsellor to students" (McDowall 2016, 343).

Rev. Laverty embodied this vision with remarkable aptitude. Known affectionately as "the Padre" within the Queen's community, a nod to his wartime service as a chaplain in Europe, he became a staple figure on campus. His approachability and understanding nature made him not only a spiritual advisor but also a mentor for students grappling with the myriad challenges of campus life. Rev. Laverty's chaplaincy skillfully balanced religious and secular elements, while maintaining a sensitivity to the multi-religious fabric of the student body. This approach laid a foundational model for the establishment of university chaplaincy across other Canadian universities.

The broader Canadian context of the late twentieth century, marked by the introduction of a points-based immigration system in 1967 and the official embracing of multiculturalism in the 1970s, led to a significantly more diverse religious and cultural landscape. By the early 1980s, while Protestant, Catholic, and Jewish voices remained prominent, the presence of Muslim, Hindu, and Buddhist students – largely from immigrant backgrounds – became increasingly noticeable. This diversity sparked a contentious debate at Queen's University from 1979 to 1982, particularly around the religious elements in convocation ceremonies.

Proponents of change advocated for a more inclusive approach, mindful of the non-Christian student body and in alignment with the secular neutrality mandated by the 1962 Ontario Human Rights Code (McDowall 2016, 348). However, Rev. Laverty advocated for the retention of traditional Protestant rhetoric and rituals. The eventual compromise reached in 1982 was indicative of a deeper realization within the university: the need to adapt to the multicultural and pluralistic values of Canadian society. This necessitated a re-evaluation and renewal of the university chaplaincy's role, aligning it more closely with the evolving demographic, religious, and cultural landscape of the student body and nation at large.

As the 1980s unfolded, the approach and worldview of Rev. Laverty began to be perceived as somewhat outdated, reflecting an unintentional paternalism and a sense of comfort with the status quo that some found to be exclusive and overly deferential to the established culture at Queen's University (McDowall 2016, 344). This perspective was indicative of a growing need for a chaplaincy model that moved away from Christian hegemony, thereby addressing the increasingly secular and religiously diverse needs of a new generation of students. This evolving context set the stage for Rev. Brian Yealland, who succeeded Rev. Laverty. Yealland envisioned the chaplain's role as one akin to a spiritual ombudsman, fostering religious pluralism and dialogue on campus. During his twenty-one-year tenure, from 1983 to 2013, Yealland endeavoured to redefine the role of university chaplaincy. His responsibilities included officiating at significant university events, such as convocations, providing assistance and support to students and staff in times of family or campus crises, and offering non-denominational counselling and support to all members of the Queen's community. This approach was distinctly non-sectarian, moved beyond the Protestant-centric model, and embraced the norm of multiculturalism.

Similar transformations also occurred in

other Canadian universities. For example, the University of British Columbia introduced a "Multifaith Chaplaincy" in the late 1980s, which emphasized representation from multiple faith groups without any specific inclination towards Christian traditions (Sherwood 2020). The University of Victoria's Interfaith Chapel – originally a joint ministry of Catholic, Anglican, and United Churches in the 1970s – expanded in the 1980s to include events such as "Learning to Meditate, Catholic Mass, Muslim Prayers, Yoga Mindfulness Meditation, Ecumenical Holy Communion, Zen Meditation, Sacred Ecology, Grief Support, Rosary Meditation, Christian Prayers, Drumming Circles, Wisdom Jesus Learning, and Baha'i conversations, along with events at neighbouring Hillel House and Luther House, as well as meals, retreats, lectures and other on- and off-campus gatherings for students" (McKenzie 2020). Additionally, the 1980s witnessed the formation of the Canadian Association of Campus Chaplains, further illustrating the trend towards a more inclusive chaplaincy model. These developments were responses to the diverse spiritual and religious needs of students, a demographic change largely influenced by the new generation of immigrants' children, who were entering universities approximately 20 years after the introduction of the points-based Immigration Act in the late 1960s and many of whom did not identify as Catholic or Protestant.

In brief, the evolution of university chaplaincy in Canada was initially driven by the need to cater to the spiritual welfare of the large number of veteran students in the aftermath of the Second World War. Its subsequent development was significantly influenced by the secularization of Canadian higher education and further refined by the societal and cultural shifts brought about by the points-based Immigration Act and the national policy of multiculturalism. This trajectory reflects a broad narrative of how Canadian universities adapted to changing societal norms and the increasingly diverse spiritual needs of their student populations.

II. The Roles of University Chaplains in Canada

The contemporary landscape of university chaplaincy in Canada is marked by a notable expansion and diversification, reflecting the nation's commitment to inclusivity and religious pluralism. Modern university chaplains are expected to cater to the spiritual needs of students from a wide array of religious backgrounds, transcending the traditional boundaries of any single faith or tradition. This inclusive approach has led to the presence of chaplains representing an array of faiths, including but not limited to Christian, Jewish, Muslim, Hindu, Unitarian, Bahá'í, Sikh, and Buddhist traditions within Canadian universities. This diversity in chaplaincy ensures that students of various faiths have access to spiritual guidance and support that resonates with their individual religious beliefs and practices. Moreover, it emphasizes the recognition by educational institutions of the importance of spiritual well-being as an integral aspect of the overall university experience. In instances where a student's faith is not directly represented by an on-campus chaplain, it is the responsibility of the chaplaincy to provide contact information and resources to connect the student with a suitable representative of their faith. This approach not only facilitates the religious and spiritual needs of the student body but also fosters an environment of interfaith understanding and cooperation.

The growing role of chaplaincy in Canadian universities is a testament to the country's changing religious demographics and the education sector's response to these changes. This highlights the commitment of these institutions to providing an inclusive environment and support for all students, regardless of their religious and spiritual affiliations. The presence of such diverse clergy in universities is a clear indication of broader social values of diversity, inclusion, and respect for cultural and religious identities.

With the growth in university enrollments and the increasing complexity of campus life, universities have developed a wide array of professionalized student services to enhance the learning experience and uphold equity. These services, exemplified by those at the University of Toronto, address a broad spectrum of student needs. Offices like the Anti-Racism and Cultural Diversity Office and the Sexual and Gender Diversity Office focus on creating a safe, inclusive environment and advocating for gender diversity. Academic Advising services, Accessibility Services, Learning Strategists, Library and Research Support, and Writing Centres assist in developing students' learning skills and providing adaptive technology for those with disabilities. The Career Centre aids in exploring career possibilities and developing job-search strategies, while the Health and Wellness Centre offers medical, nursing, health counselling, and education services. Further, the International Student Centre supports international students both on campus and those planning to study abroad, and personal counsellors are available for students to discuss life and academic issues. These professionalized services effectively meet many of the secular needs of students, roles that were traditionally part of the purview of university chaplains in the form of secular counselling. With these needs now addressed by specialized professionals, a pertinent question comes up: Which services do university chaplains continue to provide in light of these newly developed professional student services?

To gain a deeper understanding of the unique role university chaplains continue to play amidst the plethora of professionalized student services, I conducted interviews with two University Chaplains at the University of Toronto – Rev. Tim Kennedy and Ms. Jeanette Unger. Their insights offer a valuable perspective on how chaplaincy has adapted and continues to be relevant in the current university setting. The chaplains acknowledged the extensive expertise offered by other professional counselling services on campus, noting that this specialization has allowed them to concentrate more on "spiritual care." This aspect of their work specifically addresses the religious or spiritual elements of students' belief systems, an area where other counselling services may be more limited in their advice. The expansion and professionalization of student services in universities have significantly enhanced the support available to students, addressing many of the secular aspects of student life; however, some of these support forms overlap with the traditional secular counselling roles of university chaplains. In this context, the role of university chaplains has evolved to offer services that complement rather than duplicate these professional student services.

Moreover, the chaplains emphasized their focus on facilitating meaning-making with students, a process that often intersects with the domains covered by other student services. For example, discussions on faith and sexuality are areas where the chaplaincy's input is valued. This intersectionality of spiritual care with other aspects of student life is one of the reasons why chaplains occasionally receive referrals from other counsellors on campus. These referrals are indicative of the recognition of the unique contribution chaplaincy can make in addressing the holistic needs of students in areas where spiritual beliefs and personal values play a significant role. Therefore, currently, university chaplains focus on several key areas:

1. <u>Spiritual and Religious Support</u>: First and foremost, chaplains provide guidance and support for spiritual and religious exploration, offering a safe space for students to discuss faith-related issues. The chaplains also help facilitate religious rituals, ceremonies, and worship services to provide space for various faith communities on campus.
2. <u>Interfaith Dialogue and Education</u>: Chaplains play a role in promoting interfaith education and cooperation by organizing events, ceremonies,

discussions, and educational programs that foster a respectful exchange of beliefs among students of different faiths.
3. Emotional and Moral Support: While personal counsellors address psychological and life issues, chaplains offer a unique perspective on spiritual, moral, and existential questions. They guide students grappling with moral dilemmas or seeking to find deeper meaning and purpose in life.
4. Crisis Intervention and Grief Support: Chaplains are often involved in providing support during times of crisis, such as the death of a student or a campus emergency. They offer comfort and counselling to those who are grieving or experiencing trauma.
5. Mental Health and Well-Being: University chaplains also promote community engagement and social responsibility among students, coupled with a focus on mental health well-being. Their initiatives include organizing workshops on secular mindfulness practices and arranging drop-in sessions for prayer and contemplative practices to foster peace and reflection, particularly during times of global or personal unrest. Chaplains also create communal spaces for students to gather, offering solace and connection while encouraging thoughtful reflection on pressing global issues such as injustice, war, natural disasters, and challenges faced by indigenous communities. These efforts by university chaplains significantly contribute to the holistic development of students, encompassing aspects of not only their spiritual and emotional well-being but also their engagement with complex societal issues.
6. Advocacy and Referral Services: Chaplains advocate for the spiritual needs of students and can refer students to other student services or external resources for additional support.
7. Cultural Competency and Inclusivity: In the diverse and multicultural settings of modern university campuses, chaplains contribute to creating an inclusive and culturally sensitive community. Their work involves educating others about various religious and cultural practices and advocating for the accommodation of students' religious needs. This is often achieved through regular gatherings where participants can share food and discuss their respective belief systems, thereby promoting understanding and respect among students from different cultural and religious backgrounds. These activities organized by chaplains are instrumental in enhancing the campus atmosphere by making it more welcoming and conducive to intercultural and interfaith dialogue.

Thus, the modern university chaplain's role is multifaceted, extending beyond traditional religious counselling to encompass broader spiritual, ethical, and community-oriented functions. This evolution reflects the changing dynamics of campus life and the diverse needs of contemporary student populations. Chaplains now work in tandem with other professional services to ensure a holistic approach to student well-being, thereby emphasizing the importance of spiritual health as a crucial component of overall wellness.

III. Challenges Faced by University Chaplains in Canada

In his chapter from the book, *Multifaith Perspectives in Spiritual and Religious Care*, Tom Sherwood reflects on the evolving understanding of chaplaincy and ecumenism in university settings. He notes,

> "Ecumenical" was a popular 1960s church word that made sense to officials in the supportive denominational

organizations, but never made sense to students or many other members of the Carleton community. From the day I moved into the office with "Ecumenical Chaplain" on the door in August 1999, I realized that there were two problems with my job title: the two words. None of the students knew what the word "Ecumenical" meant. Some asked how to pronounce it. And except for students who had come through a religious school system, most did not know what a chaplain was.[1]

This observation is corroborated by a 2013 campus survey at McGill University, probing students' understanding of the term "chaplain." Sara Parks, then Director of the Office of Religious and Spiritual Life at McGill University, highlighted the survey's outcome: "Over 90 percent had no idea what [the word] meant. The less than 10 percent who did know thought it meant a Catholic priest" (Braganza 2017).

Sherwood's and Parks' reflections illuminate a notable disconnect in the perception and understanding of chaplaincy roles in contemporary university environments. Words such as "ecumenical" and "chaplaincy" are not only unfamiliar to numerous students since around the turn of the millennium but also carry connotations that are predominantly Christian in origin. This Christian-centric terminology may pose a challenge in contexts where chaplaincy services are intended to be inclusive and representative of multiple religious traditions.

However, as the role of university chaplaincy has undergone significant evolution since its establishment in Canada in 1947, there can be a parallel opportunity to redefine and update the understanding of the term "chaplain." The term "chaplain," originating from the Latin *cappellanu* and historically denoting a priest responsible for St. Martin of Tours' sacred cloak, has evolved in its contemporary usage to encompass a broader scope beyond its early Christian roots. The alternative term "spiritual care" has been critiqued for its broad usage, occasionally implying care that is not affiliated with any specific religious belief system based on organized principles (Harding 2005). Conversely, the term "chaplaincy" can carry a distinctly Christian connotation for some, with the belief that ordination sets chaplains apart, thereby providing them a unique authority and power to provide pastoral care in a manner that is distinct from other disciplines (Harding et al. 2008, 114). This view of chaplaincy as increasingly archaic, particularly to those who have never been religiously affiliated, reflects a trend of declining public religious affiliation (Cadge 2023).

However, what is crucial is the active promotion and education regarding chaplaincy service on campus to demystify and clarify its role. Concurrently, embracing the term "multifaith" as a more appropriate alternative to "ecumenical" aligns with the current ethos of university chaplaincy. This term aptly captures the diverse and inclusive nature of modern chaplaincy services, thereby reflecting the pluralistic reality of contemporary university campuses in which students from various religious backgrounds seek spiritual support. By adopting a multifaith ethos, universities can effectively bridge the gap in understanding and make chaplaincy services more accessible and relevant to a broader spectrum of students. This ensures that the role of chaplains is communicated clearly, thereby emphasizing their commitment to inclusivity and support for all faiths and belief systems.

A noticeable challenge for Canadian chaplains is that Canada lacks a national association for campus chaplaincy comparable to the Association for Chaplaincy and Spiritual Life in Higher Education (ACSLHE) in the United States. ACSLHE emerged from the amalgamation of the National Association of College and University Chaplains (NACUC) and the

---

1 Sherwood 2020a.

Association of College and University Religious Affairs (ACURA). Tom Sherwood attributes the absence of a similar nationwide body in Canada to factors such as limited resources, the vast geographic expanse of the country, and its relatively small population. While the Canadian Association of Campus Chaplains (CACC) was developed in the 1980s and established a constitution in 1998, it has since ceased to exist (Sherwood 2012, 82). Furthermore, Canada does not have a member association that is part of the International Association of Chaplains in Higher Education (IACHE). Recognizing the existing deficiency, Tom Sherwood established the Canadian Campus Chaplaincy Centre (CCCC) in 2008 with the aim of creating a pivotal resource and communication nexus for campus chaplaincy across Canada. However, despite this initiative, the need for a formal national association dedicated to campus chaplaincy in Canada remains a pressing and unfulfilled requirement.

Another significant challenge faced by university chaplains in Canada is the infrequency of paid full-time chaplaincy positions, a situation even more pronounced for non-Christian traditions. The appointment of the first Buddhist chaplain at Dalhousie University in 2005 was a notable development, occurring at the confluence of the general Nova Scotian population – the university's student body – and the specific ethnic and Western Buddhist communities within these groups (Woo 2005, 119). Similarly, the University of Toronto initiated a search for its first full-time Muslim chaplain in 2012 to lead its Muslim Chaplaincy program. However, this effort hinged on the Muslim community's support to raise necessary funds – approximately $70,000. Sherwood noted that of the 44 campus chaplains attending a national Canadian Association of Campus Chaplains gathering in 2002, 22 were serving in part-time capacities. This scenario emphasizes the challenges in institutionalizing chaplaincy within Canadian higher education, particularly in ensuring diverse religious representation and securing adequate funding for these vital roles.

In today's universities, where religious affiliations and participation are in decline, chaplains face the challenge of demonstrating their relevance amidst a diverse and often secular student body. This situation calls for chaplains to emphasize their unique roles in providing spiritual and moral guidance, fostering a sense of community and belonging, and facilitating interfaith dialogue. As societal shifts lead to lower the levels of traditional religiosity, chaplains must redefine and communicate the distinct value they bring to campus life, thereby ensuring that their contributions are considered essential and complementary within the broader context of university student support services.

IV. Buddhist Chaplaincy in Canadian Universities

Numerous Buddhist chaplains in North America – particularly in medical or correctional institutions – are not ordained in the traditional sense, as ordination in Buddhism typically implies becoming monastic. Most of these Buddhist chaplains are lay practitioners, challenging the definition and understanding as proposed by Harding et al. (2008). A few of them received "endorsement," rather than ordination, from local Buddhist temples. Despite not being ordained, the work of Buddhist chaplains is aligned with specific Buddhist beliefs and practices; thus, it does not fit the broader, non-affiliated definition of "spiritual care." As chaplaincy roles informed by Muslim, Jewish, Buddhist, and other religious traditions gain recognition and acceptance in Western contexts, the continued use of the term "chaplain" is justifiable, despite its potential unfamiliarity or archaic connotations for younger generations. The evolution of university chaplaincy since its inception in Canada in 1947 presents an opportunity to redefine and update the understanding of "chaplain," recognizing that terms like "ordination" have varied meanings across different religions. This evolving understanding of chaplaincy acknowledges the diverse spiritual needs and contexts in contemporary society, thereby allowing for a more inclusive and representative approach to spiritual care.

Further, multifaith chaplains informed by Buddhist traditions face unique challenges in their roles within universities and colleges. One of the primary challenges is the relatively small number of Buddhist students in North America, which results in Buddhist chaplains often engaging with individuals from various spiritual and religious backgrounds as well as those without any religious affiliation. Recent data from Statistics Canada indicates a significant decrease in religious affiliation, with only 68% of Canadians aged 15 years or older reporting a connection to a religion. Within this demographic, a mere 1.4% identify Buddhism as their religion. While educational institutions do not typically provide specific data on the religious affiliation of university students, Statistics Canada's data reveals that those between the ages of 15 to 24 years – amounting to only approximately 34,000 out of approximately 4.18 million individuals, or 0.8% of the age group – identified with a Buddhist affiliation.

The relatively low proportion of students who identify with Buddhism poses a unique challenge for Buddhist chaplains on university campuses. To effectively serve a student body characterized by diverse religious and non-religious backgrounds, these chaplains are required to develop a heightened level of religious fluidity. This involves deepening their understanding of the teachings, ethical norms, prayers, and practices of various religions. Such a broad knowledge base equips Buddhist chaplains with the necessary skills to engage in an empathetic and knowledgeable manner with students of different faiths or those who do not adhere to any religious tradition. In contrast, this challenge is somewhat less pronounced for Christian chaplains, largely due to the higher percentage of students who have been raised in a Christian environment. The greater prevalence of Christianity in the student population implies that Christian chaplains are more likely to encounter individuals familiar with their religious context, thereby reducing the need for extensive cross-religious education and outreach. This disparity highlights the need for Buddhist chaplains to be particularly adaptable and well-versed in a wide range of religious and spiritual perspectives.

The appointment of Buddhist chaplains at Canadian universities is not uniformly practiced. For example, Mount Royal University does not have a dedicated Buddhist representative among its chaplains from various faiths. However, the university does have Rev. Tim Nethercott from the United Church of Canada, who "was outside for the Church for part of his life and practiced as a Buddhist for two years." This background offers a unique interfaith perspective within the university's chaplaincy. In contrast, the University of British Columbia (UBC) has adopted a more inclusive approach towards Buddhist representation. At UBC, Dr. Ernest Ng serves as a Buddhist chaplain, a role he also fulfills at Simon Fraser University. Additionally, UBC has appointed Gareth Sironik, a former Zen monk, as a Zen Buddhist chaplain. This distinction may indicate a perception of Zen Buddhism to be less formally religious as a spiritual practice than other Buddhist traditions. Such a perspective enables a broader interpretation of spiritual guidance, potentially appealing to a wider range of students who may be seeking non-traditional or less doctrinally defined spiritual support.

In a dialogue with Ernest Ng, it was observed that Buddhist students typically manifest a relatively low engagement with religious activities on campus, in contrast to their Christian counterparts. This phenomenon aligns with findings from the 2019 report by Statistics Canada, which indicates that among Canadian adherents of Buddhism, a mere 67% acknowledge the significance of religious or spiritual beliefs in shaping life decisions, a proportion notably inferior to that recorded for followers of other faiths. In response to this trend, Ng has proactively sought to enhance his visibility and accessibility by participating more actively in student-oriented events. He further noted that many international students maintain a nominal affiliation with Buddhism, primarily through familial traditions, without fully embracing the identity of Buddhist practitioners. Ng's chaplaincy efforts are thus also directed toward facilitating a deeper comprehension and appreciation of Buddhist doctrines and practices among these students. Through this endeavour, he underscores the pivotal role of spiritual well-being as a component of holistic student health.

Further challenges for Buddhist chaplaincy are reflected in a broader trend of declining religiosity in Canada. Such a trend is more pronounced among the younger population. The observed decline in religiosity among university students raises important questions regarding the perceived relevance of chaplains in their lives, particularly in the context of counselling and guidance. Given the low percentage of students with religious affiliations who affirm the significance of religion in their daily lives, this could translate into a diminished view of chaplains as essential figures for personal guidance. This perspective is further complicated by the comprehensive professional student services available at universities, which encompass a wide range of secular needs and support, potentially overshadowing the unique role that chaplains play.

V. Conclusion

The resource constraints faced by university chaplains in Canada are a significant hurdle in their professional journey. Numerous university chaplains resort to self-fundraising through affiliations with their respective universities, while others occupy part-time positions in these institutions. The absence of a national association for university chaplains in Canada exacerbates these challenges, as it limits the support available to them in addressing the individual faith-related needs of students, faculty, and staff as well as in promoting inter-religious understanding. This role of chaplaincy is often not fully understood by the student body, which has increasingly become secular, with a diminishing percentage identifying with a religious affiliation. As fewer students seek spiritual or religious support, university chaplains are confronted with the need to distinguish the unique services they offer, particularly in the face of a broad array of student services, such as mental wellness, stress management, and other professional counselling services.

The situation presents an even greater challenge for Buddhist chaplains, given that less than 1% of the student population identifies as Buddhist. These chaplains frequently find themselves serving students whose backgrounds, religious faiths, and practices are different from their own, thereby necessitating a high degree of versatility and a broad knowledge base. This demand highlights the need for Buddhist chaplains to be adept not only in their spiritual practices but also in respecting and understanding a wide array of religious and secular perspectives, thereby enabling them to effectively serve a diverse student community.

References

Braganza, Chantal. "The Role of University Chaplain Evolves with the Times." *University Affairs*, November 10, 2017. https://www.universityaffairs.ca/features/feature-article/role-university-chaplain-evolves-times/ (accessed January 24, 2024)

Cadge, Wendy. *Spiritual Care: The Everyday Work of Chaplains*. New York: Oxford University Press, 2023.

Harding, Stephen R. "Making the Case for Theology." *PlainViews* 2, no. 10 (2005). http://www.plainviews.org/AR/i/v2n10.html.

Harding, Stephen R., Kevin J. Flannelly, Kathleen Galek, and Helen P. Tannenbaum. "Spiritual Care, Pastoral Care, and Chaplains: Trends in the Health Care Literature." *Journal of Health Care Chaplaincy* 14, no. 2 (2008): 99-117.

Lipkowitz, Scott. "The People's Solemn Burden: Queens College in the Second World War." *Queens College World War II Veterans History Project*. Queen's College Library, 2020. https://qc-cuny.libguides.com/WorldWarTwoVetsProject (accessed January 21, 2024)

McKenzie, Lyle. "Working Together for Common Good a Joyful Experience: UVic Multifaith Services – A Model for Multi-Faith Co-Operation." In Multifaith Perspectives in *Spiritual and Religious Care: Change, Challenge & Transformation*, edited by Mohamed Taher, 140. Toronto: Canadian Multifaith Federation, 2020.

McDowall, Duncan. *Queen's University Volume III, 1961–2004: Testing Tradition*. Montreal & Kingston: McGill-Queen's University Press, 2016.

Morrow, Williams S. "From Theological College to University: A Perspective from Queen's," *Studies in Religion* 51, no. 2 (2022): 156-161. doi: doi.org/10.1177/000842982110400

Queen's Journal, "ISS Executive Announces Plans," LXXII, No. 9 (November 6 1945): 1 and 6: https://archive.org/details/queensjournal72/page/n51/mode/2up?view=theater.

Sherwood, Tom. "Religion and Spirituality in Student Life." In *International Perspectives on Higher Education: Challenging Values and Practice*, edited by Trevor Kerry, 69-86. New York: Continuum, 2012.

Sherwood, Tom. "'The Carleton Model' – Change, Challenge and Transformation in a Canadian Campus Chaplaincy." In *Multifaith Perspectives in Spiritual and Religious Care: Change, Challenge & Transformation*, edited by Mohamed Taher, 149-155. Toronto: Canadian Multifaith Federation, 2020a.

Sherwood, Tom. "Chaplaincy, Religion and Spirituality in Student Life." In *Multifaith Perspectives in Spiritual and Religious Care: Change, Challenge & Transformation*, edited by Mohamed Taher, 156-163. Toronto: Canadian Multifaith Federation, 2020b.

The Queen's Review: Official Publication of the General Alumni Association of Queen's University, Vol. 20 no. 6 (August 1946), "Alumni News": 176-186: https://archive.org/details/queensreview20/page/148/mode/2up

Woo, Terry. "The Installation of the First Buddhist Chaplain at Dalhousie University." *Canadian Journal of Buddhist Studies* 1 (2005): 111-122.

16
"Buddhism Is a Whole Life Practice!" Building relationships with Asian and Asian heritage Buddhist communities to work against Neo-Orientalist tendencies in Buddhist Chaplaincy

Rev. Ivan (Kusa) Mayerhofer

Earlier this academic year, I was part of a team that invited out *The Mystical Arts of Tibet* program from Drepung Loseling Monastery of Atlanta, Georgia. During their five-day stay this group of Tibetan monks created a sand mandala, gave a lecture on compassion, and offered a performance of sacred music and instruments. Most of the events took place in the Alvarez College Union at Davidson College with the sacred music performance taking place in Tyler-Tallman Hall. The sand mandala was set up in the middle of the College Union, right next to the Davis Café. During the opening and closing ceremonies, students came and went freely, stumbling into these sacred rituals with awe and amusement, and many others talking over the chanting and horns while eating lunch. Each evening, the monks had to tear down their Tibetan Bazaar and put away their ritual implements. At the end of the week, just as the sand mandala itself was swept away, the monks themselves packed up and left the space exactly as it was before they arrived. The College Union was transformed during the week, but the space itself remained as it was: a student space with the monks as guests.

Compare this with another Buddhist ritual experience. Later this same academic year, I took a group of students to South Korea for a Buddhist pilgrimage. We stayed at three monasteries as part of the Jogye Order of Korean Buddhism's Templestay program. For each monastery, we had to take a bus into the mountains to reach the entry gate. From the bus, we walked with our bags to the Templestay lodgings. Each morning, waking up on average around 3:45 am, we then walked into the monastery from our lodgings. Once in the monastery, we waited in front of the pavilion housing the four sacred instruments: drum, bell, wooden fish, and cloud gong. By 4:30 am, a group of monastics entered the pavilion and began the morning ritual of playing the instruments to wake up all beings across the many realms. When the ritual was over, we then walked further up to the main hall for the morning ceremony, afterwards returning to our Templestay headquarters. When the week was over, we packed up and left the sacred spaces exactly as they were before our arrival. On this journey, we were the guests in spaces belonging to the Buddhists from whom we were learning. The power relation created between the Tibetan monks and the students at Davidson College was turned on its head, with clear implications for learning about Buddhist practices in general.

There is much to say about these two cases, not least of which includes the causes and conditions leading to China's colonization of Tibet leading to Tibetan monks in exile maintaining and spreading their culture through hired performances, a set of conditions not faced by

Korean Buddhist monastics. For now, I want to draw out one theme relevant for my work in Buddhist chaplaincy: it is important to take students interested in Buddhism to Asian and Asian heritage spaces, to have them meet and learn from Asian and Asian heritage practitioners, especially monastics, and to respectfully engage the cultures that have celebrated and cared for and innovated these Buddhist traditions for over 2,500 years, traditions from which many non-Asian practitioners like myself now benefit. This theme may sound obvious or easy to realize; however, it is anything but, and working toward realizing this theme has nothing to do with essentializing specific peoples in a tokenistic or harmful way. The history of Orientalism and Asian erasure informing contemporary US Buddhisms is part of the college Buddhist chaplaincy landscape. This ongoing erasure not only creates false views about Buddhist practices, rituals, and peoples, it also contributes to continuing harm for Asian and Asian heritage peoples in the United States. Realizing this theme of engagement requires deeply exploring this Orientalist past, closely investigating each of our positionalities in relation to this past, and then working closely with our local contexts to create relationships and experiences for lasting healing and liberation.

Orientalist Past, Neo-Orientalist Present

I have written at length about the Orientalist past informing contemporary USAmerican Buddhisms and the contemporary discursive strategies that are in response to this legacy of Asian erasure (Mayerhofer 2021). Those writings were from the academic point of view. In this context, I would like to address the issue from the point of view of a Buddhist teacher and chaplain in a college setting. Although some of the issues overlap, the strategies for overcoming ongoing Orientalism or, what I call, Neo-Orientalism in contemporary USAmerican Buddhisms are different for a chaplain than for an academic.

For background to Orientalism, it is essential to go back to Edward Said.[1] As theorized by Said, Orientalism is a set of power relations setting the Occident over the Orient or West over East – both of which, in their opposition, are Orientalist creations especially with regard to culture and ideology (Said 1979, p. 5). More than just an imaginative creation of the Orient in the Western imaginary, Orientalism is a hegemonic system of dominance and control consisting of (i) those who work, write, and research on the Orient, (ii) an epistemic and ontological distinction between Occident and Orient, and (iii) a set of political, educational, and economic institutions that formalize, monetize, and reify the work of Orientalists (Said 1979, pp. 2-3). As Said states, Orientalism is a "Western style for dominating, restructuring, and having authority over the Orient" (1979, p. 3). Although Said's work is primarily about the Near and Middle East, his work equally applies and has been extended into South and Southeast Asia where European scholarship and colonial extraction resulted in an Orientalist construction of Buddhism (Almond 1988, King 1999, Lopez 1995, Masuzawa 2005). This construction and its process reflect the "style" of hegemonic dominance and authority manifested by European Orientalists in Southeast Asia. This includes a turn to classical languages (e.g., Sanskrit, Pali) versus vernacular (e.g., Sinhalese, Khmer), looking toward ancient over present day practices, a predominant sense of European ownership or control over texts versus local control, a desire to remove cultural context and origins (i.e., cultural baggage) to uncover a pure and essentialized Buddhism, a greater reliance on text versus ritual (i.e., textual Buddhism), and, finally, a stripping of metaphysical, magical, and non-natural elements from the overall philosophical and religious story being created (King 1999, Lopez 1995). These strategies and tropes combined allowed Orientalists and their

---

[1] The following two paragraphs are taken, with minor changes, from my thesis (Mayerhofer 2021).

local informants and contributors to downplay diverse contemporary Asian peoples, cultural heritages, and knowledge bases, creating a context of Asian erasure.

The strategies implemented by the Orientalists contributed to a distinctive approach to studying and practicing Buddhism with lasting consequences on the transmissions of Buddhisms into the US and beyond. Text-based, classical language focused, rooted in ancient history, decontextualized and de-culturized, embedded in essential truths, this Orientalist set of strategies had far-reaching consequences, especially as they took "hold on [the] Western imagination by limiting alternative possibilities" (Iwamura 2011, p. 7) of what this religion actually was to many Asian practitioners across a diverse range of countries, cultures, languages, practices, and more. This hold has not let up as Buddhist teachings, practices, and discourses have made their way across the United States. Jane Iwamura's critical investigation into the popular discourses and representations of the "Oriental Monk" in US media shows one result of this process, a "homogenous representational effect" or "Racialization (more correctly, "orientalization")," leading her to claim that "this new form of American Orientalism is more covert than its predecessors" (Iwamura 2011, pp. 6-7). Judith Snodgrass, in her critical account of the World's Parliament of Religions in Chicago, 1893, gives the following summary of the impacts of Orientalist representations of Buddhism:

> ...[they] became part of the apparatus for dominating, restructuring, and maintaining authority over various Asian Buddhist states by defining the norm against which Buddhist practice was judged, and by which the relative value of Buddhist thought against European philosophy was measured. Western scholarship both created the object and assessed its value. Although the construct did not correspond with any Asian reality, it nevertheless functioned as the truth of Buddhism.[2]

The legacy of Orientalism, a legacy of Asian erasure and ideological control, is present in USAmerican Buddhisms, whether in the practices or the scholarship. These lasting effects can be seen in various places, one of which is in the manifestation of Buddhist chaplaincies at USAmerican colleges – the chaplains and their positionalities, where they are trained, where and how they are hired, and the kinds of programs occurring at those colleges.

The current imbalance with respect to the numbers of Buddhists and control of resources in college Buddhist chaplaincy is one example that illustrates what I call the Neo-Orientalist conditions of contemporary USAmerican Buddhisms. According to the PEW Research Center, as of 2010 the global number of Buddhist practitioners across the Asia-Pacific region was 481,290,000; North America had a total of 3,860,000 (Pew Research Center 2012b). In 2020, according to PRRI's Census of American Religion, 1% of USAmericans identify as Buddhist (PRRI 2024). Among the 1% of USAmerican Buddhists, PEW estimates that roughly two-thirds or 67% are Asian-American (Pew Research Center 2012a). This preponderance of Asian and Asian-American practitioners among USAmerican Buddhists is clearly reflected in the long history of Buddhisms in the US. First arriving on the western coast of North America in the 1800s due to labor and other forms of migration, Japanese, Chinese, and Korean peoples brought Buddhist traditions, practices, and cultures, established temples for multiple generations, all the while facing intolerance, prejudice, and racist acts of violence. One might expect (from the standpoint of historical presence alone) that this long history would lead to greater numbers of Asian and Asian-American Buddhists entering Buddhist vocations. However, a recent

---

2 Snodgrass 2003, pp. 7-8.

survey published in *Mapping Buddhist Chaplains in North America* reported that 61% of Buddhist chaplains identify as white (or 85% identify as White, Other POC, Prefer Not to Say) whereas 15% identify as Asian/Pacific Islander (Giles, C., & Sanford, M. 2022, p. 21). The researchers pose the question, "Why are so many Buddhist chaplains white?" Given the historical context and ongoing presence of Neo-Orientalism in USAmerican Buddhisms, I would pose the question as follows: "Why are so many Buddhist chaplains not of Asian or Asian-heritage descent?" Among the many factors, the history of Orientalism – especially the way in which resources and knowledge systems are controlled by a select minority for ideological and hegemonic purposes – in USAmerican Buddhisms provides one explanation.

Returning to the methods of Orientalism, methods that are text-based, classical language focused, rooted in ancient history, decontextualized and de-culturized, embedded in essential truths, Neo-Orientalism's presence in college Buddhist chaplaincy can be explored via the varieties of Buddhist programs. Consider Davidson College's Buddhist chaplaincy. When I first entered the job three years ago, there were five types of regular programs: Davidson Dharma, a student-led Buddhist affiliated group; Davidson Mindfulness, a student-led secular mindfulness group; a yearly public lecture coordinated by the Buddhist chaplain; a yearly meditation retreat; and as-needed engagement with various college groups regarding Buddhism and Mindfulness practices. Davidson Dharma, the one regular Buddhist group, consisted of a guided meditation and Dharma talk usually based on a scriptural text. Mindfulness consisted of body-centered breathing and physical practices for the cultivation of mindful awareness without inclusion of the Asian heritages from which mindfulness practices originate. The yearly lecture series consisted of non-monastic, predominantly white teachers. The yearly meditation retreat was held at a non-Buddhist retreat center and primarily centered around vipassana or insight practices as developed in the non-monastic USAmerican Theravada lineages from Jack Kornfield, Sharon Salzberg, Joseph Goldstein, and others (Wilson 2014). In other words, the programs were text-based, de-contextualized and de-culturized (from Asian and Asian-heritage culture, not White American culture), embedded in a mood of getting at the essential truth, and, because of the reliance on scripture outside of living commentaries, rooted in history rather than a living presence of ongoing Buddhist cultivation across Asian and Asian-heritage communities. What was missing were rituals, devotional practices, experiences of temples and living Buddhist communities, engagement with monastics, retreats in Buddhist sacred spaces, and more. These elements, when introduced, have the potential to disrupt ongoing Neo-Orientalist practices and, ideally, work to end past harms from occurring again and again.

Some Issues to Consider when Developing Strategies for Countering Neo-Orientalism in College Buddhist Chaplaincy

As a college Buddhist chaplain, there are specific ways I work to counter Neo-Orientalist tendencies in contemporary USAmerican Buddhisms. Two ways I will discuss here include site specific visits to Asian and Asian heritage Buddhist locations, and meeting with Asian and Asian heritage practitioners, whether lay or monastic. Before providing a detailed example from my work at Davidson College, I want to discuss some general issues and approaches that guide my working processes. These include working with your local context, laying the groundwork through relationship building, and examining one's intersectionality and related privileges in relationship to Neo-Orientalist Buddhist practices as a means to creating programs that effectively transform the current context in the direction of liberation for all.

Regarding local context, two quick anecdotes will illustrate the ways in which

Neo-Orientalist tendencies blind us to the living and vibrant presence of Buddhist communities in our own local contexts.[3] While planning an interfaith event, I was in discussion with a Buddhist monastic who identifies as white about other possible monastic invitees. The monastic, without hesitation, claimed that they were the only Buddhist monastic in town that could be present for the event. After kindly making clear that this was false – there were Vietnamese monastic communities in that area that go back to the early 1980s alongside a number of monastic temples of Cambodian, Loatian, Burmese, and Vietnamese descent – the monastic corrected themself saying that they were the only English-speaking monastic in town (again, most likely false) and that these centers were more cultural centers than Buddhist temples. This only perpetuates Orientalist tools of Asian erasure (turn to cultural vs. authentic dharma, gatekeeping on the appropriate languages for Dharma expression), indeed failing to see the large Asian heritage Buddhist community presence right in front of us. In yet another city in which I lived, similar examples were all too commonly experienced. A close friend and mentor of mine is a Vietnamese Buddhist monk and there were many times when someone wanted a Buddhist presence at an event and they would ask me, even if the Vietnamese monastic was right beside me, preferring my presence to a monastic's presence. Again, a history of erasure, of seeing "our" Buddhism as authentic, of seeing monastic and ritual practice as superstitious and backwards, blinds some of us to the human presence before our eyes, to the cultural diversity and living practice of Asian and Asian heritage Buddhists in our very communities.

With this in mind, my first approach is to work closely with the local context. Identify the Buddhist communities and more specifically temples in the area. Search both your local city and surrounding cities. If doing a Google search, use terms like 'temple' and 'monastery' as opposed to just 'meditation' or 'Zen' or 'Insight'. Or put in a general search for Buddhism and then click on all the available red pins, even those written in languages you may not understand (use Google translate to help you navigate the temple names). When I first arrived in the greater Charlotte region in the summer of 2021, I identified more than ten Asian and Asian heritage Buddhist communities, temples, and monasteries. The numbers increased when I broadened my search to include both North Carolina and South Carolina. Overcoming our Neo-Orientalist present does not require looking to distant places for a truth that is out there; as with Zen practice, the living suchness of practice is right before our very eyes, sometimes in our very backyards.[4]

Once local Buddhist communities have been identified, the second step becomes even more crucial than the first, especially given the histories of erasure and devaluing that examples like the ones I gave above bring to light: laying the groundwork through relationship building. In its briefest form, this may look like contacting an organization first and meeting someone from that community. When I took students to Atlanta for an interfaith social justice pilgrimage, we visited The Temple, a synagogue with a long history of social justice and civil rights work. First, we contacted The Temple via email, let them know the intentions of

---

3 In an effort to balance two aims – (i) working with the precept of not speaking ill of others misdeeds and (ii) also speaking out about situations that are harmful, especially structural ways – I will present situations as in the following paragraph in general ways, using third person pronouns, and general characteristics and traits that match the qualities of people I have interacted with, without singling out anyone in particular.

4 Chenxing Han and Andy Housiaux created a similar initiative called "Listening to the Buddhists in our Backyard". I first encountered this project through an online presentation in the Spring of 2022. Visit their website at https://www.l2bb.org/ to learn more about the essential and wonderful work they are doing.

our visit and requested permission for a visit, as well as a zoom meeting with one of the rabbis. When speaking with one of the rabbis online, they were a little surprised. In their words, "You know we are a public space? You don't need to talk with us to visit." Yes, and we want to make sure our visit doesn't disrupt community, that others know why we are present, and that we are respectful of the community when we visit. When I first decided to take students to a lunar new year celebration at a Buddhist temple, I reached out to a local Vietnamese Buddhist community: Chùa Liên Hoa of Charlotte, North Carolina. I picked this community because of my background with Vietnamese Buddhist communities, practices, and ritual forms. First, I contacted the community via email and made formal greetings as well as stated my intention to eventually bring students. In this case, I wanted to meet someone at the temple and, if appropriate, practice with them at various services. After meeting with a lay member of the community and spending a Sunday service in practice with them, the idea of bringing students for lunar new year or Tết Nguyên Đán felt appropriate. From my arrival in Charlotte in the summer of 2021, I first brought students to Chùa Liên Hoa for Tết in 2023. Establishing relationships, trust, and mutual understanding was more important than taking students to a community as if I simply had the right to show up unannounced.

These relationships depend on a third step that is specific to each individual: an ongoing close look at one's specific positionality across many variables of identity formation and across a number of relational, material, and historical contexts. Consider my case: I am the child of immigrant parents, a Mexican-German born in Southern California. I grew up in a Latinx community, and I am white-skinned, meaning I racialize as white while still being Latinx and German and US American. My parents were both of lower economic class origins, but because of immigrating to the United States during the 60s, they were able to build a modest household without debt. I benefited from this growing intergenerational wealth by moving through school with modest debt and not much concern for future jobs. I grew up Catholic in a Mexican Catholic household, where the Virgen means as much if not more than Jesus Christ. Due to my mother's illness, I moved across Southern California evangelical churches and then no church as a staunch atheist until I eventually joined a Buddhist temple to learn how to meditate. As a white racializing German-Mexican US American child of immigrants, well educated, cis-gendered heterosexual man, of economically mobile class status, I enter Buddhist spaces with this (and more, this is only a fraction of the matrix) informing my presence and my relationality to others.

All of this identity work is dynamic, of course. In the temple where I am an affiliated teacher, a Korean lineage and predominantly white Buddhist temple, I take part in services in my official robes and *kasa* without question. When I am taking part in services at a Vietnamese temple with a monastic culture, I don't wear my ceremonial robes because it would be elevating myself to a status on par with the monastics, a community of which I am not a part. However, in the same city where my Vietnamese monastic mentor and friend, Thay, resides, they don't feel comfortable wearing their robes outside the temple because of the anti-Asian racism they face, strengthened by being a Asian Buddhist monastic, and so doubly outside white USAmerican culture. In the same city, I can walk around with my ceremonial robes and become an object of interest, not derision, because as a white racializing Buddhist practitioner my Buddhist markers are indications of a control of information that belongs to white culture, a sign of ongoing Neo-Orientalist tendencies impacting everyday consciousness.

This dynamic background is essential to continue to explore and understand, on my part, because when I begin to form relationships with Asian and Asian heritage communities, I must understand the context within which I am working. If a Vietnamese community has been present for forty years and the current Buddhist scene doesn't know they exist, there is a history to this absence, a history of neglect, erasure, and anti-Asian racism, as well as a history of ownership where non-Asian practitioners feel entitled to be authorities of Buddhism based on Neo-Orientalist knowledge formation practices. I cannot simply enter into these communities and assume I am welcome or that my presence is not a source of suffering for others. Indeed, quite the opposite! In order to work with one's local context and form deep relationships with Asian and Asian heritage communities, it is essential to do ongoing individual identity formation understanding, to break down one's positionality, to understand the dynamics of relational identity formation practices and histories and materialities, and to do all of this with humility and joy. Why joy? Because it is a joy to see where suffering arises, and the causes and conditions of that suffering, so one can work to remove those causes and conditions for the benefit and liberation of all beings!

Case Study: Buddhist Pilgrimage to South Korea

I referenced my work with a local Vietnamese Buddhist community above as one example of how to form deep relationships when working with a local Asian or Asian heritage community. That is one example of how to create a Buddhist chaplaincy program that works against Neo-Orientalist currents and against ongoing Asian erasure in our Buddhist communities in the United States. When possible, I find that forming deep relationships with local Asian and Asian heritage communities does indeed work against Neo-Orientalist tendencies in Buddhist programming, programs that may typically focus on text-based events, on ancient history rather than living present realities, and decontextualized and de-culturized Dharma teachings rather than the dynamic and deep ways in which cultural diversity breathes ongoing life into Dharma for this present moment. This last academic year, I had the great fortune of taking this local context to an international level through a Buddhist pilgrimage to South Korea. Here is how I made this trip possible, in the hopes that describing this process will inspire other college Buddhist chaplains to form deep relationships with Asian and Asian heritage communities but also to inspire others to work against Asian erasure in our Buddhist chaplaincy programs and promote a deeply liberative and engaged Buddhist practice for all.

When I entered the job at Davidson College three academic years ago, I had the unique benefit of having an overflow of funds from a lack of programming during the pandemic. I decided to pursue an international Buddhist pilgrimage trip, the first of its kind at Davidson College. The initial suggestion was to take students to India and Nepal to visit the main Buddhist pilgrimage sites such as Lumbini, Bodh Gayā, Sarnath, and Kushinagar. However tempting this was for me, it was important to me at that time that the trip did not become a Buddhist tourist trip, but had significant Buddhist cultural and practice impact for the students, myself, and those hosting us. I am an ordained Dharma and meditation teacher in a Korean Sŏn Buddhist lineage. As part of my seminary training and ordination, I took a vow to be well-educated about Korean Buddhist history and its present. Indeed, our founding teacher, the Ven. Samu Sunim, encouraged us in this vow because, in his view, we could not become Dharma teachers in a Korean lineage and without having a deep immersion in Korean Buddhist teachings, practices, and history. Although India is significant for Buddhist pilgrimage, it did not resonate with my identity and spiritual formation as a Buddhist teacher. I felt more called to give back to the teachers and ancestors who inform my lineage – by bringing students to their temples, their places of practice, their Dharma halls – and encourage a deep exchange between the students on the trip and the monastics we would meet. With this in mind, I pursued a pilgrimage trip to South Korea.

It was also essential that, from the beginning, I work with and alongside Korean teachers and practitioners to make this possible. Although I practice in a Korean heritage tradition, I don't speak Korean nor am I myself Korean. Bringing students to Korean temples and places of devotion and practice would require working closely with Korean monastics, practitioners, and others in the Jogye Order (the predominant order of the Korean Buddhist orders), especially since the Jogye Order runs the primary vehicle for staying at temples, the Templestay Program administered through the Cultural Corps of Korean Buddhism. In the spring of 2022, I connected with a college Buddhist chaplain colleague and, through a series of connections, I was finally put in touch with a representative from the Cultural Corps of Korean Buddhism. Since the Spring of 2022 through the trip this last May of 2024, I have worked with this representative via WhatsApp chats and eventually Kakao Messenger, planning a trip, submitting applications for grants, and just connecting on an individual basis about the unfolding possibilities. At the time I didn't know it, but we were forming deep relationships throughout, not just individually, but institutionally as well. This created a sense of mutual respect and responsiveness to one another, so that the Davidson students were not only partaking in a pilgrimage to Korea; they would be giving back to the Jogye Order through reflections, writings, and other cultural offerings.

Preparation for the trip involved reading and Buddhist practice, but it was important that both reading and practice focused on the present traditions the students would be encountering. Students were instructed to read documents provided by the Jogye Order via their website regarding temple practices, artifacts, and etiquette. I also provided students with some Dharma talks by recent and contemporary teachers such as T'oe'ong Sŏngch'ŏl and Samu Sunim, as well as video clips from the critically acclaimed film *Spring, Summer, Fall, Winter...and Spring*. For practice, we engaged some forms of meditation, but more important was prostration practice, especially because of its central role in Korean Buddhist forms. It is common to start the day with 108 prostrations, to do prostrations when entering a Dharma hall, meeting a senior teacher, for repentance and purification, and more. Learning about and doing prostrations before our trip was an essential learning requirement, more important than decontextualized meditation practices for peace of mind and other English language sources on Buddhism. This helped prepare students for the ritual forms of Jogye Order Korean Buddhism.

Regarding the pilgrimage itself, I worked with one of my colleagues from Religious Studies who specializes in Tibetan Buddhism. We traveled with nine students and stayed at three monasteries during our ten-day trip, each one with a different focus and flavor of practice. Beomeosa, near Busan, is a major Sŏn (Japanese: Zen) training center. Golgulsa is primarily known for its 9th century rock-carved Buddha and its focus on *Seonmudo* training, a specifically Korean Buddhist martial art. Haeinsa, located high up in the mountains of Gayasan National Park, is one of Korea's Triple Jewel Temples, specifically the Dharma Jewel Temple because it houses the Buddhist teachings in the form of the UNESCO World Heritage *Tripiṭaka Koreana*, a set of 81,258 woodblock carvings from the 13th century. We finished our week of Templestay with a weekend in Seoul, including a food tour of local markets.

Regarding undoing Neo-Orientalist practices, this pilgrimage, defined as a journey, especially a long one, made to some sacred place that can lead to a personal transformation, indeed worked to that end. After journeying 11 to 14 hours by plane, we took a five-hour bus ride to reach our first monastery. To get to the main Buddha hall, we hiked around a river and then up a steep meandering pathway through three gates: the One Pillar Gate, the Gate of the Four Guardians, and finally the Gate of Non-Duality. We climbed further to enter the Buddha hall, making three prostrations out of gratitude for this precious life of ours and for the many opportunities we have to help ourselves wake up and be of service to all beings! At Haeinsa, we hiked up even further, up one mountain to visit a 1,000 year old rock-carved standing Buddha and up another mountain to visit the hermitage of the late Korean Sŏn master Sŏngch'ŏl Sunim. Our days started around 3:45 am with morning services and prostrations. We ended around 9 pm in noble silence. We transformed and reshaped our lives into the schedule of the monasteries and monastics from whom we learned. The order of control and knowledge acquisition was reversed. This is just one of many ways in which this pilgrimage physically and materially worked against Neo-Orientalist currents.

The impacts of this trip are many, but the most clear and moving way in which this trip impacted our students' understanding of Buddhism is summed up by one student's reflections. Before the pilgrimage, this student only studied Buddhism in classes, through books and podcasts and lectures. This student in particular had attended a weekly meditation session, but even there the student commented that this was compartmental, something they plugged in to a busy schedule. After the pilgrimage to South Korea, the student came away transformed. They experienced first hand that, for Buddhist monastics there in Korea, Buddhism is a full-time endeavor, a whole life practice, a 24-hour commitment and vow. The student didn't get this from texts, lectures, or podcasts. Even if the student felt like they knew Buddhism before, this was only under a Neo-Orientalist lens that privileges harmful forms of knowledge acquisition. After this pilgrimage, their mind and heart were transformed, shaped by the prostrations, the hikes, the chanting, and the numerous smiles and bows from Korean monastics and lay practitioners.

Conclusion

The Buddhist Pilgrimage trip to South Korea was a humbling coming together of causes and conditions that felt like lifetimes in the making. And yet, it should not be considered a model for other college Buddhist chaplains to follow since it requires a lot of resources and time, both of which are not part of the college Buddhist chaplain material landscape. Also, this kind of international trip should not be considered a model because many of us, if not all of us, college Buddhist chaplains are living next to communities of Asian and Asian heritage practitioners in our cities, neighborhoods, and backyards. As college chaplains, we should be forming deep relationships with our neighbors, working to undo Neo-Orientalist practices that encourage Asian erasure in favor of a liberative model of mutual care and responsibility. By looking deeply into our own intersectionalities, biases, and privileges, by learning from and giving back to local communities of Buddhist practitioners, by making our students aware that, as is definitely the case for me, most Buddhist practitioners do not look like me or practice like some of us were taught to practice, we honor a past and thriving present that makes our jobs and spiritual livelihoods possible in the first place.

References

Almond, Philip C. 1988. *The British Discovery of Buddhism*. Cambridge: Cambridge University Press.

Giles, C., & Sanford, M. 2022. *Mapping Buddhist Chaplaincy in North America*. Chaplaincy Innovation Lab.

Han, Chenxing. 2021. *Be the Refuge: Raising the Voices of Asian American Buddhists*. Berkeley: North Atlantic Books.

Hsu, Funie. 2016. "We've Been Here All Along." *Buddhadharma: The Practitioner's Quarterly*, 2016. https://www.lionsroar.com/weve-been-here-all-along/.

———. 2017. "Lineage of Resistance: When Asian American Buddhists Confront White Supremacy." *Buddhist Peace Fellowship: Buddhism + Social Justice* (blog). May 8, 2017. http://www.buddhistpeacefellowship.org/lineage-of-resistance/.

———. 2018. "Let's Continue Aaron's Work." *Lion's Roar: Buddhist Wisdom for Our Time*. November 20, 2018. https://www.lionsroar.com/lets-continue-aarons-work/.

Iwamura, Jane Naomi. 2011. *Virtual Orientalism: Asian Religions and American Popular Culture*. Oxford: Oxford University Press.

King, Richard. 1999. *Orientalism and Religion: Post-Colonial Theory, India and "The Mystic East."* New York: Routledge.

Listening to the Buddhists in our backyard. N.d. https://www.l2bb.org/

Lopez, Donald S., Jr., ed. 1995. *Curators of the Buddha: The Study of Buddhism Under Colonialism*. Chicago: University of Chicago Press.

Masuzawa, Tomoko. 2005. *The Invention of World Religions: Or, How European Universalism Was Preserved in the Language of Pluralism*. Chicago: University of Chicago Press.

May we gather. N.d. https://www.maywegather.org/

Mayerhofer, Ivan. 2021. "Emergent Orientalisms in Contemporary US Buddhisms and Buddhist Studies." Boulder: University of Colorado, Boulder. https://www.proquest.com/openview/145be677c4fea5b5028f529f43f8fa1a/1?pq-origsite=gscholar&cbl=18750&diss=y.

Pew Research Center. 2012a, July 19. *Asian Americans: A mosaic of faiths*. https://www.pewresearch.org/religion/2012/07/19/asian-americans-a-mosaic-of-faiths-overview/#_ftnref19

Pew Research Center. 2012b, December 18. *Buddhists*. https://www.pewresearch.org/religion/2012/12/18/global-religious-landscape-buddhist/

PRRI. 2024, February 23. *2020 PRRI Census of American Religion*. https://www.prri.org/research/2020-census-of-american-religion/

Said, Edward W. 1979. *Orientalism*. New York: Vintage Books.

Snodgrass, Judith. 2003. *Presenting Japanese Buddhism to the West: Orientalism, Occidentalism, and the Columbian Exposition*. Chapel Hill: University of North Carolina Press.

Williams, Duncan Ryuken. 2019. *American Sutra: A Story of Faith and Freedom in the Second World War*. Cambridge, Massachusetts: The Belknap Press of Harvard University Press.

Wilson, Jeff. 2014. *Mindful America: The Mutual Transformation of Buddhist Meditation and American Culture*. Oxford: Oxford University Press.

17
Managing and Transforming Conflict
Nathan Jishin Michon

Introduction

A student enters your chaplains' office at the university. They are fed up with the administration. They exasperatedly describe how campus wages have been stagnant for students for years despite increasing housing and general cost of living in the area, not to mention tuition increases. After a few months of trying to contact administration and organizing other students to protest in front of admin buildings, they express exhaustion at the effort. As you listen further, it becomes clear that the feeling that nobody is even listening in the administration has both intensified the frustration, while leading to deeper general exhaustion with the efforts. You also hear how three of this student's close friends have either quit the university or taken extended leaves of absence due to financial hardship, further increasing stress over the matter.

Although your position involves spiritual care and counseling, it also involves student advocacy. You make no promises for results, but you tell them that you will explore the issue further speaking directly to some of the administration. You also work with them to hear further stories of students who had been protesting and struggling with financial issues of their own.

At first, you struggle getting your own appointments with the CFO and a dean, but an ombudsman helps organize the meetings. It is by no means a quick process, but you let the students know you have meetings set up and are advocating to present their issues. Meetings with the dean and CFO both reveal similar positions and attitudes: both express some initial compassion towards student struggles, but point out how lower enrollment numbers in recent years make it nearly impossible to make significant additions in budget areas like pay for student jobs. However, further discussion at least opens the door for administrators to meet with student leaders. You and the ombudsman work together in helping to coordinate and facilitate the meetings.

A few student protesters, along with two representatives from student government, join and examine the budgets with administration. The meetings reveal some significant expenditures on student activities that student representatives say are either old unneeded traditions that are poorly attended or other resources that current students rarely make use of. The student government offers to help produce a survey for the student body that not only explains budgetary constraints, but asks for student input on their priorities.

In the end, surveys show widespread support to the administration for areas where cuts can be made; an outside organization helps with some of the local housing issues, and student wages receive their first significant raise in years. The administration allows student government representatives on a few administrative committees for the first time to ensure longer-term communication lines remain open. The story is reported in local papers and the morale boost on campus is felt. Moreover, the campus experiences its best student retention numbers going into the next academic year.

Of course, not every situation will fall into place as ideally as this case did. But it is more possible than many realize and represents a few key principles of conflict work that will be explored in greater depth throughout this chapter – patience through the process, hearing all sides, perceiving conflict for its potential positive change, and coming to creative both/and solutions that no party might have initially foreseen.

Introduction and Basics of Conflict

Conflict may be uncomfortable and difficult, but it is not necessarily negative in itself. The energy of conflict can produce change and, if skillfully managed, we can at least try to work with those around us to make that change as positive as possible. The key is to understand that conflict itself is not the enemy. What we truly want to avoid is violence, whether in thought, word, or deed; and whether that violence is physical, structural, or societal. When we are better able to distinguish conflict from violence, we have a greater opportunity to help turn that conflict into change, and hopefully reduce, prevent, or eliminate the violence of the situation.

The field of conflict transformation theory and practice meshes particularly well with Buddhist thought and practice. The four noble truths and teachings on karma help bring a deeper and thorough sense of understanding to the field and Buddhist practices can complement those extant conflict transformation practices. Just as Buddhism often teaches us to face suffering and look to its roots, these same principles can help us face and work with conflict in productive ways. With that in mind, it can be first useful to more thoroughly examine a few basic terms and concepts.

Conflict itself is a neutral and broad term that refers merely to how an issue remains unresolved. Sure, it could refer to major land disputes with warring nations on either side. Or it could simply be indecision about which park to go to for a walk or whether to wear the blue or yellow shirt. Conflict resolution refers to the process of bringing those conflicts to a close. However, in some circles, this term gained a negative connotation for how "resolving" a conflict might leave the underlying causes in place. A more holistic perspective in treating conflict along with all its depths and perspectives is referred to as "conflict transformation."

One of the pioneers of the field, John Paul Lederach, said conflict transformation is "to envision and respond to the ebb and flow of social conflict as life-giving opportunities for creating constructive change processes that reduce violence, increase justice in direct interaction and social structures, and respond to real-life problems in human relationships" (J. Lederach, 2003, p. 14). Lederach emphasizes that we can see conflict as a gift and opportunity. There is often a certain energy to conflict. It stirs the pot. That energy creates latent potential for change. Of course, when left to the whims of strong emotions, anger, and self-centered desires, the energy of conflict can create havoc. Yet, if harnessed with open heart and willingness to listen to all sides of a situation, looking past initial concerns into root issues, dealing with the uprooted issues can be an opportunity to sustainable change that leaves all parties in better conditions.

What we really want to avoid is not the conflict itself, but any violence, whether or not it stems from the conflict in question. Violence can have numerous forms. Direct violence is the harm done directly from one person or group to another, whether physical or verbal. This covers everything from a slap or a bomb explosion to a racial slur or angry yell. Structural violence refers to those societal structures that create poverty, oppression, exploitation, and other systematic causes of distress. Cultural violence lies even behind these other forms of violence within paradigmatic assumptions of the world; it is produced by symbols in our surrounding ideologies, languages, art, literature, media, law, education, and other facets of our accumulated unconscious archetypes.

Conflict transformation ideally deals with conflict in ways that avoid all forms of violence and helps to undo violence that is occurring. Detailed conversations with compassionate presence, deep listening, and internal exploration may uncover forms of structural or cultural violence that no parties involved even realized were present.

As Roger Fisher and William Ury suggest, people in conflict can often think of the issues as a negotiation and think about what they can gain or lose. There are typically two approaches:

> Soft or hard. The soft negotiator wants to avoid personal conflict and so makes concessions readily in order to reach agreement. He wants an amicable resolution; yet he often ends up exploited and feeling bitter. The hard negotiator sees any situation as a contest of wills in which the side that takes the more extreme positions and holds out longer fares better. He wants to win; yet he often ends up producing an equally hard response which exhausts him and his resources and harms his relationship with the other side.[1]

As a chaplain, being aware of these two tendencies is important, since you may be in a role of balancing them out or even helping people become aware of their place on such a spectrum. As the *Sutta Nipāta* states, "Winning gives birth to hostility; Losing, one lies down in pain; The calmed lie down with ease, having set winning and losing aside" (SN 3.14). In a sense, neither attitude would be "right view" from a Buddhist perspective, and both can ultimately be more stressful to the individual in conflict than they might even realize.

Getting to those points in between can require plenty of both *imagination* and *creativity*. Internationally acclaimed conflict transformation specialist Johan Galtung suggested these two skills might be more important than any others when working with conflict (Galtung, 2004, p. 1). The parties involved might have initial goals in mind that cannot mesh. Yet helping people pay deeper attention to their true needs and seeing the ways in which those might overlap and fit together can make everyone happier in the end. We often need to not only step "out of the box" ourselves in that process, but help invite others to step out of the box as well. As the story above showed, there were ultimately alternative ways around the simple give-and-take within the original debate.

Another point to be wary of in facilitating, navigating, or exploring such processes is the values that others and ourselves bring to such situations and how we *structure* and *prioritize* such values. Marc Gopic astutely points out:

> We are particularly prone to generate conflict by our stereotypical expectations of and sensitivity to what we think are the worst qualities of our enemy. Conversely, when reconciling with an enemy – an extremely difficult moment for the human psyche – we offer what we consider to be our best qualities of prosocial engagement, our ideal selves, and utterly reject the methods and character of what we perceive to be our enemies' worst traits. Most important, we expect our enemies to do exactly the same thing. But here is the catch! We expect them to engage in peaceful gestures that reflect our own highest selves, not theirs. And here the tragic failings in communication occur.[2]

There are many cases in which two or more parties in extended conflict actually have very similar values. But how everyone prioritizes those values may differ. If one person sees value A as fundamental, they may feel uncompromising

---

[1] Fisher & Ury, 2000, p. 71.

[2] Gopin, 2005, p. 147.

in saying "Of course, A, B, and C are important. But without A, there's no way we can bring B or C to the table." If another party thinks similarly about value B, not being able to offer anything else of themselves unless value B is foundational in talks, then you might lose your starting points.

Of course, most people don't consciously label and list their personal values in order. But being aware of such issues and pointing them out can help people come to greater understanding of each other when talks are at a standstill. Having individuals consciously list and prioritize those values may bring such unconscious priorities into consciousness and help people move forward.

We must also keep in mind that not all conflicts are meant to be "resolved." Not all people have to agree to come peaceably together in conflict situations. Let's explore this issue within another case study:

Student A enters your office asking to talk about some general troubles at school. They are a freshman and were a good student in high school, but have been struggling with various adaptations to college life. They are especially concerned about grades, as a couple of recent midterm exams had much lower scores than they had hoped for. A couple of meetings reveal that they are a relatively quiet and introverted student, but making some friends. Studies are valued and they do feel some pressure related to parental perceptions of their academic performance. However, while listening and asking numerous reflective questions, the end of the second meeting with the student reveals they are not sleeping well, often feeling exhausted. You agree to meet a third time to explore this more.

It finally comes out that, although Student A generally gets along with their assigned roommate, they have very different lifestyles. The student takes early classes and prefers going to bed around 11 pm, only using the dorm room for study and sleep. Their roommate, Student B, regularly invites friends in, drinks in small groups, and stays up until 2:00 or 3:00 am on a regular basis. Student B agrees to come in and speak with you separately, and you have a good conversation. Student B tries to be quiet when their roommate falls asleep, but also expresses a little frustration through the effort. "We'll only get this college experience once. I wish Student A would at least live it up a little. I don't have any classes 'til afternoon anyway. Ten is freakin' early to go to bed. I wanna relax a bit, chill with some friends at night." Both students try to respect the other and don't have particularly ill feelings. But the frustrations in their different lifestyle preferences are apparent. In the end, you talk with student life coordinators on campus, and the students are placed with new roommates. They are both happier with the new situations.

Of course, there are many roommate situations in which students simply have to learn a little give and take. Yet in some cases – not only for roommate situations, but conflict in general – trying to bring two parties together can be more complex than its worth. Finding a way to live amicably apart might be the better solution for all involved. Those involved in conflict can sometimes become so attached to bringing parties together that they lose sight of these alternate options. Trying to make sure our minds and hearts remain truly open to broader possibilities is part of our own constant practice in facilitating any explorations of conflict.

This story also further emphasizes the value of listening and reflective questions in exploring conflict. In this case, Student A themselves wasn't even fully cognizant or open about the true impact of the roommate situation on different areas of their lives. Helping people explore those deeper underlying causes is an important role we can regularly help fulfill; and it may often lead to the need to contact other members within the university to collaborate with in more fully dealing with the conflict situation.

It can also be helpful to remember the Buddha's advice regarding Right Speech. For example, in the *Aṅguttara Nikāya*, the Buddha states, "Monks, a statement endowed with five factors is well-spoken, not ill-spoken. It is blameless and unfaulted by knowledgeable people. Which five? It is spoken at the right time. It is spoken in truth. It is spoken affectionately. It is spoken beneficially. It is spoken with a mind of good-will" (598). Being mindful of each of these factors while facilitating between those in conflict, or even posting them in the room visible to self and others can be a useful reminder. The first factor in particular is an important reminder. Even when our words are truthful and spoken with the best of intentions, it might not necessarily be the proper time. In so many sutras about right speech, the Buddha emphasizes this point; finding the appropriate time to speak is important and, if it is not yet that time, simply being quiet and listening can be the best form of right speech.

Luckily, this a point where Buddhist principles mesh well with both conflict transformation and chaplaincy skills. The deep listening involved in right speech is such a key part of most chaplains' background and training, but is also so critical to helping different parties find their deeper needs in conflict and the new ways of engagement in which all people involved might be more free from the even the subtler forms of violence or dukkha within a situation.

Larger Conflicts and Circle Processes

Conflicts can sometimes be far more complex and involve multiple people or groups. It should be kept in mind that many times sizable conflicts are not simply between two parties. Even when it seems there is a split between two sides of a conflict, closer listening and attention reveals many gray areas, third parties, and textures to the social fabric that may be hard to place; there may also be people who are not as directly involved, yet feel deeply impacted by the conflict at hand. The conflict ripples out into the community and surrounding people. When sizable fissures result in part of the campus culture, a broader circle process might be advisable for all people to hear each other out, to uncover the various dynamics of what is occurring, and to try to heal together.

Let's think back to the above example that opened the chapter, between protesting students, administration, and the student government. Imagine, under such circumstances, that there had also been building distrust over the lack of response from administration, mixed feelings from students about the student government and the complexities of members' relationship with the administration, and numerous other issues that compounded the situation. In the midst of it all, imagine you are the chaplain helping to convene this circle process.

You have invited and brought together main representatives from the protesters, the student government, and the administration. A few students who were not a part of either group, as well as a couple of staff members, a school counselor, a faculty member, and a parent of a student on leave of absence all hear about the process, and inquire about joining. You welcome their perspectives into the circle and they appreciate the opportunity to join and share their own experiences related to the conflict.

On the day of the circle process, all participants sit in chairs arranged in a circle, and you greet all individuals as they arrive. When everyone is present, you politely and kindly ask them to take a seat. The circle process might go like this:

1. The circle begins with a brief ceremony or sacred act that opens the process. You might choose lighting a candle at the middle of the circle. Everyone bows their heads in a short moment of silence, while you instruct them to connect with their breaths and seek to find their best selves for this moment. You can adjust the act as you see fit, but it should be a religiously or spiritually neutral act (unless all parties are part of the same tradition) that helps

not only mark the beginning, but creates some sense of serenity. There may be many nerves, angst, or numerous feelings coming in, and not all people are going to become completely calm. Yet to even calm the room a little with a sense of sacred presence can help set the tone and assist in creating better group dynamics that follow.

2. You then remind everyone of the purpose of the gathering. Make it a short, but succinct statement that summarizes the main points.

3. All information shared within the circle shall be considered confidential, and you should clearly let people know and stress this point. It will ultimately help with the sense of safety and security within the space. Please note, however, exceptions to confidentiality include mention of intent to harm other humans or commit a crime, for which contacting appropriate professionals and authorities can be legally required of a facilitating chaplain. Also clarify any time restrictions on the gathering, so such limits can be properly respected.

4. You begin by helping the group as a whole identify shared values and guidelines for the circle. Although you yourself could suggest such things as open-mindedness, caring, honesty, and deep listening, the more that participants come up with these points themselves, the better they tend to follow them. A single talking piece should be used to identify who has the right to speak at any given moment and nobody should speak over them or interject. Whether people have as long as they need or if there are certain time constraints, the group and circumstances can help determine those factors. The guidelines, as much as possible, are agreed upon by consensus. You also maintain a visible record of all agreed upon discussion guidelines, whether on a chalkboard, projector, or other device.

5. As indicated above, the group uses a talking piece which designates the speaker. Generally, no one else may speak while the speaker holds the piece. The one exception is the facilitator, who may intervene occasionally to provide instructions, notify participants of established time limits, or remind people of rules within the circle. You might be the facilitator. But if it is another, you should clearly introduce them. If not established by the group themselves, some further points about discussion with the talking stick should be established. There is no obligation to speak while holding the talking piece, nor should participants be pressured to speak; they may choose to have a pause while finding words, offer a period of silence, or quietly pass it to others. In a physical space, the talking piece usually moves around the circle from one person to the next. However, if meeting in an online space, the order of the "circle" should be clearly noted at the outset.

6. Before the process begins, even if points have been established, it can be helpful to remind participants to be respectful of the holder of the talking stick: participants should be asked to practice attentive listening as much as possible, not only by not speaking out of turn, but by trying to fully listen with body, heart, and mind. Nobody should feel they must agree with the words of another, but we can all respect their time and space within the circle. In other words, while another holds the talking stick, ask participants to try to also avoid gestures, grunts, or vocal expressions, and strong facial signs of judgement upon others which may interrupt and/or disrupt the person with the talking stick. Conversely, respectful listening should be open-minded, open-hearted, attentive, and avoiding preconceived notions as much as possible.

7. The holder of the talking piece should be asked to avoid "you" statements and speak as much as possible in "I" statements when referring to any feelings or intent. It is a time to tell *one's own* story. Participants should avoid assuming the thoughts, emotions, or intentions of another. In other words, a statement about an event might be "When [name] said ____, I felt _____," maintaining an emphasis on one's own thoughts, feelings, reactions, and perceptions. When a person begins assuming another's thoughts or emotions, especially if that person is in the room, it might be all the more difficult for that individual to remain silent, and if you let such "you" statements continue, it could lead to far more difficulty in keeping order within the circle. If you are the facilitator, this point may simply require a consistent occasional, yet gentle reminder.
8. Even if participants know each other, begin with a round of self-introductions. This may include a short ice-breaker question focused on a positive-values each participant adheres to.
9. Begin at least two rounds with all participants having an opportunity with the talking piece. This is the time when they may speak their own truths of their own experiences. The first round is to more generally speak about feelings on the issue. The second round may be in response to items of the first round. If time remains for another round(s), focus on primary themes of the first two rounds. If you believe guidelines need to be re-addressed after the process begins, you may pause the circle sharing to begin a discussion about following the guidelines.
10. 15-20 minutes before closing, ask all participants to share final thoughts and conclusions from their experience in the circle.
11. You or a separate facilitator finally summarizes the experience and the final thoughts.
12. If it seems like a further meeting might be necessary, agree on an appropriate time.
13. Conduct a brief closing ceremony.

Of course, this example is only a model and you may adapt any parts of it to fit your own situation and circumstances. The example above is imagined with a larger group of people, with a primary purpose of coming to greater, rounded understanding about all of the underlying issues and feelings. With a larger group, such a process can take significant time on its own. In this case, further steps were probably necessary and the hopes for such a future meeting and the process for that could have been decided during step #12. If everyone has poured out their emotions and listened to others over a significant amount of time, there is typically little energy left to go into more than those basic details of further steps during the current circle process. Any larger decisions a group tries to make during such a state could run the risk of being inadequate representations of people's true thoughts, feelings, and intentions; it could even run the risk of fraying some of the progress that was made.

However, with a smaller group of people or if individuals come to an understanding while still having time to proceed, you may want to include more detailed expression of 'next steps' within this circle discussion. Generally, it is best for this process to have decisions made by consensus. Numerous models can be found on generating consensus. It is best to search and read through several such processes to choose the one that best fits your group. You might enter "consensus-based decision making" or "Martha's rules" into a search engine to begin exploring those options.

If you are facilitating a circle for the first time, it might be helpful to facilitate a practice run with a few close friends and/or colleagues; it is best to be comfortable with the process before running it in a situation over a tense issue. And of course, most importantly, do what you need for your own self-care and heart care prior to and after such an exercise.

If you are facilitating a circle for the first time, it might be helpful to facilitate a practice run with a few close friends and/or colleagues; it is best to be comfortable with the process before running it in a situation over a tense issue. And of course, most importantly, do what you need for your own self-care and heart care prior to and after such an exercise. Facilitating a circle about an issue that has led to intense conflict can be exhausting, but can also be rewarding when it leads to lasting positive change. The opportunity to simply have a voice in front of others can relive a lot of pressure that builds up under the surface within a school community. The chance for all involved, whether directly or indirectly, to be heard and seen can be so beneficial. Even if people do not agree with all the perspectives provided, simply having more understanding about where other are coming from can also provide important steps in the community's broader healing process. We cannot truly face problems unless we are first aware of them.

Buddhist Tools and Returning to Right View

Buddhism not only echoes this critical importance of awareness, but provides numerous tools to both accentuate that awareness, and to deal with even the most subtle forms of violence that we may become aware of. This is the whole basis of Right View and the Four Noble Truths. Some people think of the Four Noble Truths more as a zero-sum game: it's all about full awakening, and that's it. But this set can be more usefully applied to the minutiae of daily stress and suffering that arise in our lives from moment to moment.

When we notice the truth of suffering and stress that exists somewhere, we are taught to examine it. The stress might exists physically, mentally, socially, structurally, or culturally. But as calmly and equanimously as might be possible, we look into that; we face it and observe it. By coming to understand it deeper, we realize the cause. This leads directly the second noble truth: the origin of stress and suffering. Our duty here is to let it go. In this case, we find those ways to help the people involved or the broader community let go of that suffering. Whether through ritual, listening, conversation, or other tools at our disposal, we do what we can to help people leave that original cause behind. By doing away with the cause, there is a cessation to the suffering. We notice this difference and reflect on how we arrived here. We can even take a moment to enjoy the little victories. But then we return to the path: Right view, intention, speech, action, livelihood, effort, mindfulness, and concentration.

The Four Noble Truths can create positive feedback loops. In the case of college and university-based conflict, we explore points of stress and suffering within the community. Finding and releasing those factors, we also end up broadening our overall awareness of the community and its web of interconnections. This increased awareness can highlight further and deeper points of the conflict which cause violence, maybe in previously unrealized ways. Yet by continuously facing them and expanding our awareness of the situations, we have that capacity to see ever deeper and handle more.

> When embraced,
> the rod of violence
> breeds danger & fear:
> Look at people in strife.
> I will tell of how
> I experienced
> terror:
> Seeing people floundering
> like fish in small puddles,
> competing with one another –
> as I saw this,
> fear came into me.
> The world was entirely
> without substance.
> All the directions

were knocked out of line.
Wanting a haven for myself,
I saw nothing that wasn't laid claim to.
Seeing nothing in the end
but competition,
I felt discontent.
And then I saw
an arrow here,
so very hard to see,
embedded in the heart.
Overcome by this arrow
you run in all directions.
But simply on pulling it out
you don't run,
you don't sink....
Whatever things are tied down in the
   world,
you shouldn't be set on them.
Having totally penetrated
sensual pleasures,
sensual passions,
you should train for your own
unbinding [nirvana] (SN 4.15).

May all beings in conflict find the ways to use that energy to unbind the violence within and around them, and may we listen to those stories in ways that assist them in that process.

Further Reading

Amstutz, L.S. (2009). *The Little Book of Victim Offender Conferencing: Bringing Victims and Offenders Together in Dialogue*. Good Books.

Karp, D.R., & Armour, M. (2019). *The Little Book of Restorative Justice for Colleges and Universities: Repairing Harm and Rebuilding Trust in Response to Student Misconduct* (2nd edition). Good Books.

Kraybill, R. (2007). *Cool Tools for Hot Topics: Group Tools to Facilitate Meetings When Things Are Hot*. Good Books.

Lederach, J.P. (1998). *Building Peace: Sustainable Reconciliation in Divided Societies*. United States Institute of Peace.

Pranis, K. (2005). *The Little Book of Circle Processes: A New/Old Approach to Peacemaking*. Good Books.

Glossary

Circle Process: Also known as "peacemaking circle" and by many indigenous names. These processes of community peacemaking use simple circular listening structures that try to ensure equity of expression and opportunities for individuals to share and reveal their truths with the present community.

Conflict Transformation: Envisioning and responding to the ebb and flow of social conflict as life-giving opportunities for creating constructive change processes that reduce violence, increase justice in direct interaction and social structures, and respond to real-life problems in human relationships.

References

Fisher, R., & Ury, W. (2000). Getting to YES. In D.P. Barash (Ed.), *Approaches to Peace: A Reader in Peace Studies* (pp. 70-76). Oxford University Press.

Galtung, J. (2004). *Transcend and Transform: An Introduction to Conflict Work*. Pluto Press.

Gopin, M. (2005). *Holy War, Holy Peace: How Religion Can Bring Peace to the Middle East* (Revised ed. edition). Oxford University Press.

Lederach, J. (2003). *Little Book of Conflict Transformation: Clear Articulation of the Guiding Principles by a Pioneer in the Field*. Good Books.

Pranis, K. (2005). *The Little Book of Circle Processes: A New/Old Approach to Peacemaking*. Good Books.

Part IV
Upaya

Part IV: Upaya

Introduction

While Buddhist teachers in retreat settings can counsel a path of renunciation, the college chaplain's work is to confirm that an enlightened person does belong within this world. Like a traditional Zen cook, we can work with all the ingredients at hand, so that, as Zen Master Bernie Glassman put it, "our life is the supreme meal." Each of the contributors in this section has offered precious methods for preparing that meal within the context of students' lives and learning.

One particularly resonant theme of this section is bodymind integration. Victor Gabriel offers prayers that operationalize a Queer Buddhist theology, practices which revalorize Buddhist icons and scriptures to affirm LGBTQ+ identities and lives. In traditional temple settings, very little advice is given on sex, love and relationships. Gabriel offers gathas that support the bringing of one's wholeness to the use of dating apps, to coming out, to sexuality. I am reminded of Carl Jung's teaching, "The attainment of *wholeness* requires one to stake one's *whole* being. Nothing less will do; there can be no easier conditions, no substitutes, *no compromises*." Gabriel's mindful awareness of sexuality and intimacy has been enthusiastically adopted by the college students with whom I have worked during the editing process, who served as a test audience.

Harrison Blum expands upon this awareness of the relational realm through improvisational movement and dance, peer-to-peer dialogue and spontaneous prayer. He cites the rich history of Buddhist movement practices, as well as the recent evolution of Dharma art and movement. Blum then describes a singular and valuable contribution to this field, his own métier, as *Dharma Jam*. This mindful-movement journey has three phases: *Tune In*, which leads the participant into conscious embodiment, *Get Down*, which welcomes explorations of Dharma as joy and authenticity, and *Join Up*, which explores movement as a path of interconnection with Sangha. This mindful-movement serves as a foundation for the exploration of the Three Marks of Existence: *anicca* (impermanence), *anatta* (non-self) and *dukkha* (suffering). Dharma Jam is effectively a ritual that bridges the sacred and secular. However, as Blum notes, "In a world with sacred potential in every moment, every action carries the potential to be ritual. Dharma Jam is neither inherently functional nor sacred. It simply names the sacred as possible and invites a doorway into that space." Blum then generously provides instructions for the facilitation of Dharma Jam.

Reverend Mark Unno shows us the path of practice expressed through calling and vocation, using three examples from Nikaya Buddhism and three episodes from Mahayana texts. Within both systems, Unno notes, we can access a dynamic web of interdependence. Within Nikaya Buddhism, there has always been flexibility of response: we see this within the Buddha's own adaptation of the teaching according to the capacity of his followers. In Mahayana Buddhism, the skillful adaptation of Dharma to circumstances is described through the concept of *upaya-kausalya*, skillful means. Unno then provides us with a nuanced and careful consideration of the interplay of calling and career within our modern world, pointing to the need for balance, and the need "to live in society (form) but aspire not to be defined by it (emptiness)."

Jessica Thomas invites personal and intergenerational wellness through the contemplative use of genograms, a skillful means based in family systems theory which emphasizes interdependence as well as awareness of the patterns and dynamics within the web of life. This pathway of critical self-reflection makes it possible for students to be mindful of both the connectedness of all life and the differentiation of our own precious human life. Through this meditation on the "threads of the family tapestry," family systems can be navigated in a conscious and mature way. Thomas integrates this systemic work with contemplative photography and deep listening practices so that clients can access a deeper level of emotional awareness and systemic healing.

18
Queer Buddhist Prayers
Dr. Victor Gabriel

I wrote this chapter because when I was in my teens in the 1980s in SE Asia, I could not find any resources for myself. The following queer Buddhist prayers were written in collaboration with Benson Pang, Daryl Toy, Oliver Lim, and Syd Yang. They brought to these prayers a more contemporary lived experience of being queer. These prayers were not meant to be definitive or extensive. These prayers do not attempt to capture the beautiful tapestry of the intersectionality of queer lives. These prayers were meant to support the readers' successful exploration of Buddhist prayer that is meaningful and relevant to contemporary LGBTQ+ lives.

I knew early that I was queer, but I had no understanding what that meant. Later, neither school nor temple provided any positive direction or understanding of what it means to be queer. As this was during the AIDS pandemic, the wider community did not provide any environment where one could have future dreams. It was only much later when I arrived in the USA that I allowed myself to dream big.

As a Buddhist academic, these prayers represent one possible way to operationalize what I would like to call a Queer Buddhist theology. Scholars Jose Cabezon and Roger Corless have noted its foundations in non-duality, interdependence, and Buddha Nature. These prayers revalorize Buddhist scriptures, icons, and practices to affirm LGBTQ+ identities and lives. Lay Buddhists are seldom given any guidance by traditional dharmology (Buddhist theology) of sex. Traditional discussions on sex and relationships privileges the male monastic experience. The little advice there is on sex, love and relationships is vague or overly determined by cultural contexts. This includes the historical stigmatized third and fourth gender categories of the *paṇḍaka* ("gender-deficient," culturally thought of as "male-deficient") and the *ubhatobyañjanaka* ("both-sexed"). Both categories do not map unto contemporary queer identities, causing anguish, confusion, debate, and discretion in contemporary Buddhist cultures.

From the perspective of a Buddhist practitioner, these prayers can be used as stand-alone prayers. In more formal contexts, these prayers can be preceded by imagining that Bodhisattva Avalokiteshvara or Guan Yin is truly present. In the *Lotus Sutra*, Avalokiteshvara, the expression of compassion itself, makes a vow to manifest in whatever gender to benefit beings. They represent a numinosity that cannot be essentialized to the male/female binary. This is followed by the Refuge prayer and the Four Immeasurables prayer. Next, light rays stream down from the crown, throat, and heart of Avalokiteshvara bringing compassion, wisdom, and power to the practitioner. The practitioner imagines that this has actually happened. This is followed by one of the prayers given here. Finally, the session is concluded with a dedication of merit. Through this merit, may all readers become truly free.

A Prayer for Coming Out

O Compassionate Avalokiteshvara,
As I take steps to come out and share my truth,
I know that my ultimate truth is my perfect Buddha Nature;
Yet coming out is my truth in this dream-like conventional life.
Help me overcome my stress, fear and anxiety that hiding my sexuality has caused.
May I find the strength to know myself beyond the fear of others,
As I take this step
Bless me with a life that is happy and free.
May my coming out awaken more truth in myself and others.
May these stresses and anxieties I am experiencing,
Transform into loving-kindness and compassion for myself and others.

A Prayer While Transitioning

O Compassion Avalokiteshvara,
My mind, this ever-present awareness, is pure.
Through the power of interdependence, I have received this precious human life,
This precious human mind, this source of Buddha Nature has no physical form.

My mind knows depths that do not always make sense to me and others.
Yet it knows when I take a chance on this unfolding,
My body carries the wisdom of the Buddhas and guides me into the unknown
Grant that my physical form mirrors the expansiveness and beauty within me.
Grant me the power and bravery to fully be myself.
Give me patience to be brave in small steps and bold ways.
In becoming may I be free.

A Prayer before using a Dating App

O Compassionate Avalokiteshvara,
As I search for a compatible and loving partner,
Grant me the courage to be vulnerable enough to open myself to another in love,
Help me to see the Buddha Nature in each person on this dating app.
To treat them with dignity and respect rather than as objects for my pleasure.
I pray that you grant me the wisdom and eloquence to represent myself well on this dating app,
So that I can recognize me from my words.
Bless me with patience and persistence so that I may continue my search for love and companionship.

A Prayer before a First Sexual Experience

O Compassionate Avalokiteshvara,
You have always been with me.
Through the heartache and the happiness in my search for companionship.
I have longed for this moment for so long.
May I experience connection of the physical,
May I connect with the Buddha Nature of others.
May all who desire intimacy have their wishes swiftly fulfilled.

A Prayer before Testing for HIV

O Compassionate Avalokiteshvara,
You who hear the prayers of the anxious and afraid,
You who have heard the prayers of my parents, of my ancestors,
I feel scared, numb, and overwhelmed,
May these results be unstained as my innermost nature.

Whatever the results may be, help me face each day bravely.
My life may be different, but it is far from over.
May whatever stress and anxiety I feel be of benefit to others.
I bow to those who made this test possible,
For those who came before me,
Their protest, their dreams,
These now protect me.
May all beings be free of illness and prejudice.
May all have access to healing of body, speech, and mind.

19
SANGHA SYNERGIES:
DANCE AND PRAYER AS DHARMA MODALITIES

Harrison Blum

Excerpts used with permission from Blum, Harrison. "Buddhists, Get Your Prayer On" as found in Gustafson, Hans, ed. (2018). *Learning From Other Religious Traditions: Leaving Room for Holy Envy*. London: Pallgrave Macmilan.

Across my twenty-five years of Buddhist practice, I have continually been impressed with the detail and efficacy of Buddhist insight tools. Through meticulously described techniques of meditation and self-reflection, Buddhism teaches practitioners to refine their present-moment awareness of sensations, thoughts, and emotions. From this foundation of clarity, the tradition describes exact procedures to train one's intentions to produce fruitful thoughts, statements, and actions. Beyond vague and societally in-vogue concepts of Buddhism as cool or peaceful, the religion presents a rigorous path demanding discipline and persistent attention to our shadow sides and less-than-life-giving desires. Indeed, it is through gentle observation of our mental and emotional process – especially their sharp edges – that we come to learn a better way of being.

Amidst the tradition's wisdom and teachings, Buddhism's internal focus can create deficits in the relational realm, its utilization of silence can undermine the power of the spoken word, and its embrace of measured observation can cast into irrelevance, if not disapproval, prophetic voice, and artistic creation. Buddhism harbors advanced spiritual technologies for cultivating awareness and a growing edge for bringing that awareness into fuller expression.

From these observations, for the past fifteen years, I have sought to expand the modalities of Buddhist practice, first through improvisational movement and dance, then peer-to-peer dialogue, and, more recently, spontaneous prayer. Each of these approaches has, in turn, expanded who is practicing while also deepening insight and benefit. I have found this to be particularly true on college campuses.

Moving Bodies as Dharma Practice: Laying the Ground

If one perceives the Dharma with one's own body…then one is indeed an upholder of the Dharma. – *The Buddha*.

Both Buddhism and dance invite the practitioner into present-moment embodiment. The Buddha states in the *Anguttara Nikaya*, "There is one thing that, when cultivated and regularly practiced, leads to deep spiritual intention, to peace, to mindfulness and clear comprehension, to vision and knowledge, to a happy life here and now, and to the culmination of wisdom and awakening. And what is that one thing? Mindfulness centered on the body." Within "this fathom-long body," he taught, "is the cosmos."

Similarly, movement and dance training foster continuous mindfulness of the body. Artists in these fields spend decades fine-tuning their awareness and control of subtle sensations and movements. In the *Satipatthana Sutta*, the Buddha's pivotal teaching on the Four Foundations of Mindfulness, the First Foundation focuses on the body. Practitioners are guided to cultivate mindfulness of their breathing, postures, and movements. When "going forward and returning...looking ahead and looking away...when flexing and extending...when eating, drinking...when walking, standing, sitting, falling asleep, waking up, talking, and keeping silent" the practitioner is to maintain continuous mindfulness. This list encourages embodied awareness in everything we do, in all our moments. Movement and dance artists practice, create, and perform in this realm. They are masters of the First Foundation.

Amidst this inherent synergy between Buddhist and dance practice, the climates of Buddhism and dance are aligning in new ways that offer unprecedented opportunities for cross-pollination. Most Western Buddhists are lay people. As such, there are now multiple generations of Western Buddhists who have deep Buddhist practices alongside other life pursuits. There are practitioners sitting intensive Buddhist retreats and meditating daily as they work as choreographers, dance teachers, theater directors, and bodyworkers. There are also Buddhist lamas, nuns, teachers, chaplains, and professors integrating movement forms into their Dharma teaching. While Buddhism has always focused on the body, embodied practice modalities are now increasing and spreading in novel ways; there are many movement practices emerging alongside walking meditation as alternatives to seated meditation.

Amidst current innovations, there is a rich history of movement and dance as Buddhist practice, a connection shared by most religions across time and culture. Tibetan Buddhist Cham dance, performed by monks, dates back over a thousand years. Writing in the 15th century, Japanese Nōh theater master and devout Buddhist Zeami Motokiyo claimed, "The fundamental properties of dance and song have always arisen from the Buddha-nature that is stored in all sentient beings." A century later, Japanese samurai and Rinzai Zen master Takuan Sōhō wrote of a state of pure perception that "applies to all activities we may perform, such as dancing."

Drawing upon these artistic traditions that had been part of Buddhist lineages for millennia, 20th century Buddhists illuminated the connection between Buddhism and the arts in Western contexts. Anagarika Govinda wrote Art and Meditation in the 1930s. A few decades later, D. T. Suzuki, whose work greatly popularized Zen in the West, wrote that with a spontaneity born of presence, "all arts merge into Zen." Jump forward another few decades to the 1970s, and Sangharakshita, founder of the Friends of the Western Buddhist Order in the UK, was writing of a "religion of art" grounded in "the expansion of consciousness beyond the boundaries of selfhood." Naropa University and Shambhala lineage founder Chögyam Trungpa Rinpoche spoke of Dharma art as "art that springs from...the meditative state." Also, in the latter half of the 20th century, Buddhist teacher Ruth Denison loosened the structures of meditation retreats and incorporated movement and dance. Reflecting in the 1980s on her approach to teaching, Denison shared, "When there is strong awareness, one can be creative. A new approach is no problem."

Sacred and therapeutic dance in the West, meanwhile, has blossomed. The turn of the 20th century saw individual dance performers, such as Isadora Duncan and Ruth St. Denis, focusing on the sacred element of their work. As modern dance gave way to post-modern dance in the 1960s, some dance artists began to embrace a process-over-product orientation. This shift was best exemplified by the Judson Dance Theater, which grew out of classes taught by Robert Dunn, a student of Buddhist *Abhidharma*.

Movement and dance have also become widely available as spiritual practices for untrained dancers, with programs hosted in venues that include large retreat centers and the yoga studio around the corner. Some of this momentum arises out of yoga's growing popularity. The Kripalu Center for Yoga and Health, for example, has offered multiple yoga-dance fusions, from "Let Your Yoga Dance" to "Salsa and Yoga" to "Shake Your Soul: The Yoga of Dance." Artists in contemporary dance are also contributing. JourneyDance, 5Rhythms, Soul Motion, and Spiritweaves are examples of visionary movers formalizing and sharing their practices of sacred dance. Some of these even offer teacher trainings in their respective forms.

The field of Dance/Movement Therapy (DMT) has emerged as another arena of conscious movement and dance, harnessing the therapeutic potential of the moving body. Originating in the 1940s, DMT arose "out of the merger of the modern dance movement with existing theories of group and individual psychology and psychotherapy." Distinct from talk therapy or technical dance training, DMT honors and examines expressive embodiment as a source of insight and healing. In a move toward professionalization, the American Dance Therapy Association was established in 1966 and began with 73 members. Their online directory currently lists over 1,000 members.

Perhaps most noteworthy in the current landscape of dancing with Dharma is the ever-growing popularization of mindfulness meditation. In 2014, amazon.com listed two thousand books for sale with the word "mindfulness" in the title. As of December 2023, there are over 50,000 hits for that same search criteria. A 2006 study by the National Institutes of Health stated there could be as many as "one million new meditators every year" in the United States. That number has continued to grow, with the Centers for Disease Control reporting a tripling of the number of adult meditators in the United States from 2012 to 2017. Meditation by children over that time increased by a factor of nine.

In many settings, mindfulness meditation is not being taught or practiced in an explicitly Buddhist context. In his book *Evolving Dharma*, scholar, and contemplative Jay Michaelson states that "in the last quarter century, the dharma has evolved by disappearing: it's been taken out of its religious context, abstracted, and now appears in any number of secular (and multi-religious) forms instead."

While high-profile figures, from the Dalai Lama to Oprah Winfrey, have supported the rise of meditation outside of Buddhism, mindfulness has largely been popularized by clinical application and research drawing directly from Buddhist practices and teachings. Mindfulness-Based Stress Reduction founder Dr. Jon Kabat-Zinn and Mindfulness-Based Cognitive Therapy co-founder Dr. John Teasdale both credit Buddhism, specifically the Insight Meditation tradition, with influencing the establishment of these therapeutic models. Buddhism stands to continue gaining attention in the West as mindfulness continues to grow in popularity.

The rise of Western Buddhism, sacred dance, and Dance/Movement Therapy, along with the mindfulness meditation boom, offer unprecedented opportunity for Buddhism to inform movement and dance practices, and for Buddhist practice to be shaped by movement and dance artists. Such interweaving is already well underway, as documented by the 27 contributors to my 2016 *Dancing with Dharma: Essays on Movement and Dance in Western Buddhism* (McFarland). As incubators of inspiration and innovation, college campuses are ideal testing grounds for such new developments.

With this foundation now laid on the synergy and context of Buddhism and dance, I will bring you into the first format I created to fuse the two.

Dharma Jam:
A Modern Buddhist Dance Liturgy

Choreographer-philosopher Sandra Horton Fraleigh writes, "The present-centered moment...[is] the vital moment of both art and religion." Dancing with Dharma inhabits that vitality shared by spirituality and expression in the present moment. Since 2008, I have sought to host that experience for others in Dharma

Jam – a format I have led at colleges and divinity schools that integrates mindful movement and sacred dance as Dharma practice.

Jams are divided into three phases: Tune In, Get Down, and Join Up, corresponding with the Three Gems of Buddha, Dharma, and Sangha. Tune In affords time and space for personal arrival. We begin in seated meditation, followed by a standing meditation, and then slow movement. Spacious music invites us to let go of the busyness of the day and show up in our bodies. We observe our impulses to move and then allow our movement to have momentum. We begin to dance with our partners of breath and balance, honoring our human potential and Buddha nature.

Get Down welcomes a greater range of motion and speed. The music gains intensity, and we blur the line between movement and dance, holding dance as being playful and curious about movement. We focus on how we feel more than how we look. We continue to breathe and know that we are breathing. We follow our joy and authenticity, welcoming the ways in which truth, the Dharma, enters our lives.

Join Up expands the focus from me to we. We enter the collective ritual by paying more attention to how others are moving around us. Small similarities in dance gestures and styles bridge our individual dances into a group creation. Music remains mid to high-tempo and opens into a more playful tone as we celebrate our shared practice, our Sangha. These three phases close with a dancing dedication and a seated reflection circle.

Undergirding this choreographic progression is a Dharmic process infused with what the Buddha called the Three Marks of Existence. These are impermanence, non-self, and the suffering that arises when we live in resistance to these first two. Anicca, anatta, and dukkha in Pali.

We live as mortal beings in a changing world. Change is a constant, from the vibrations of molecules to the slow erosion of mountains. As the world changes, we change with it, down to our bones. Every seven years, even our skeletons are made up of completely different cells. While we may feel and act as separate beings, apart from the rest of the world, indeed, we are more interconnected than separate. This built-in interconnection is what Buddhism calls non-self. Much of the suffering that Buddhism is so well known for discussing arises when we push against these natural laws of change and interconnection. The word dukkha originally referred to an axle that didn't fit well – quite literally, a square peg in a round hole. We experience dukkha when we try to live in an unchanging world as separate beings when we do not surrender to what is.

Dharma Jam offers a format for this surrender. By tuning in with awareness to our body's impulses to move, we contact the impermanence of sensation (*anicca*). A few moments of observing our physical sensations show us that our body itself is a constantly changing landscape. In receiving more than creating our movement, we release concepts of "me" or "mine" (*anatta*). Our dance is happening without our needing to drive it – dances without a dancer. As we align with change and selflessness in this way, we also align with the natural order of things. We ease that square peg away from the round hole (*dukkha*). We become like the bees the Buddha mentions in the *Dhammapada*, drinking the nectar without harming the flower. We are present without needing to attain or defend anything. Our dance thus becomes a ritual offering. We return two of our most precious possessions – time and ourselves – to the universe. We offer these as we realize they are not ours to begin with. We offer the universe back to itself.

In holding Dharma Jam as a ritual practice, I resonate with anthropologist Edmund Leach, who located ritual in a continuum. Writing in the 1950's, he stated:

> At one extreme, we have actions that are entirely profane, entirely

functional...[and] at the other we have actions which are entirely sacred, strictly aesthetic.... Between these two extremes we have the great majority of social actions which partake partly of the one sphere and partly of the other. From this point of view technique and ritual, profane and sacred, do not denote types of action but aspects of almost any kind of action.

In a world with sacred potential in every moment, every action carries the potential to be ritual. Dharma Jam is neither inherently functional nor sacred. It simply names the sacred as possible and invites a doorway into that space. It is upon each participant to accept the invitation to surrender to our fluid interconnection.

Religious studies scholar Catherine Bell coined the term *ritualization*, pointing to how the qualities of action assign meaning to the acts, as opposed to actions possessing inherent meaning. Bell speaks of the "ritualized body [as] a body invested with a 'sense' of ritual," and holds that with practice one may attain "'ritual mastery'": [whereby] 'schemes of ritualization' come to be embedded in the very perceptions and dispositions of the body." Dharma Jam invites practitioners to re-pattern their perceptions and dispositions, shifting away from desire, aversion, and delusion into a direct embodiment of clear awareness.

When I tell people about doing work with Buddhism and dance, a question I often get is, "What does Buddhist dance look like?" My answer points to each mover's experience on the inside. The Buddhist part of the dance happens internally, in how we perceive and respond to experience. At any given moment in a Dharma Jam, different participants dance quickly and slowly, gracefully and spastically, with others and alone. There is also usually at least one person in stillness or stretching. Amidst this eclectic dance floor, it is each mover's experience that makes it Buddhist, or spiritual, or transformative. Northeastern University student Katy Davis shared her thoughts after a Dharma Jam I held for the campus Buddhist Group. "Dharma Jam was the first time my mind and body felt completely in sync. Even being a dancer for my whole life, I had never moved so freely and spiritually as I did there. There was no disconnect between what I felt and how I moved."

Leading a Dharma Jam

Dharma Jam is a two-hour Buddhist dance liturgy. It has been impactful for dancers trying on Buddhism, Buddhists coming to dance, and those not identifying as either. This template is offered as a model for replication or a foundation for revision. One important disclaimer: You don't need to be an impressive dancer to facilitate a Dharma Jam. Your role is more about confidence and presence than aesthetics and ability. You are there to be a host and a guide and to hold space for the experience. Present the structure clearly and sincerely. Be the facilitator and also a participant.

Arrival: Creating Sacred Space

The tone of the Dharma Jam should be signaled before one enters the room. A sign placed outside the entrance to the Jam can welcome people to enter quietly and mindfully. The Jam space should consist of a large, open room with meditation cushions (if possible) and chairs circling the perimeter. Feel free to decorate or beautify the room as you like. You might arrange a simple altar or centerpiece in the middle of the floor. Dimming overhead lights or using rope lights can help create ambiance. A pleasant space can add to dancers' experiences, but all that's needed are props to sit comfortably and space to move freely.

Once Jam time arrives, play an extended track of ambient music. (Collaborating with live musicians can also work well, although I will describe the process using recorded music here.) This music continues the invitation of the welcome sign, supporting a period of personal arrival into one's body and the room. As people arrive, let them know they can move or be still as they like and that the Jam will begin shortly.

Fifteen minutes in, formally begin the Dharma Jam by inviting participants to walk through the space with different qualities – slowly, quickly, toward open space, leading with different body parts, reaching and stretching as they go, etc. This brief "milling" period serves both to open participants' range of motion in their bodies and within the room itself. As appropriate, comments throughout the Jam can be tailored to people of different physical abilities.

After a few minutes, ask the group to form a standing circle – close enough to reach out and take hands, though not yet doing so. This refuge circle sets the tone and intention for the Jam. It is a time to honor our human potential (Buddha), paths of truth (Dharma), and practice community (Sangha). Speak to each of those briefly in your own words. This is also a good opportunity to speak to and normalize the range of emotions people may feel at the Jam, and the importance of creating a safe space together. You might welcome people to hold hands (as they are comfortable) during the Sangha phase of refuge.

Move on by inviting participants to drop their hands and take a seat on a cushion or chair around the edges of the room. During this transition from standing to sitting, it is timely to now turn the music down or off. Once people are settled, offer an overview of what is to come. Having a rough idea of the Jam phases can help put participants' curiosity at ease and aid presence in the moment. Simply outline the main phases of the Jam – Tune In, Get Down, and Join Up. Tune In begins with a seated meditation, moves into standing, and then gentle movement. Get Down invites a fuller range of movement style and tempo, supported by increasing intensity of music. Join Up shifts the focus from the individual to the collective creation. The Jam will close with a dancing dedication and seated reflection circle.

Buddha: Tune In

Begin the seated meditation by offering a few words on the Jam's theme. This could be a line or two from a Buddhist text you are drawing from, or an image or metaphor – something short, accessible, and tied to the sparse facilitation comments you'll be offering throughout the rest of the Jam. This is less a mini-Dharma talk and more a Dharma seed. Brief meditation instructions can then be shared as the last spoken words before you ring a bell, signaling the beginning of the meditation.

Ring the bell after ten to fifteen minutes to signal the end of the seated meditation and invite participants to stand (as they are able), continuing their meditative attention. Once all are standing, call their attention to the felt sense of the standing body. Speak to the mutual presence of stillness and movement in the body. They are standing, one of the four traditional meditation postures taught by the Buddha (in addition to walking, sitting, and lying down). Standing is a posture based on consistency of form, on the still body. Standing is also referred to by contact improvisation dance founder Steve Paxton as "the small dance," the dance of breath and balance, the dance of small movements within relative stillness. Call attention to these seeds of movement and dance present within the standing body.

This is a good point to turn the music back on, with the next 20 minutes or so building gradually from a slow to medium tempo. I like to keep music selections instrumental during this phase, with the exception of explicitly spiritual or prayerful lyrics.

Guide participants to notice the body's impulses for movement, beginning to allow slow movement while still keeping both feet planted on the floor. Ask that after some moments of moving, they return to stillness in some new position when their moving gesture feels complete. Draw attention to the details of starting and stopping a movement and the feeling of each new shape of relative stillness. Continue in this way for some minutes, giving participants time to alternate between slow movement and stillness. Next, invite them to allow more momentum to the movement, coming back to stillness only when it feels wanted or needed, when there is no impulse for movement. Give permission for this expanded movement to bring people's feet off the floor and to move them through the space.

For the remainder of Tune In, it can be good to offer occasional facilitation comments, encouraging practitioners to allow whatever the body needs. Stillness, slow movement, stretching, lying down, walking, and moving in place are each welcome. There is no right or better way to move. As the seated meditation attended to fostering beginner's mind, this phase is a dedicated time for cultivating beginner's body – a felt presence received anew in each moment. In focusing on and supporting the beginner's body, Tune In provides the crucial foundation for lifting up how the moving body feels over how it looks.

Dharma: Get Down

The next phase of the Jam permits fuller movement while letting go of expectations. Let participants know that the music pace will start to build and that they can stay with movement that feels natural and honest, with their dance partners of breath and balance, movement and momentum. There is no need to match the speed or style of the music. Encourage participants to blur the boundary between movement and dance, perhaps thinking of dance as being playful with movement. Slowness and stillness are always available. We follow our joy, or whatever comes up, wherever it leads us.

As bodily activity increases, facilitation comments can be sprinkled throughout this phase to welcome expanded movement and maintained attention to the breath. While the pace and range of motion may increase for most people, the focus is still mainly inward. Remind them to lean away from controlling and toward receiving, to dissolve into rather than build up their dance. Your facilitation is a welcome into ritual dance space, where movers become the universe dancing with itself. As participants navigate their own authentic paths from stillness into movement and dance, so too should you.

The music for Get Down continues from the mid-tempo of Tune In and progresses gradually toward faster, more dance-able tracks. As with the previous one, this and the next section should each last about 20 minutes.

Sangha: Join Up

Join Up increases connection by broadening attention from the individual to the group journey. Welcome awareness to shift from the personal to the collective dance, trusting the sincere practice each person has been doing during the Jam. State that this expanded attention is an orientation, not a requirement for movement. Participants do not need to copy anyone else. They don't need to dance with anyone. They don't even need to make eye contact, although all of these may happen. Invite practitioners to simply notice the qualities of movement around them, welcoming a sense of resonance and togetherness, even if only through peripheral vision.

With increasing connection comes the second aspect of this phase – increasing safety. Knowing that increasing relation can bring up issues of comfort and safety for people, ask participants to pair their widened attention with a heightened sensitivity to the needs of others. Cue them to body language as an indicator of how interactive another practitioner wants to be. Together, you continue the shared work of making the Dharma Jam a safe space.

This phase can be fun and playful. By this point in the Jam, most people's comfort levels will have increased. Your clear permission to be only as relational as each person wants will free people up to exchange without obligation. Some will pair up for extended dances. Others will orbit each other more briefly, one person's spin momentarily aligning with a neighbor's curving arm or turning head.

Join Up blends the meditation hall with the dance club. You've spent the last eighty minutes or so establishing a strong mindfulness foundation for the Jam. During this phase, the tone shifts from contemplation to celebration. Choose music that reflects this shift. The pace can remain mid to fast tempo, taking care to stagger your selections so as not to wear people out. At this point, it can be great to dip into more popular tracks, such as oldies, Motown, hip-hop, etc. Whereas lyrics could have posed a distraction during Tune In or Get Down, they can now be a positive addition to the celebration, even something to sing along to. As this phase nears its end, giving dancers a heads-up when the last track is beginning can be good.

Closing: Dedicating and Reflecting on the Practice

The dedication tracks are a time for practitioners to return to their center while sending the benefit of their practice outward. The music shifts from fast to slow tempo, lending toward prayerful or inspirational tracks. Speak again to their partners, their allies, of breath and balance. Call them into attunement with the world's suffering. They might think of all sentient beings, or a specific community in crisis, or of just one person. That person might be oneself. The dance, or stillness, is now an embodied solidarity with this suffering, as the practice is dedicated to the wellbeing of others and all our relations.

I give one to two tracks for this moving dedication. When the music ends, there will be a power in the silence. Give that silence time to be heard. After some moments, invite people to gather in a seated circle. This is a time to share spoken words about the practice if anyone is inclined. Depending on the context, this can be followed by saying names around the circle and making brief community announcements.

Dharma Dialogues and Spontaneous Prayer as Skillful Means

While experiences with Buddhism vary greatly across people and schools, I suspect that elements of my experience resonate with larger trends, at least among convert practitioners in the West. I've practiced mostly within the Insight Meditation tradition in the United States. Insight Meditation is almost 50 years old as a Western Buddhist tradition, though it traces its lineage to traditional Southeast Asian Theravada Buddhism. It was founded by Western practitioners who studied in Asia, mainly with Thai and Burmese Buddhist masters, in the 1970s and then brought the teachings back (initially to the U.S. East and then West Coast), setting up their own retreat centers. Theravada lineages base their teachings on the Pali Canon – the oldest surviving complete written accounts of the Buddha's teachings, which themselves were written hundreds of years after the Buddha gave them. I've also practiced at Shambhala centers, Goenka vipassana retreats in Nepal and the U.S., and Tibetan Buddhist retreats in Northern India.

Throughout these contexts, the majority of time was spent in silent meditation practice or listening to a teacher deliver a Dharma talk. These two approaches are invaluable, yet also represent just two of the Three Jewels of Buddhism – Buddha (as an example of our human potential), Dharma (the laws of nature, or teachings of the Buddha), and Sangha (spiritual community). In meditation we touch into our Buddha nature. In listening to a teacher, we are reminded of the Dharma. Sometimes, though, we may forget about the Sangha, and the importance of sharing notes with fellow practitioners as we walk the path together.

I've observed a number of ways in which sangha groups have revitalized their connections with each other. Some young adult, or 35 and under, retreats and practice groups gather in a circle instead of rows and include conversation or council practice. In 2007, Gregory Kramer published *Insight Dialogue: The Interpersonal Path to Freedom* – a wonderful adaptation of silent Buddhist practice into a dialogical model. In the Insight Meditation tradition, the *Kalyana Mitta* (spiritual friends) group format is growing, in which practitioners meet for meditation and discussion, often in people's homes.

In my own work advising college Buddhist groups, first at Northeastern University, then at Emerson College, and most recently at Amherst College, I structured the weekly meetings largely around conversation. After a check in and guided meditation, we spent about half our time in discussion of the week's Dharma topic. Centering this relational form of practice and reflection enhanced both individual participants' understanding of the concepts as well as connection and cohesion of the group itself.

Likewise, in my work as a Staff Chaplain on an acute inpatient adolescent psychiatric unit, a good portion of my daily mindfulness meditation groups were reserved for patient feedback about the experience. After each guided meditation, I asked, "What happened?" The floor was then open for these teenagers to speak about what they noticed with body sensations, thoughts, and emotions during the practice. More than just giving patients a chance to articulate to themselves what happened, this post-meditation sharing often emerged into full conversations with both patients and staff validating and normalizing each other's experiences in meditation, and life more broadly. Clinical research into these groups found that patients' state anxiety decreased a statistically significant amount regardless of age, sex, or previous experience with the practice.

While Buddhists and meditators may be starting to talk with each other more in Western practice contexts, we are not necessarily speaking from a prayerful place. A classic Buddhist prayer model is *metta*, or loving-kindness, meditation. In its traditional form, a practitioner offers a series of well-wishes for another or themselves in the format of: "May you be happy. May you be peaceful." Certain words traditionally end these wishes or blessings, though practitioners might alternatively choose the words that feel most needed. While metta practice thus offers something of an opportunity for improvised prayer, the practice is most often done in silence, with the focus more on cultivating the practitioner's intentions than impacting those being prayed for.

When such words are uttered out loud and in community, they are often delivered with a calm voice and even cadence, perhaps by a teacher modeling the practice or closing a meditation period. These expressions too often strike me as the mind's wishes for the heart, but not the heart itself given voice – the steady mind speaking to the quivering heart rather than offering a listening ear. They are also typically addressed to a universal audience – attempting the inclusion of everyone to a degree while risking the embrace of no one fully. "May all beings live with ease. May all beings be free of suffering." Certainly, these prayers may be deeply held, but there is something sacrificed, something lost, by addressing our transcendent truths without also planting our heels, our prayers, in our mundane realities. The general wish for ease and wellbeing likely does not go far enough to acknowledge, validate, and encourage the specifics of someone who has just lost a job or experienced a microaggression or simply had a hard day.

A Zen master was once asked about the goal of spiritual practice. "An appropriate response," he answered. Growing up in the Reform Jewish tradition for the first half of my life, and practicing Theravada Buddhism for the second, spontaneous prayer has not often been modeled for me within my own traditions. Largely through my Clinical Pastoral Education (CPE) chaplaincy training, especially participation in or leading of Christians in prayer, I have become convinced of the appropriate response improvised prayer can offer. Indeed, it has been within Christian prayer circles that I have shared some of my most sacred moments with others, a space that has modeled for me how heart and mind can join body and spirit in the spoken word.

There's a qualitative shift that occurs in the transition from conversation to prayer – a shift into a space that is simultaneously more internal, more connected, and more transcendent. Monotheists might ascribe the power of that space to the presence of God, and for all I know they may well be right. My own Buddhist, agnostic sensibilities, however, are also able to furnish attunement, empathy, and expansion through prayer.

As Buddhists, it's this third aspect of prayer – its transcendent or expansive quality – that we may stumble upon. We're well trained to see into ourselves and hold others with compassion. Invoking a power beyond ourselves, though, could be outside our comfort zone. Who, or more likely *what*, would we be addressing our prayers to? For those Buddhists facing this predicament, a bridge to authenticity can be found in the Buddhist view of non-self, or *anatta*, described above. Prayer invites the speaker to be both less and more than their personal self. In prayer, we become a vessel for grace – the mysterious blessings of ease upon heart and mind. In the *Satipatthana Sutta*, among other places, the Buddha advises us to reflect on the body as comprised of the four elements: earth, water, fire, and air. Prayer invites the speaker to give voice as nature aware of itself. In prayer, we empty the self, join with each other, and dissolve into what is. In prayer, we become nature, blessing nature. Buddhists chaplains might find the prayerful voice to be an underdeveloped skillful means, both for responding to students' needs and for connecting them to each other.

Expanding the Synergies Through Embodied Mandalas

To close, I'll share about the most recent and emerging shape of my work with Dharma and ritual arts. Though I have yet to bring what follows to a college community, I foresee doing so and believe it holds promise as the type of intermodal experience that can entice more and different people to taste the Dharma on our campuses.

In a January 2020 four-week series I led at Insight Western Mass (IWM), I began blending the elements of seated and walking meditation, movement and dance, and spontaneous prayer into an embodied mandala format. With the unifying theme of taking practice off the cushion, we proceeded through classes on mindfulness-based movement and dance, spontaneous prayer, and reflections on Extinction Rebellion's use of the Four Noble Truths to frame their climate activism.

The most experimental aspect for me, the class on prayer, proved to be the most powerful. My curiosity over whether practitioners would gravitate toward spontaneous prayer with strangers was answered as we split up into triads of rotating roles – one person expressing challenge, another then praying for them (i.e., reflecting what they'd heard and then speaking wishes for ease, wellbeing, resolution, etc.), and a third sharing what it was like to witness the exchange at the end. The depth of struggle shared by one in my own triad was well matched by the exquisite, responsive prayer of another. Scanning the room to keep time and assess the group, the murmurs and tears and smiles I observed told me my group's experience was not unique. Indeed, in our closing debrief, many shared that they had been craving this type of extemporaneous prayer among fellow yogis.

The final class culminated in a four-sphere movement and prayer mandala – an outer circle of seated meditation, a ring of walking meditators within that, open space for movement and dance taking up much of the middle of the room, and a small altar in the center where practitioners could offer spoken prayer. As with the Join Up phase of Dharma Jams, there was a palpable sense – spoken to in our closing circle – of us each being a part of a larger collective creation, or offering, happening in the space.

Pivoting from the success of this series, I recently offered just the closing mandala portion at Body-Time: A Silent Somatic Retreat at the Earthdance retreat center. Resonating with the synergies I'd been weaving into Dharma Jams, this retreat sought to wed contemplative and expressive practices in a mostly silent container over a few days and multiple modalities. For my part, I framed the mandala score as more of a ritual container than I had previously at IWM. With the same successive circles from outside in of seated meditation, walking meditation, movement/dance, and prayer, I evoked the imagery of fire – with seated meditators as the fuel, the walking meditators as circulating air, movement and dance as the flames, and those praying in the center as the tip of the flame. I guided an opening reflection, setting the intention to sit, walk, move, and pray as witness to human, animal, plant, and planetary suffering, and to sit, walk, move, and pray as aspiration toward human, animal, plant, and planetary flourishing. I framed the practice as one of ritual acknowledgment, solidarity, and rejuvenation. This time, I included a prayer bell on the center altar with the invitation to ring the bell once finished with silent prayer. The only other instruction was to spend time in each of the four spheres at some point.

What ensued was breathtaking. Bodies used to seated meditation danced, dancers at home in movement practiced stillness, and everyone made at least one visit to kneel in silent prayer – what I suspect was, for many, the first time they'd been publicly witnessed while engaged in prayer. The image of eight or so people kneeling in prayer while dozens more danced and meditated around them still burns clear in my memory, as does the sound of prayer bell gongs punctuating the space, prayer after prayer. Many commented on the power of that session afterward and how it set the tone for the days that followed. There were also appreciations voiced for how the mandala practice gave form and expression to spiritual needs and religious sensibilities that often go unmet in an increasingly secular and even post-religious culture.

While the myriad additional ways that Buddhist, or Buddhist-inspired, practices meet such needs are beyond the scope of this chapter, the examples described herein serve as a basis for consideration and exploration in college and university contexts. As readers will have observed themselves, alongside those raised in Buddhist familial or cultural contexts, many participants in college-based Buddhist groups are often not strictly Buddhists themselves but rather spiritual seekers, searchers for a set of wisdom teachings that are testable by, and beneficial to, their own lived experience. Thus, we as Buddhist chaplains invite a broad swath of former, current, and emerging religious affiliations and spiritual persuasions when we put out our shingles. Various mindfulness practices have harnessed Buddhist wisdom technologies to benefit audiences from diverse backgrounds. Similarly, incorporating movement and dance, peer dialogue, and spontaneous prayer into college Buddhist groups could help expand and diversify participation, nurture connection among participants, and support deeper grounding in participants' human and spiritual potential, as students hunger for such embodied communal practice spaces. There is a profound relationship between the inquiring mind and the expressive mind; the still, quiet, and insightful mind is also the source of poetry, painting, and dance. Wherever you are situated in your college or university context, may you find inspiration in this connection as you embody the Dharma in your own way for your community.

20
Buddhism and the Calling of No Calling
Mark Unno

Republished with permission from *Calling in Today's World: Voices from Eight Faith Perspectives*, edited by Kathleen A. Cahalan and Douglas J. Schuurman, 2016.

Buddhist "Calling" in Comparative Context

The concept of "calling" may be applicable to Buddhism, but generally not in as straightforward a manner as in other religions due to the nature of Buddhism as a religion, basic assumptions about "calling", and the logic implicit in these assumptions. For instance, calling in the Abrahamic traditions illuminates the relationship between God, a transcendent being, and the followers. Whether understood literally or metaphorically, God is often depicted in personalized terms, making "calling" an ideal term to describe the relationship to the Divine: God "calls" to his believers. The divine-human relationship generally reflects a "two-worlds" worldview, a qualitative difference between God and a Divine realm, on the one hand, and human beings and an earthly, mundane realm, on the other. Calling bridges these two qualitatively different worlds that diverge in the very nature of their existence. In contrast, Buddhism tends to emphasize *awareness* and awakening, such as karmic awareness and *awakening* to no-self, emptiness, and oneness in compassion.

Buddhism, in its roughly 2500-year history, has had many twists and turns, so many, in fact, that it can be difficult to make generalizations about how Buddhists would generally interpret the idea of "calling." Buddhism's diversity can be compared with the Abrahamic religions in one example. In each of the three Abrahamic traditions, there is significant agreement about central, canonical religious texts: the Hebrew Bible in Judaism, the Old and New Testament in Christianity, and the Qur'an in Islam. Imagine a religion in which there are hundreds of sacred scriptures, all attributed to the same founding figure, and scores of sectarian developments, and equally multitudinous ways about speaking about the nature of reality, with little overall agreement. Such is the case with Buddhism.

Nevertheless, I will draw some broad historical strokes. The historical development of Buddhism can be divided into two large movements: Nikaya Buddhism and Mahayana Buddhism. Nikaya Buddhism is represented in the Nikaya literature, the earliest layer of Buddhist scripture recorded a few centuries after the passing of the historical Buddha Śākyamuni (ca. 6th–5th century BCE), focusing on his exploits and the lives of his followers: monks, nuns, and laity. One form of this school remains today: the Theravada, which is found throughout much of South and Southeast Asia, including Sri Lanka, Thailand, and Burma. Mahayana Buddhism, the Buddhism of the "Great Vehicle," is based on scriptures compiled from the beginning of the Common Era onwards and is found in North (Tibet, Nepal, and Mongolia)[1] and East Asia (China, Japan,

---
[1] Buddhism in North Asia—Tibet, Nepal, Mongolia—recognizes a third major development, the Vajrayana, the Diamond Vehicle, above the Mahayana, but in general considers Mahayana the umbrella term.

and Korea).² Mahayana Buddhists have referred to followers of the earlier Buddhism as "Hinayana," the "Lesser Vehicle," but as this is a derogatory term, some scholars use the more neutral descriptor, "Nikaya Buddhism."³

In the early Buddhism of the Nikaya literature, the center of the stage is largely occupied by Śākyamuni Buddha as a human figure teaching his human followers, both renunciants and laity. He emerges as a figure that has rejected and left behind the Hindu religious order, which includes the structure of society in a hierarchical caste system, overseen by the all-encompassing deity Brahman. The Buddha does not emerge as a divine figure himself, and does not exhort others to follow him based on his personal authority, but rather tells them to serve as "lamps unto themselves," illuminating their realization of the Dharma, or teachings. The path of the Buddha in this early account in some ways represents a rejection of religion, understood theistically. The Buddha responds neither to a god who calls nor to a singular higher principle, nor does he wield the authority of the divine, as he sought peace and repose in an otherwise tumultuous world filled with suffering.

Mahayana Buddhism, initiated with the compilation of a new set of scriptures that were attributed to the historical Buddha centuries after his passing, consists of hundreds of deities, and numerous world-systems, somewhat like the many galaxies that have been found to populate our physical universe, but each with its own cosmic buddha. Ultimately, cosmic buddhas do not inhabit a different level of being from humans. The nature of everything is said to be 'emptiness,' devoid of any intrinsic, conceptually identifiable essence. Mahayana Buddhism, adopting forms of logic from Hinduism, operates on the basis of a nondiscursive logic: "both/and," "neither/nor," such that the cosmic buddhas are ultimately empty: they are both personal and impersonal, both exist and do not exist, ultimately neither exist nor do not exist. In a word, reality as such is "beyond words."

One of the largest developments of East Asian Buddhism, Pure Land Buddhism, refers to the "call of Amida Buddha," the cosmic buddha of infinite light. The practitioner of Pure Land Buddhism responds to the "primal vow of Amida," the vow to bring all sentient beings to awakening or enlightenment. Yet, as will become evident, Amida is not a transcendent deity, and shares the nature of emptiness with everything and everyone else: Amida is both personal and impersonal, exists and does not exist, just like the sentient beings that are to be saved by Amida's primal vow. This is, as it were, the call of no-calling, of the voiceless voice.

In Nikaya Buddhism and Mahayana Buddhism, including Pure Land Buddhism, there is no God as a singular, ultimate reality. Buddhism has generally not subscribed to a two-world's worldview as the theistic religions have. Instead, everything is interrelated, more like a web or net, where a change in any one aspect affects all others. Interrelatedness does not mean that a sense of calling cannot be distilled from the history of Buddhism. Yet, because of the diverse range of practices, conceptions, and deities within Buddhist history, and its vast web of interrelations, the account given here is necessarily selective and episodic. Within the development of both Nikaya and Mahayana Buddhism, specific moments have been chosen

---

2   Vietnam, although geographically in Southeast Asia, has been shaped more by Mahayana Buddhism coming from China and elsewhere rather than Nikaya Buddhism.

3   "'Nikaya Buddhism' is a coinage of Professor Masatoshi Nagatomi of Harvard University who suggested it to me as a usage for the eighteen schools of Indian Buddhism, to avoid the term "Hinayana Buddhism," which is found offensive by some members of the Theravada tradition. Robert Thurman, "The Emptiness that is Compassion: An "Essay on Buddhist Ethics." Religious Traditions, 4, no. 2 (Oct-Nov 1981): footnote 10. See, for example, Peter Harvey, *An Introduction to Buddhism: Teachings, History, and Practices* (NY: Cambridge University Press, 1990), pp. 9-27.

to illustrate what in Buddhism might resonate with a sense of calling. In Nikaya Buddhism, the primary goal or calling is to awaken to the tranquil repose of nirvana, and thereby attain liberation, *mokṣa*, from the bonds of suffering in human existence. Secondarily, those who have attained nirvana are called to teach others the path to nirvana. Three episodes have been selected to illustrate early Buddhist notions of calling: the Buddha's leave-taking on his spiritual quest for awakening, the moment of his awakening and the beginning of his teaching career, and the entry of the Buddha's son Rahula into the Sangha, the monastic community.

In Mahayana Buddhism, the order is reversed: the primary calling is to manifest compassion for all beings in order to bring them to awakening first, and only then attain awakening for oneself. I have selected three episodes to illustrate Mahayana senses of calling: one from the *Vimalakīrti-nirdeśa-sūtra* (*The Holy Teaching of Vimalakīrti*), involving a lay spiritual teacher; one from the *Liuzu Tanjing* (the *Platform Sutra of the Sixth Patriarch*), of Chan/Zen Buddhism, describing the transmission of the Dharma-seal of awakening from one Zen master to another; and one from the life of Shinran, the founder of Shin Buddhism, the largest sect of Pure Land Buddhism in Japan, in which he declares himself to be "neither monk nor layman." Before recounting the episodes, however, I will introduce key Buddhist concepts relevant to calling.

Buddhist Teachings: Key Concepts

Nikaya Buddhism

Four sets of categories can be helpful to understand the Nikaya literature: the Three Treasures, the Three Baskets of sacred literature, the Four Noble Truths, and the Three Marks of existence.[4]

The Three Treasures are: Buddha, the awakened one, Dharma, the teaching, and Sangha, the community of monks and nuns. The Three Baskets of sacred literature are Sutra, the sayings/teachings of the Buddha; Śāstra, the commentary that explains the teachings of the Buddha; and Vinaya, the rules and regulations governing the Sangha, the monastic community.

The Four Noble Truths are: suffering, cause, end, and path. First, life is filled with suffering, which is, second, caused by human attachment to preconceptions of how things are, or how they should be. Third, there is an end to this suffering that can be attained by following the Eight-fold Noble Path, broadly applicable to both renunciants and laity, which includes right thought, right intention, right speech, right action, right livelihood, right effort, right mindfulness, and right concentration.[5] Cultivating this path leads to the purification of karma and the attainment of nirvana and awakening. After awakening, this path continues as the expression of the life of enlightenment.

Although there is not room here to explain all eight aspects of the noble path, it is worth highlighting "right livelihood," as it has a direct bearing on calling. It generally means undertaking wholesome and virtuous livelihoods, ones that demonstrate cardinal precepts such as honesty and care for the life of sentient beings, and that are conducive to realizing nirvana. It also means avoiding unwholesome livelihoods, in particular those that involve

---

[4] For a more detailed explanation of early Buddhist teachings and categories, see, Peter Harvey, *An Introduction to Buddhism: Teachings, History, and Practices* (NY: Cambridge University Press, 1990). Harvey also provides the original vocabulary for various terms in Pali, which is the language of the Nikaya literature.

[5] It is problematic to attribute the Eight-fold Noble Path to all Buddhists. Mahayana Buddhists, for example, reject any pan-Buddhist doctrine or dogma as absolute. East Asian Buddhists since the medieval period widely rejected this path also as too 'gradual,' and instead advocated the path of 'sudden awakening.' Pure Land Buddhists, in particular Shin Buddhism, rejects the idea that human beings can follow this path, especially in the corrupt age, including ours.

harm to sentient beings and the taking of lives: weapons makers, slave traders and purveyors of prostitution, those who raise and slaughter food-source animals, producers of intoxicants and poisons. The underlying rationale is karmic: livelihoods entailing destructive actions lead to impure karma, taking one further away from enlightenment.

The early Buddhist view of right livelihood brings complications, however. Most people in India ate meat, so that butchers were essential to society, yet they were regarded as karmically impure and inferior. The same is true for weapons makers, who were needed for warriors, who were considered noble. The Buddha himself came from the warrior class. Thus, right livelihood potentially reintroduced a class-based system of karma that the Buddha is said to have rejected.

The Three Marks of Existence are: suffering, impermanence, and no-self. Suffering recapitulates the first of the Four Noble Truths, accentuating its significance. Attachment causes suffering because everything, without exception, is impermanent. According to this view, even the Buddhist teachings will someday disappear, only to reappear in a new form. The heart of the problem for human beings is that the very self is impermanent, which is to say, there is no eternal essence or soul of any kind, nothing that one can cling to within oneself. Even "Life" and "death" are illusory labels that fall away in the attainment of nirvana. If one were to place this in the context of "calling," then, the Buddhist is called to seek liberation from the illusory opposition of life and death and to realize that there is no permanent or eternal self, a calling of no-calling from the self of no-self.[6]

Mahayana Buddhism

Mahayana Buddhists continued to use the categories of Nikaya Buddhists but in a more flexible manner. The keys to understanding Mahayana Buddhism can be found in the following three notions: the two-fold truth, *upāya-kauśalya* or skillful means, and the bodhisattva ideal.

The two-fold truth was articulated by the first philosopher-master of Mahayana Buddhism, Nāgārjuna.[7] It consists of conventional truth and highest truth, which are like two-sides of the same coin rather than two separate truths. Often rendered as form and emptiness, respectively, form refers to the world understood through the filter of words and concepts; it is the world understood through the human conventions of language. Emptiness, *śūnyatā*, characterizes the highest truth beyond words. It is reality freed from the divisions and separations imposed by categorical thinking. There is nothing wrong with the categories of language *per se*, but true awareness of reality beyond words can only be attained by the mind emptied of dogmatic attachments and preconceptions. Once free of dogmatic preconceptions, reality as such (Skt. *tathatā*)[8]

---

6 Early Buddhists, including Mahayana, are not called to sustain life per se. Buddhism is generally not life-affirming (nor life-denying). The goal is awakening and liberation from having to live or having to die (cycle of life and death). Ultimately life and death turn out to be illusory. Human life is specifically cherished, not for its own intrinsic value, but because human beings are well disposed to attaining awakening and liberation. This shows a significant difference between Buddhism and some other religions regarding basic existential assumptions. The precept on not-harming life (ahimsa) has more to do with self-contradiction (taking life to sustain one's own) than it does affirmation of life. The real problem is attachment to life, as well as attachment to death. Relative to some other religions, Buddhists may appear to be aloof for these reasons. Buddhists are not detached, but seek to live in non-attachment, since life and death are illusory, not intrinsically real. Ultimately, reality, nirvana, is said to be "unborn" (*asaṃskṛta*) in the sense that "coming into existence" is regarded as illusory.

7 Nāgārjuna, born in present-day Sri Lanka, was a monk of the second or third century. Several treatises are attributed to him, but the main work is the *Fundamental Verses on the Middle Way* (Skt. *Mūla-madhyamika-kārikā*). Nāgārjuna is recognized as the first Mahayana master by all Mahayana schools and sects.

8 "Skt." is an abbreviation for "Sanskrit," the language

discloses itself as a dynamic web of interdependence in which all beings and things coalesce in each moment as a self-expression of the empty cosmos. Phenomena arising in interdependent co-origination (Skt. *pratītya-samudpada*) is the positive expression of emptiness, disclosing the oneness of reality in its vivid unfolding.

Emptiness is similar to no-self, *anatman*, in Nikaya Buddhism, in which the self has no conceptual essence but is nevertheless unfolding dynamically as an impermanent self. However, there is a difference between *anatman* and *śūnyatā*. Nagarjuna formulated emptiness in part as a criticism of what he perceived to be the dogmatism of the Nikaya Buddhists. While they may have understood that the self is without any conceptual essence, they seemed to him to set up dogmatic orthodoxies concerning the Buddhist teachings, the Dharma. Thus, Nagarjuna developed the emptiness critique in part to target attachment to religion as much as attachment to self. He warned that one should not even become attached to the concept of "emptiness," and thus taught the "emptiness of emptiness," *śūnyatā-śūnyatā*. In one form or another, virtually all schools of Mahayana Buddhism subscribe to the two-fold truth: conventional and highest truth, form and emptiness.

The bodhisattva ideal, in one of its classical formulations, states that the bodhisattva, as a seeker of enlightenment, refuses to attain enlightenment by him or herself unless all other beings first attain enlightenment. The philosophical basis for this lies in emptiness. If the true nature of reality including the self is emptiness, then the true nature of the self is empty of any categorical oppositions: male/female, self/other, human/non-human, and so forth. In emptiness, all conceptual distinctions lose their holding power, the separation created through the use of words and concepts dissolves, thus giving way to the flow of a oneness beyond words. The true nature of the self turns out to be emptiness/oneness in which all beings are inseparable from oneself. In such a view, it makes no sense for one person to attain awakening before everyone else. For the true self to attain awakening, all beings must attain awakening. Putting other beings before oneself, as the bodhisattva is said to do, assures that the seeker of enlightenment does not render an egalitarian view in which one sees oneself as slightly "more equal" than others. The call to bodhisattvahood, if it can be described as such, is to realize the self of emptiness, which is also the self of oneness with all beings, in which they are all led to liberation from attachment.

Skillful means, or *upāya-kauśalya*, refers to the skillful adaptation of the Dharma beyond words to the specific circumstances of the moment: the varying capacities of practitioners; the changing circumstances of time, place, and culture; and the various factors of diversity for which the Dharma must be adapted. For Mahayana Buddhists, it was more important to be faithful to what they perceived to be the wordless spirit of the Buddha's awakening rather than the literal categories of the Nikaya Buddhists, which may have been appropriate for the time of the historical Buddha but were not suitable for later centuries and other cultures. Yet, even within the Nikaya literature, the Buddha is touted for his ability to adapt his teachings according to the differing capacities of his followers. If the call of bodhisattvahood is to become one with all beings in liberation, then skillful means is the wide array of approaches available to this realization.

Narratives of Calling

Nikaya Buddhism

The origin story of the Buddha is well known and widely considered to have a substantial basis in history.[9] Born Siddhartha Gautama of the Śākya clan in Northern India, he was a member of the *kṣatriya* or warrior class or

---

of classical India and of Mahayana Buddhism. The Buddha is said to have spoken in Pali, related to Sanskrit, and the language of the Nikaya scriptures.

---

9 See, Harvey, *An Introduction to Buddhism*, pp. 9-27.

caste, princely heir to the throne. At the age of twenty-nine he abandoned what would have been his calling within the existing Hindu caste system in favor of an individual quest for awakening. Overly protected within the royal palace where he had spent his entire life, he was overcome with a sense of dis-ease in the face of the illness, old age, and death that awaited him. For six years he wandered among philosophers, ascetics, and various religious teachers in the coalescing śramaṇa culture of holy seekers lying outside the boundaries of the traditional caste structure, until at the age of thirty-five, he attained bodhi, awakening, and the realization of an unconditioned truth, nirvāṇa, that released him from the continual cycle of rebirth and existence. Thenceforth, he came to be known as Śākyamuni Buddha, the Awakened One, the Sage of the Śākya Clan, and commenced a teaching career that spanned forty-five years until he entered into ultimate nirvana, or parinirvāṇa (Pali: parinibbāna), at the age of eighty.

Although there is no God who calls, one could say that Siddhartha set out on his spiritual journey due to an inner calling rooted in his deep dissatisfaction with life, not from the exhortation of an external authority. His story shares some features of what Kathleen Cahalan describes concerning calling in the Catholic tradition in the sense that there is a special life of sacrifice for which Siddhartha is called. On the one hand, he could be accused of being selfish for abandoning not just his princely status but also his familial obligations: to this father, his wife, and his newborn son. On the other hand, his departure can also be seen as a great sacrifice in the service of a higher religious life. One could imagine that the youthful prince agonized over his decision, that he loved his family and suffered all the more knowing the pain his departure would cause them. He had no assurance that his quest for spiritual peace and repose would ever be fulfilled. He could easily die of injury, illness, or starvation. Yet, he risked everything because he could not suppress his spiritual yearning.

Soon after attaining awakening, the Buddha realized that the illusory bonds of the self had been forever broken and liberation attained:

> Through many a birth in saṃsāra have I wandered in vain, seeking the builder of this house (of self). Repeated birth is indeed suffering! O house-builder, you are seen! You will not build this house again. For your rafters are broken and your ridge-pole shattered. My mind has reached the Unconditioned; I have attained the destruction of craving.[10]

He did not then proceed immediately to show others the path to liberation. Rather, his initial thought was to spend the rest of his days in repose and peace, and then attain final nirvana, never having to be reborn again. The truth he had awakened to was unconditioned, beyond literal description, and could not easily be taught; in fact, he would likely have to contend with the confusion and misunderstanding of others:

> When the Blessed One was newly Self-awakened…this line of thinking arose in his awareness: "This Dhamma that I have attained is deep, hard to see, hard to realize, peaceful, refined, beyond the scope of conjecture, subtle, to-be-experienced by the wise…. For a generation delighting in attachment, …this/that conditionality and dependent co-arising are hard to see. This state, too, is hard to see: the resolution of all fabrications, the relinquishment of all acquisitions, the ending of craving; dispassion; cessation; Unbinding. And if I were to teach the Dhamma

---

10 Acharya Buddharakkhita, trans., *Dhammapada*, verses 153-154, accessed January 7, 2012, http://www.accesstoinsight.org/tipitaka/kn/dhp/dhp.11.budd.html.

and if others would not understand me, that would be tiresome for me, troublesome for me."[11]

This doubting about his ability to convey the path of liberation to others is in turn presented as a moment of decision as to the question of the Buddha's calling:

> Then Brahmā Sahampati, having known with his own awareness the line of thinking in the Blessed One's awareness, thought: "The world is lost! The world is destroyed! The mind of the Tathagata, the Arahant, the Rightly Self-awakened One inclines to dwelling at ease, not to teaching the Dhamma!" Then, just as a strong man might extend his flexed arm or flex his extended arm, Brahmā Sahampati disappeared from the Brahmā-world and reappeared in front of the Blessed One. Arranging his upper robe over one shoulder, he knelt down with his right knee on the ground, saluted the Blessed One with his hands before his heart, and said to him: "Lord, let the Blessed One teach the Dhamma! Let the One-Well-Gone teach the Dhamma! There are beings with little dust in their eyes who are falling away because they do not hear the Dhamma. There will be those who will understand the Dhamma."

Brahmā Sahampati is a deity that descends to appeal to the Buddha's sense of compassion.[12]

An invention of Buddhist writers, this deity in modern terms could be said to represent the Buddha's conscience. In the early Buddhist scriptures, however, it represents the second moment of his calling: the first, to rise up and seek the spiritual path, and the second, to go forth and teach out of compassion for other suffering beings. Spreading his teaching marks the beginning of the sangha, the Buddhist community of monks and nuns.

The third moment of calling involves his son Rāhula. As mentioned earlier, when Siddhartha Gautama renounced his status as prince and set out as a wandering seeker, he had already been married and had had a child, a baby boy named Rāhula.[13] Thus, he abandoned not only his princely calling but also his calling as husband and father. Years after he attained awakening and became the Buddha, he returned to the Sākya Kingdom when his son was a full- grown adult. Inspired by the spiritual presence of his father, Rāhula declared that he, too, wished to renounce his status as princely heir to the throne to join his father's sangha. The Buddha's father King Śuddhodana (Pali: Suddhodana), by now elderly, strongly objected; he had already lost his son, and to lose his only grandson was too much to bear. The Buddha insisted, however, that his son's wishes be respected and that he be allowed to join the sangha. Yet, recognizing his father's anguish, he told the king that he would grant any wish that he could fulfill, other than returning the grandson Rāhula. King Śuddhodana then made one request, which the Buddha granted, became codified in the vinaya, and still holds true in many Buddhist cultures today: If a son wishes to become a Buddhist monk, then he

---

11 Thanissaro Bhikkhu, trans., "Ayacana Sutta," *Samyutta Nikāya* 6.1, http://www.accesstoinsight.org/tipitaka/sn/sn06/sn06.001.than.html, accessed January 7, 2012.

12 This is not the Brahman, the all-encompassing deity of Hinduism, but rather one of many possible deities presented as the voice of compassion and conscience. In fact, Sahampati is unknown outside this particular reference, a momentary narrative creation that brings the Buddha's mindset into relief.

13 See, for example, Bhikkhu Bodhi, "The Buddha and His Dhamma," accessed March 6, 2015, http://www.accesstoinsight.org/lib/authors/bodhi/wheel433.html.

must receive the permission of his parents.[14] In today's world, this often extends to parents of other faiths or normative commitments. For example, if a man wishes to renounce his social ties and become a Buddhist monk, and his Christian parents object, then there are Buddhist orders that will not ordain him because it goes against the vinaya. Thus, the suffering of the King, as father and grandfather, was transformed into compassion for the suffering of other parents (and grandparents).

In these stories of early Buddhism, we thus find at least three kinds of calling: the calling to seek enlightenment in the renunciant path of a monk or a nun, the calling to teach other renunciants the path to awakening, and the calling to extend compassion and the teachings to lay people. All three kinds of calling can also be found in Mahayana Buddhism, but the Mahayana brings into view a whole other set of concerns including types and dimensions of calling, the status of lay versus ordained, and the dissolution of core categories for defining Buddhism as a "religion."

Mahayana Buddhism

Whereas early Buddhism emphasized anātman, no-self, as the lack of any fixed, essential conception of selfhood, Mahayana emptiness extended this to all phenomena, negating the reification of all concepts, including religious dogma, even emptiness itself. Philosophically, this was intended to dissolve barriers and oppositions, including those involving religious hierarchies of ecclesiastical status and gender. While historically, the male monkhood continued to dominate Buddhist institutions into modern times, ideologically the Mahayana reflects a movement away from the monastery-centered perspective towards a more lay-oriented ideal.

The following three narratives provide a sampling of what might be considered calling in the Mahayana scriptures: one from the *Vimalakīrti-nirdeśa-sūtra* (*The Holy Teaching of Vimalakīrti*),[15] that of the illness of Vimalakīrti the merchant; an episode of the illiterate woodcutter from the *Liuzu Tanjing* (*Platform Sutra of the Sixth Patriarch*)[16] of Chan (Jpn. Zen Buddhism); and an autobiographical moment from the life of Shinran, the founder of Shin Buddhism, the largest sect of Japanese Pure Land.

The Holy Teaching of Vimalakīrti, an early Mahayana sutra that was likely composed in the first couple of centuries of the common era, became widely read and influential, especially in East Asia, and is cited by various schools of Buddhism including Faxiang (Skt. Yogācāra) and Chan/Zen. It begins with Śākyamuni Buddha instructing his disciples go pay their respects to a lay bodhisattva named Vimalakīrti, a merchant, a householder, and a family man. He has fallen ill, and the Buddha is sending his disciples to wish him well. They refuse, however, complaining that Vimalakīrti always exposes their deficient understanding. Finally, Mañjuśrī, the wisest of the bodhisattvas, agrees to go, and the others follow him to Vimalakīrti's residence. There, after conveying his sympathies, Mañjuśrī asks Vimalakīrti a series of questions that Vimalakīrti answers from the standpoint of emptiness. Finally, Mañjuśrī asks him about his illness.[17]

> Mañjuśrī: Householder, of what sort is your sickness? Vimalakīrti: It is immaterial and invisible.
> Mañjuśrī: Is it physical or mental? Vimalakīrti: It is not physical, since the body is insubstantial in itself. It is not mental, since the nature of the mind is like illusion.

---

14 Richard F. Gombrich, *What the Buddha Thought* (London: Equinox, 2009), p. 177.

15 Robert A.F. Thurman, trans., *The Holy Teaching of Vimalakirti* (University Park: Pennsylvania State University Press, 1987).

16 Philip Yampolsky, trans., *The Platform Sutra of Hui-neng* (NY: Columbia University Press, 1967), pp. 125-153.

17 Thurman, Vimalakirti, p. 44.

Mañjuśrī: Householder, which of the four main elements is disturbed—earth, water, fire, or air?

Vimalakīrti: Mañjuśrī, I am sick only because the elements of living beings are disturbed by sicknesses.

Mañjuśrī: Householder, how should a bodhisattva console another bodhisattva who is sick?

Vimalakīrti: He should tell him that the body is impermanent, but should not exhort him to renunciation or disgust. He should tell him that the body is miserable, but should not encourage him to find solace in liberation; that the body is selfless, but that living beings should be developed; that the body is peaceful, but not to seek any ultimate calm. He should urge him to confess his evil deeds, but not for the sake of absolution. He should encourage his empathy for all living beings on account of his own sickness, his remembrance of suffering experienced from beginningless time, and his consciousness of working for the welfare of living beings.... Thus should a bodhisattva console a sick bodhisattva, in such a way as to make him happy.

In their exchange, Vimalakīrti tells Mañjuśrī that the suffering of all beings is the source of his own suffering, such that his illness is his expression of emptiness, oneness, and great compassion.

While Vimalakīrti is a fictional, idealized character, it is not as if he is merely depicted as a seamless, superhuman figure. Particularly in the last statement cited above, Vimalakīrti describes what it means to abide both in the highest reality of emptiness/oneness and this world of vicissitudes: that to live the truth of emptiness is in fact to live in the very depths of this suffering world itself.

For example, one should be aware of the inherent instability of embodied existence and its attendant ills; yet, one should not retreat into a solipsistic meditative state: "He should tell him that the body is miserable, but should not encourage him to find solace in liberation." Implied in this is a criticism of early Buddhist monasticism and its retreat into renunciation and solitary meditation. Rather, one should balance living in this world of suffering with having one's center in the depths of meditative tranquility.

One should be aware that "body" is merely a social construction, a human convention, and does not actually exist in any reifiable sense; nevertheless, one should honor and respect the empirical body as the conduit to awakening: "The body is selfless, but ... living beings should be developed." That is, the process of religious awakening involves the transformation of consciousness, from a view of the body as 'real,' something that is the possession and 'property' of the ego self, to a view of the body as an open conduit of compassion to the human and larger sentient community.

The realization of emptiness gives rise to the awareness of others' suffering as inseparable from one's own, and the unfolding of great compassion in bodhisattva service: "He should encourage his empathy for all living beings on account of his own sickness, his remembrance of suffering experienced from beginningless time, and his consciousness of working for the welfare of living beings."

In this Mahayana vision, the bodhisattva ideal is based on the loosening of conceptual boundaries and the realization of oneness through compassion. As such, religious calling comes not at the behest of a transcendent absolute but arises from profound suffering immanent to life itself; this is the impetus behind the bodhisattva vow. Vimalakīrti also represents an inversion of the prior monasto-centric hierarchy. He is a layman, a family man, a lowly merchant; he enters into places of commerce, drinking establishments, homes of friends and family, but he is not perturbed, does not lose his equanimity or composure. Ordinary daily life becomes the realization of the inseparability of samsara and nirvana, the life of vicissitudes and the truth that liberates. Yet, this does not mean he is unfeeling or detached. His *modus operandi* is *nonattachment*, neither attachment nor detachment, in which the karmic awareness of the suffering of others becomes Vimalakīrti's own, only to be transformed into great compassion.

Above all, the fact of Vimalakīrti's illness illustrates the bodhisattva ideal of Mahayana Buddhism: He refuses to be liberated from suffering until all beings attain liberation. Vimalakirti the layman represents a philosophical overturning of the earlier Buddhist monastic hierarchy, displacing it with a demonstration of bodhisattva compassion. Vimalakirti, along with other characters of early Mahayana literature, began to emerge around the first or second centuries.

In turning to the episode of the illiterate woodcutter from the *Platform Sutra of Huineng*, a Chan/Zen Buddhist scripture likely compiled during the eighth century, we find another such overturning. The protagonist of the *Platform Sutra* is an illiterate woodcutter who is a "southern barbarian," a trope for the uneducated and uncultured.[18] One day, on one of his work errands, he hears a monk reciting verses from the Diamond Sutra, and immediately inspired, seeks out the monk's master Hongren, the Fifth Patriarch, or fifth-generation Chan master as counted from the founder Bodhidharma. Hongren tells the young woodcutter that he cannot become a monk as he is uncultured and illiterate, but entreated by the aspirant, allows that he can be a servant of the temple, preparing firewood and engaging in other manual tasks; already at this point, Hongren glimpses the woodcutter's superior realization. As Hongren is also preparing to retire, he must name a successor. To make a long story short, it is the illiterate woodcutter who demonstrates his keen intuition and superior wisdom. Deciding that the woodcutter is the one capable of becoming his true successor, Hongren bestows him with the Dharma name Huineng (wise and capable), and presents him with the transmission of the seal of awakening in the form of his robe and begging bowl.

However, Hongren knows that this will cause problems. His monks will be incited to jealousy and raise objections. He instructs Huineng to escape at night and stay out of sight, and only much later re-emerge to take the Dharma throne as the Sixth Patriarch after things have calmed down. Although he follows his master's instructions, Hongren's monks eventually find out and go in pursuit of Huineng. Finally, one of the monks by the name of Huiming catches up to him and demands the return of the bowl. Huineng points out that Huiming is not really after the bowl, that his true desire is for genuine awakening, and guides Huiming to realization.

Huiming departs gratefully, leaving Huineng unharmed. Huineng lives for some years in the woods, suffering from isolation, deprivation, and difficult circumstances. Along the way he instructs hunters and others he encounters, and finally emerges to take his rightful place as the Sixth Patriarch.

Here again, there is an implicit criticism of the monastic intellectual elite. An illiterate woodcutter turns out to be more enlightened than all of the monks who have been engaged in Buddhist practice for many years. Yet, when they pursue him out of their jealousy, Huineng does not criticize them or put them in their place; instead, he compassionately brings Huiming to his own awakening. Unlike Vimalakirti, however, Huineng does become a monk and is in fact anointed as the Sixth Patriarch. This brings us closer to the historical reality of Mahayana Buddhism, which for all its scriptural valorization of laity and women continued for most of its history to place great importance on the authority of male Buddhist masters and their institutional authority.

---

18 Yampolsky, *The Platform Sutra*, pp. 126-135.

The third episode of calling in Mahayana Buddhism is taken from the life of Gutoku Shinran (1173–1262). He was the founder of Jōdo Shinshū, known as Shin Buddhism in the West, which became the largest sect of Japanese Pure Land Buddhism. Whereas in Zen Buddhism, the central practice is seated meditation, in Shin Buddhism, the central practice is the invoking or chanting of the Name of Amida Buddha. The Name consists of the six-syllable phrase, Namu Amida Butsu, which is a transliteration of the Sanskrit, Namo Amitābha Buddha, meaning, "I bow and entrust myself to the Buddha of Infinite Light." The "Namu" or "I" in this case refers to the practitioner who is filled with the blind passion of attachments. "Amida Butsu" refers to the manifestation of emptiness as infinite light or illumination. Since the illumination of emptiness is a dynamic unfolding from moment to moment, the Name might be better rendered, "I entrust myself to the awakening of infinite light." The repetitive invoking of this name is a kind of contemplative practice, but because it arises from emptiness, the chanting of the Name is said to arise not from the ego's own self power but from "other power," meaning the power that is other than ego, or the true nature of the self as emptiness. A respected lay Shin Buddhist teacher from the modern period, Wariko Kai, composed a poem that expresses this well. She states,

> *Mihotoke no na wo yobu waga koe wa*
>   The voice with which I call Amida Buddha
> *Mihotoke no ware wo yobimasu mikoe nari keri*
>   Is the voice which Amida calls to me.

This is the voiceless voice of the boundless compassion of emptiness arising to embrace and dissolve the foolish attachments of the practitioner. Thus, we have here a genuine sense of calling, yet because of being based in emptiness, it is a calling of no-calling.

As Shinran states, Amida Buddha turns out to be upāya, a skillful means of leading the practitioner to compassionate liberation from the bonds of attachment, just like Vimalakirti's illness, and the illiterate woodcutter showing the learned monks the path to awakening.

According to Shinran,

> What is called the unsurpassed Buddha has no form. Due to having no form, it is called the spontaneous dharma-nature [jinen hōni].... We learn to listen deeply [to the voiceless voice of] Amida in order to be led to the awareness of formlessness. Amida Buddha is the skillful means for us to realize [this formless] spontaneity.... One should not be constantly thinking about this matter of spontaneity. If one thinks about this spontaneity too much, one will take the meaning of what has no meaning [i.e. emptiness], and turn it into something that appears to have [some specific] meaning. This is the inconceivable buddha-wisdom.[19]

Shin Buddhism arose in medieval Japan as a lay-centered movement, outside the control of the established sects. As it gained popularity, it posed a threat to the established ecclesiastical authorities, and they were successful in petitioning the Japanese emperor to defrock and banish its leaders, including Shinran who was exiled into the countryside. He had broken protocol by openly marrying, having children, and working along with his wife Eshinni, who took a nun's name, wore robes, and worked as Shinran's partner in ministering to peasants in outlying regions.

At the very end of his main philosophical work, Shinran states, "Thus, I was neither

---

19 Shinran, *Mattōshō*, in *Shinran chosaku zenshū* (SCZ), ed. Daiei Kaneko (Kyoto: Hōzōkan, 1964), p. 587.

monk nor layman."[20] This was a historical statement describing his situation as an outlaw monk living like a layman. In addition, it was a statement of Mahayana philosophy, going beyond the false distinction between clerics and laity. Furthermore, it can be taken as Shinran's own confession as a foolish being filled with attachment, unworthy to be regarded as a good monk or a good layman, and thereby embraced, illuminated, and dissolved into the flow of boundless compassion and infinite light. This final statement is reflective of Shinran's entire life, called by Amida Buddha from the depths of his own being, and like so many episodes in Mahayana Buddhism, upsetting the apple cart of conventional religious expectations.

Practices Sustaining Calling of No-Calling in Asian and Western Buddhists

In the West, in particular in Europe and North America, the image of Buddhism has been closely associated with seated meditation including participation in workshops and retreats held at Buddhist centers. Historically and into the present, the vast majority of Asian Buddhists do not engage in seated meditation and associated yogic practices. For laity, contemplative practice is much more likely to take the form of chanting the Name of Amida Buddha, other cosmic buddhas, or prayers that invoke a range of Buddhist deities. While monastics continue to wield a great deal of institutional authority, lay teachers and practitioners, men and women, have also played prominent roles in contexts other than yogic practice.

In the US, Buddhists constitute about one-percent of the population, and among them, there are more lay-based movements – such as Shin Buddhism and Soka Gakkai International, with their central practices invoking cosmic buddhas, bodhisattvas, and scriptures through chanting their names – than those movements that rely on some form of seated meditation practice and related practices derived from monastic traditions, such as Zen, Tibetan Vajarayana, and Vipassana-based mindfulness. However, in the US, even in the case of teachers coming from monastic traditions, most of the American teachers have not been celibate, with the majority married or in committed partnerships. In some Asian cultures, such as Japan, the majority of priests are married even in monastic traditions such as Zen, but in monastically-derived traditions, they will have trained for some time in single-sex monasteries or convents, anywhere from six months to several decades.

While in Asia, there are Buddhist temples, in the US, there are both temples and "centers," the latter a Western innovation, in which there are usually just a handful of full-time religious teachers in residence, and lay people participate in weekly, monthly, and other periodic services, workshops, and retreats. These centers tend to be based on models of individual practice with some degree of community, and centers are often run entrepreneurially to attract and cultivate followers. A particular feature of these centers is that they are mixed-gender, unlike Buddhist monasteries in Asia that are segregated similar to Catholic monasteries and convents.

Sexual scandals involving Buddhist teachers and their students, especially involving the abuse of religious authority, have been of particular concern in the mixed-gender setting of American Buddhist "centers" (although such scandals have not been limited to heterosexual relations).

The part-time center participation model stands in contrast with ethnic Asian "temples." These ethnic temples are generally community-based, with weekly services but many other group activities throughout the week such as study classes, Buddhist choir practice, and sports clubs. As an example, in Japanese American Shin Buddhist temples in the early- to mid- twentieth century, members donated to their temples upwards of fifty percent of their often extremely modest household income, and

---

20 Shinran, *Kyōgyōshinshō*, in *SCZ*, p. 340.

the ministers themselves were sustained purely by dāna, or religious donations. In turn, the temples functioned almost like extended families that provided all manner of spiritual and material support to families in need. In effect, the temple members, although lay, necessarily lived lives of renunciation with the religious life as the core. This is no longer the case as temple ministers have become modestly salaried, and youth leave for college and/or work, often never returning to the temples.

There is a relatively small yet growing percentage of Shin temples that have become ethnically and racially more diverse, sometimes incorporating aspects of both "temple" and "center" cultures. In terms of "calling," early ethnic temples were more communal, with members called in service to temple life, and centers more individualistic in the way each practitioner is called to practice, following the beat of his or her own drum, with consequently higher turnover rates in terms of center participation.

Modern Challenges and Opportunities: Calling Versus Career

Buddhism in the contemporary US faces particular challenges, especially in relation to the center model, of which teacher-student sexual concerns is only one example. More generally, the combination of intensive meditation practice, including retreats of a week or more, on the one hand, and the demands of lay life, on the other, can be especially stressful. The traditional system of monastic training was not designed to facilitate the transition back-and-forth between the hustle and bustle of lay life and the deep quietude of the intensive retreat setting. As Willoughby Britton has documented, the result is often difficulty both in transition and in the practice itself, with a number of students falling into disturbing mental states as a result.[21]

The renunciant path of monastics looks very different from the life of laity, despite exemplars depicted in sacred writings such as Vimalakīrti the layman; the path of yogic practice that involves far more than seated meditation is not for the faint of heart. One way of understanding the complexity faced by those who feel called to the life of intensive Buddhist practice in the West is to place it in the larger context of the work of religious calling versus the work carried out in one's career.

The life of religious calling for a monk or a nun in principle entails renunciation of mundane desires—for family, material success, social status, and the like. Alms-begging, a practice common to monks and nuns in much of Asia, is emblematic of this renunciation. In Japan, for example, Zen monks are not even allowed to touch alms with their hands but extend their kesa, a cloth mantle symbolic of their entire robes, heads bowed, to receive ofuse (Skt. dāna) in humility. Moreover, these alms are not their own to keep individually but used to sustain the entire monastic community.[22]

In contemporary American culture, such a way of life would amount to the renunciation of a career that entails self-promotion, the search for social recognition, and the accrual of wealth. Yet, the life of alms-begging is not really possible for even monks in the US, since we do not live in a culture that recognizes alms-begging as a culturally acceptable practice.

If the ideal of the life of a monk or a nun is based on renunciation, the career of a contemporary layperson is based on acquisition: the proactive accumulation of all forms of symbolic capital – social and material – that

---

21 Willoughby Britton, "Meditation Nation," *Tricycle*, accessed June 28, 2015, http://www.tricycle.com/blog/meditation-nation, http://www.tricycle.com/blog/meditation-nation.

22 In actual practice, monks in Japan have other sources of income, such as "donations" (Jpn. *ofuse*) received for performing funeral and memorial services. The example of alms-begging is simply given as an example that illustrates the principle of renunciation, not the historical reality.

constitutes a significant marker of success. Unlike monks and nuns in the vision of traditional Asian Buddhist cultures, Buddhists in the US live and work in a culture defined by individual entrepreneurship. It is difficult to sustain a Buddhist center or career as a Buddhist teacher without self-promotion through social media, charging fees for workshops and retreats, and active recruitment of students and followers. Contemporary Asian Buddhist monks, nuns, and priests have also had to develop similar strategies, and it is not as if they did not actively pursue the accumulation of symbolic capital within their traditional, pre-modern contexts. However, there are significant differences between traditional Asian ideals of religious calling and the way that Buddhist practice has come to be promoted in the contemporary US and in the West generally.

Three examples help to illustrate the complex intersection of calling and career for contemporary American Buddhists. One comes from an interview with Grace McLeod (1907–2006), a pioneering lay Buddhist who helped to nurture Shin Buddhist temples through many efforts including creation of English-language teaching materials in the early- to mid-twentieth century. Another comes from a question posed to His Holiness the 14th Dalai Lama, Tenzin Gyatso (b. 1935), on the occasion of his special lecture at the University of Oregon in 2013, regarding the balance between work and religious life. The third is taken from the life of author, feminist, and social activist Natalie Goldberg (b. 1948), and her attempt to negotiate her life as a writer and her devotion to Zen Buddhist practice.

Born in Anacortes, in Washington State, and raised Catholic, Grace McLeod encountered Japanese Buddhists in her twenties in the Seattle area and converted to Buddhism in 1948 along with her husband Hugh McLeod.[23] Although little-known outside of her own circle of associations, she made major contributions to Buddhism internationally. Streams of prominent Buddhist teachers from high ranking Tibetan lamas to Zen masters visited her in Seattle as she produced volumes of teaching materials for American Buddhists before it became popularized in the 'sixties and 'seventies. For nearly four decades, several of her publications were circulated to all of the Shin Buddhist temples in the US.

McLeod was in her seventies when the 16th Karmapa, one of the highest-ranking Tibetan lamas, came to visit her from his renowned Rumtek monastery in Sikkim in North India. He asked her to visit him there, saying, "I have work for you." When she eventually arrived, he introduced her to the nuns there, calling her their "mother." In time, she helped to establish an international Buddhist convent in Sikkim, helping to raise the funds almost single-handedly. Gail Kaminishi, herself a long-time contributor to Seattle Betsuin temple and American Shin Buddhism, said of Grace, "She is truly like a bodhisattva, very committed to being in this world, helping others when and how she can."[24]

One wonders about the lack of wider recognition for McLeod's work, but she herself seemed to prefer it that way: "The problem," she said, "is that Western Buddhists have such a hard time not being proud of the teachings they receive, even though this is counterintuitive."[25]

For McLeod, her calling to be a Buddhist was to be without ego, which comes very close to the meaning of Buddhist "no-self" and "emptiness." Since the passing of her husband Hugh in 1978, Grace had lived mostly alone, had very few needs or possessions other than

---

23 The following account of Grace McLeod's life is taken from: Keith Ervin, "Grace McLeod, World Traveller, Potent Advocate for Buddhism," *The Seattle Times*, August 27, 2006, accessed July 2, 2015, http://community.seattletimes.nwsource.com/archive/?date=20060827&slug=mcleodobit27m; and Sienna Craig, "Under the Magnolia Tree: Days with Grace McLeod," unpublished essay, 2006.

24 Craig, "Under the Magnolia Tree," p. 3.

25 Craig, "Under the Magnolia Tree," p. 9.

her modest early twentieth-century home in Seattle, and in many ways, she had become like one of the nuns she had helped so much. Her Buddhist way of life was especially remarkable considering that she became a Buddhist when it was not fashionable, indeed when it made her the friend and ally of an oppressed ethnic, racial, and religious minority. Her life was one of calling, albeit a calling of no-calling, as it arose from no-self, non-ego, and returned quietly to no-self and to vast emptiness.

Grace's comment about Western Buddhists having "such a hard time not being proud" was directed, not so subtly, at the individualistic, self-promoting, entrepreneurial character of the many Western Buddhists she had encountered, especially in recent decades. While this criticism certainly seems valid, one could argue that it can be difficult to maintain and develop Buddhist centers in the US without this entrepreneurialism, without fee-based retreat centers, advertisements in *Tricycle: The Buddhist Review*, Buddhist center-related businesses such as organic eateries, paraphernalia stores, and the like. At what point does the life of a Buddhist teacher cease to be a life of religious calling and become a career? Can the two co-exist, or are they mutually incompatible? These questions also arise for lay Buddhists, as the next episode shows.

After nine years of cooperative planning between Maitripa Tibetan Buddhist College in Portland, Oregon; the Eugene Sakya Center; and the University of Oregon (UO), His Holiness the 14th Dalai Lama arrived for one afternoon lecture presented to a packed audience of 12,000 at Matthew Knight Arena at the UO, along with events at our partner institutions. After concluding his presentation on "The Path to Peace and Happiness in the Global Society," for which the Dalai Lama received a long, standing ovation, he responded to three pre-taped video questions from those who were in attendance. One was from Jennifer Burton, staff member at the UO Center for Multicultural Academic Excellence:

Sometimes in professional life aggressiveness and self-centeredness are rewarded more than compassion and care for others. Since it is not possible because of financial and family obligations for the average person to withdraw from the professional world, how can people be altruistic and maintain bodhicitta, the aspiration for enlightenment, and still thrive in their jobs?[26]

The response from the Dalai Lama was brief yet to the point,

In order to help others more effectively, ...to help other...people, first you yourself [must] be healthy. If you, yourself [are] sick, then how [can you] care for other sick people?... So, in order to help other people, you yourself must be fit, ...including economic condition [finances].... Balanced with sense of concern [for] others' well-being.

This exchange is telling, both in terms of the question and the answer. The question went to the heart of the problematic intersection of calling and career. The answer addressed the need to develop spiritual resources and a balanced approach. Jennifer Burton, identifying herself with the Buddhist teachings, was asking how one could be giving and selfless when career and job often seemed to require self-promotion and selfishness. The Dalai Lama's response did not directly answer her question. Instead, he seemed to suggest that one must be spiritually and financially robust enough (healthy enough) to be able to give to others, and that one must balance concern for others with concern for self.

---

26 The Fourteenth Dalai Lama, Tenzin Gyatso, "The Path to Peace and Happiness in the Global Society," University of Oregon, May 10, 2013, accessed July 2, 2015, https://www.youtube.com/watch?v=LW42SqUqbjM, 1:12:33.

Religions including Buddhism often tout virtues such as generosity, unselfishness, love and compassion for others, that is, a life of renunciation that entails abandoning selfish concerns in order to cultivate a life of religious virtue. Yet, as Burton indicates, success in lay society often entails competition and self-promotion, a point that is especially poignant for her, as she advocates for minority students whose needs go unrecognized, and voices unheard.

For lay people who spend a large proportion of their time at work, and attempt to derive meaning from it, a meaningful career is difficult to disentangle from success in a competitive marketplace. Unselfishness can be an important virtue in the workplace, but being a good team player or listing volunteer work on one's resumé is of a completely different order of unselfishness from Buddhist no-self or the realization of emptiness. The former is ultimately based in self-interest, the latter in non-self.

In the context of calling and career, the Dalai Lama's response may be understood in at least two ways: 1) One must have enough in reserve – spiritually, emotionally, materially – to be able to give without suffering compassion fatigue; 2) For lay people, it is unreasonable to renounce personal desires for self, family, and friends. Instead, one needs to strike a balance between one's calling as a Buddhist and one's work and career that entail some degree of selfishness, including the job of simply feeding one's family. The balance between life in society that is necessarily competitive, on the one hand, and a life of Buddhist calling that entails renunciation of personal desires and socially-defined success, on the other, continues as a prominent theme in the following episodes, taken from a memoir by Natalie Goldberg, writer and Zen Buddhist practitioner.

Best-selling author Natalie Goldberg recounts her path to becoming a writer as well as Zen Buddhist practitioner in her memoir, *A Long Quiet Highway*. Both are presented as paths that take one deep into the truth of the self. Even her Zen master Dainin Katagiri seems to think the writing life can be a practice like Zen Buddhism:

> "Make writing your practice," Roshi [my master] told me.
> "Oh, no, I can't. My brain," I pointed to my head, "I can't shut it up."
> "If you commit to it, writing will take you as deep as Zen," he told me.[27]

Eventually, Katagiri tells her she will have to make a decision: Choose writing or Zen.

> Once I went to Roshi when I lived in Minnesota and told him, "When I'm at Zen center, I feel like a writer. When I'm with writers, I feel like a Zen student."
> "Someday you will have to choose. You're not ready yet, but someday you will be. Writing and Zen are parallel paths, but not the same."
> We never spoke about it again. I continued to write; I continued to sit [in meditation practice at Zen center]."
> Three months after I finished [composing Writing Down the] Bones, I went camping alone one weekend in August by the Chama River....
> I made breakfast of brown rice and roasted nuts over a fire and then packed up....
> Pink cliffs shot up from the dry desert to my left and the Chama River and its valley spread out to my right.
> I'd gone about three miles when suddenly I burst out crying.... I repeated over and over: "I chose being a writer. I chose being a writer. I chose being a writer," and sobbed

---
27 Natalie Goldberg, *A Long Quiet Highway: Waking Up in America* (New York: Bantam Books, 1993), p. 183.

and sobbed. Before that moment I had no idea that that question had been working in me so deeply....

Why did I have to choose? I don't know if we do really choose. Eventually, I think something chooses us and we shut up, surrender, and go with it. And the difference between Zen and writing? In writing you bring everything you know into writing. In Zen you bring everything you know into nothing, into the present moment where you can't hold onto anything.[28]

As a woman and a Jew growing up in places and at a time when she felt displaced in the dominant culture, writing was a way for Goldberg to find her voice, to establish her identity in society, in the world of form. Zen practice was her way of going deep within, connecting with her deepest, truest self, which for her was the self of emptiness and oneness with everyone and everything. Writing and Zen were close but not the same. Writing was a way to bring her depth out into the world; Zen was a way of freeing herself from the oppressive world and finding her true self, beyond words. Writing became a meaningful career for Goldberg, but she would likely object to the characterization of her writing life as a "career." It carries a much deeper meaning for her than what is usually thought of as a successful career, one that brings financial success and social status.

Neither Goldberg nor Katagiri ever make clear why she had to choose Zen or writing. Goldberg continued her Zen practice even as she chose the path of writing, so the choice was not to eliminate one in favor of the other. Rather, the decision seemed to be a matter of commitment. One cannot truly deepen one's practice unless one commits to a vehicle that will take one to greater realization. It can be likened to the fact that it is very difficult to become a virtuoso violinist and pianist at the same time; you can play both, but you have to commit to one.

Still, writing as a path and Zen as a path are not the same in the way that becoming a violinist or a pianist might be regarded. Writing is an inherently social activity, an act of human communication that entails some degree of competitive success. It just wouldn't have been the same if no one bought Goldberg's books, attended her writing workshops, or followed her on Facebook, validating her voice, "I'm here, and people recognize my existence." Of course, one can be recognized as an accomplished Buddhist practitioner, but many great Buddhists go nameless, their virtue inconspicuous. Nevertheless, Katagiri tells Goldberg that writing can take her as deep as Zen practice, that it can be a kind of Buddhist practice without carrying that label: "If you commit to it, writing will take you as deep as Zen." The art, discipline, or vehicle itself is not as significant as one's commitment.

Whether going from form to emptiness deep in Zen practice, or from emptiness to form bringing the depths out into the light of day in writing practice, as human beings both Katagiri and Goldberg have to live in society (form) but aspire not to be defined by it (emptiness). In fact, both Katagiri and Goldberg end up being Zen practitioners and writers, each publishing books, each getting married, each continuing Zen practice throughout their lives, each needing students to be teachers of their art. The life of a writer and that of a Zen teacher are vastly different, but also not so different, according to Goldberg and Katagiri, if one goes deep enough into either one. Both carry dimensions of calling and of career, each path with its need for social recognition, and equal aspiration to be free of this need. It could be that both 'writer' and 'Zen master' as defined by the voices in *A Long Quiet Highway* contain profound self-contradictions that are embedded in their respective paths, and possibly in human life itself.

---

28 Goldberg, *A Long Quiet Highway*, pp. 190-192.

The Dalai Lama takes a view similar to Katagiri, that the choice of the path itself is less significant than the commitment to cultivate it, whether Buddhist or non-Buddhist, or even religious or non-religious. Of his consistent emphasis on compassion as the basis for genuine human existence, he states, "I am convinced that everyone can develop a good heart and a sense of universal responsibility with or without religion."[29] In this sense, a specifically religious sense of calling is less significant for these Buddhist teachers than a clear view of human life and death, and a truth that is free from ideological attachments.

Conclusion

As can be seen from the discussion above, there are a number of ways in which dimensions of Abrahamic conceptions of calling resonate with Buddhist notions. At the same time, there are significant differences. In a view of selfhood that emphasizes no-self, emptiness, and great compassion, it may be more significant to think about what is most helpful for a given person within the context of the moment, than about any one specific aspect of their lives, including religious calling or even religious identity. Or, one might say, religious calling can be an important component of considering what can be said and done for a person given the karmic limitations and possibilities of the moment.

Making one's faith explicit seems foundational to a life of religious calling in the Abrahamic traditions. As an example, for a Christian, being called to faith in Christ can be the most defining moment of the formation of their religious identity. In contrast, to be a real Buddhist, it may be necessary to forget that one is a "Buddhist." The path to being Buddhist, to realizing no-self, can be understood as forgetting the self, to loosen the boundaries between self and other, Buddhist and non-Buddhist, religious and non-religious. According to the Zen Master Dōgen (1200–1253), "To study the Buddha Way is to study the self. To study the self is to forget the self."[30] Or, as the Vietnamese monk, socially and environmentally engaged activist Thich Nhat Hanh states,

> The way of nonattachment from views is the basic teaching of Buddhism.... We are determined not to be idolatrous about or bound to any doctrine, theory, or ideology, even Buddhist ones. Buddhist teachings are guiding means [upāya] to help us learn to look deeply and to develop our understanding and compassion.[31]

"Calling" can be a helpful category for thinking about the life of a Buddhist, but it is not a primary concept in the way it might be for Abrahamic religions. Especially in Mahayana Buddhism, it can be seen as one component within a larger, fluid, contextual view of empty Buddhist teachings as upāya or skillful means. This consideration of calling in a Buddhist framework has been necessarily selective, episodic, a constructed account. It will have more than served its purpose, however, if it provides a basis for further exploration.

Resources

Chadwick, David. *The Life and Zen Teaching of Shunryu Suzuki*. New York: Harmony Books, 2000.

Dalai Lama. *Ethics for the New Millenium*. New York: Riverhead Books, 2001.

---

29 The Fourteenth Dalai Lama, Tenzin Gyatso, "Nobel Peace Prize Acceptance Speech," accessed July 3, 2015, http://www.dalailama.com/messages/acceptance-speeches/nobel-peace-prize.

30 Dōgen, "Genjōkōan," *Shōbōgenzō*, vol. 1, ao 319-0, annotated by Yaeko Mizuno (Tokyo: Iwanami Shoten, 1993), p. 54. Norman Waddell & Masao Abe, tr. "Shobogenzo Genjokoan," by Dogen Kigen, *The Eastern Buddhist* 5:2 (10/1972): 134.

31 Thich Nhat Hanh, *Being Peace* (Berkeley, CA: Parallax Press, 1987), pp. 90-91.

Dresser, Marianne. *Buddhist Women on the Edge: Contemporary Perspectives from the Western Frontier.* North Atlantic Books, 1996.

Goldberg, Natalie. *A Long Quiet Highway: Waking Up in America.* New York: Bantam Books, 1993.

Guenther, Herbert. Translator. *The Life and Teaching of Naropa.* Boston: Shambhala, 1995. Nhat Hanh, Thich. Being Peace. Berkeley, California, 1987.

Haas, Michaela. *Dakini Power: Twelve Extraordinary Women Shaping the Transmission of Tibetan Buddhism in the West.* Boston: Snow Lion, 2013.

Kaye, Les. *Zen at Work.* New York: Three Rivers Press, 1997.

Kornfield, Jack. *After the Ecstasy, the Laundry.* New York: Bantam, 2001.

Kotler, Arnold. *Engaged Buddhist Reader.* Berkeley, California: Parallax Press, 1999.

O'Halloran, Maura Soshin. *Pure Heart, Enlightened Mind: The Life and Letters of an Irish Zen Saint.* Boston: Wisdom Publications, 2007.

Unno, Taitetsu. *River of Fire, River of Water.* New York: Image, 1998.

21
A Contemplative Approach to Family Systems
Jessica Thomas, PhD, LMFT

In this chapter, we delve into the fusion of family systems theory with a contemplative approach, particularly within the realm of Buddhist college chaplaincy. We explore how these complementary frameworks intersect to provide profound support for students navigating the complexities of higher education and family dynamics. At the heart of family systems theory lies the recognition that the "self" is intricately entwined within a larger familial context, emphasizing the relational nature of identity. This notion resonates deeply with Buddhist philosophy, which underscores the principle of mutual causality or interdependence. Both systems advocate for understanding patterns and dynamics shaped by interconnections.

As students embark on their educational journey, they are immersed in a myriad of experiences – peer interactions, intellectual discourse, personal introspection, and exposure to diverse perspectives. Through these encounters, they gradually expand their awareness, confronting inherited beliefs and familial paradigms. By integrating family systems theory with Buddhist principles and contemplative practices, chaplains can provide invaluable guidance to students traversing this path of transformation. Drawing from the wisdom of both traditions, chaplains facilitate spaces for students to engage in mindful reflection, fostering a deeper understanding of their familial histories, roles, and relationships. By embracing the interconnectedness of self and family, students gain insight into the dynamics that shape their lives, empowering them to navigate challenges with resilience and compassion. In essence, the contemplative integration of family systems theory and Buddhist philosophy equips chaplains with a holistic approach to supporting students' growth and self-discovery within the intricate tapestry of family systems and university life.

First, we will explore key concepts of both family systems theory and contemplative therapy. We then examine how combining contemplative therapy with the creation of genograms offers a unique and holistic approach to exploring family dynamics, relationships, and intergenerational patterns. By integrating contemplative therapy principles into the creation and interpretation of genograms, chaplains can provide a deeper and more nuanced exploration of family dynamics, relationships, and intergenerational patterns. Second, we will explore the use of photovoice, whereby students and their families bring images to a family session to reflect on their significance, meaning and stories. Photovoice is facilitated by the chaplain as a family intervention to invoke compassion, insight, healing, and growth within the family system. Although photovoice is often applied in social action research, it can also be a method that encourages families to reflect on the interdependent nature of family life and galvanize necessary changes (Feen-Calligan., et al, 2023).

Finally, we will present a case study in which a university student named Sarah seeks guidance from her university Buddhist chaplain. This case study demonstrates how the integration of family systems theory, contemplative therapy, and photovoice might contribute to a shift in Sarah's life through increased compassion and insights both within herself and her family system.

Family Systems Theory

Family systems theory was inspired by general systems theory, which was proposed by biologist Ludwig von Bertalanffy in the mid-20th century. Bertalanffy's theory suggested that systems can be understood by examining their components and their interactions as a whole, rather than just studying their individual parts separately (Bertalanffy, 1968). Family systems theory applies this concept to the family unit, considering the family as a system composed of interconnected individuals, each influencing and being influenced by the others. It emphasizes understanding family dynamics, communication patterns, roles, and relationships within the context of the entire family system rather than focusing solely on individual members.

In essence, family systems theory views the family as a complex system with its own unique structure, rules, and processes, and it seeks to understand how these elements interact and influence one another over time. In this view, the family unit is an interconnected system where each member's behavior affects and is affected by the functioning of the whole. Developed primarily by psychiatrist Murray Bowen in the 1950s and further expanded by theorists like Salvador Minuchin and Jay Haley, family systems theory proposes that individuals cannot be fully understood in isolation from their family context (Titelman, 2014). Family systems theory is applied in various contexts, including therapy, education, and organizational consulting, and chaplaincy, to understand and address relational dynamics, communication patterns, and systemic issues within families and other social systems.

Key concepts of family systems theory include:
1. <u>Interconnectedness</u>: Emphasizes the interdependence and interconnectedness among family members. Changes in one part of the system can ripple throughout the entire family.
2. <u>Hierarchy and Boundaries</u>: Families have hierarchies and boundaries that regulate interactions and relationships between members. Healthy families maintain flexible boundaries that allow for both autonomy and connection.
3. <u>Patterns and Dynamics</u>: Families develop patterns of interaction and communication that shape their functioning over time. These patterns can be adaptive or maladaptive, influencing family members' behavior and emotional well-being.
4. <u>Differentiation</u>: Refers to the degree to which individuals can maintain a sense of self while remaining emotionally connected to the family. Higher levels of differentiation enable individuals to navigate family dynamics with greater autonomy and emotional maturity.
5. <u>Triangulation</u>: Describes a dynamic where tension between two family members is alleviated by involving a third party. Triangulation can disrupt healthy communication patterns and perpetuate conflict within the family system.

One of Bowen's most notable methods in understanding a family system is through a genogram. Creating a genogram can be a valuable tool to visually represent relationships, dynamics, and patterns across multiple generations (McGoldrick, M., & Gerson, R. Shellenberger, 1999). More than just a chart of names and dates, a genogram is a window into the heart of a system, revealing the patterns and dynamics that define it. The process is like painting a picture of your family's story, tracing the lines of relationships and connections that span generations. Similar to a family tree, a genogram brings awareness and insights about who we are, where we come from, and how we relate to one another. It presents a powerful therapeutic tool for promoting insight, understanding, and communication within relational systems. Creating a genogram with a client or university student can be multipurpose as it can enhance the joining process, serve as an assessment tool, and an intervention that inspires new understandings.

As you work together to create a genogram, students might share stories and memories, laughter, and tears. They uncover hidden connections and surprising revelations, finding new understanding in the familiar. When the genogram is complete, your student will step back to marvel at the intricate web of relationships that have been woven together. It's more than just a chart – it's a living document of a family's story, a testament to the bonds that bind together across time and space. As students reflect on their genogram, they gain new insights into themselves and others, seeing themselves and their family in a whole new light. It's a powerful tool that can guide students on a journey of self-discovery and healing as they navigate the complexities of a transformative experience in university life. In the end, a genogram is more than just a piece of paper – it's a symbol of a shared history and identity that is marked by the recognition of each generation's contribution to the past, present and future. At the end of this chapter, we will explore the use of a genogram through a case study where a university chaplain supports a student in exploring the unique interpersonal challenges that arise as a first-generation immigrant.

Contemplative Therapy

Contemplative therapy is an approach to psychotherapy that integrates mindfulness, meditation, and other contemplative practices into the therapeutic process. It emphasizes the cultivation of present-moment awareness, self-reflection, and compassionate acceptance to promote healing and well-being. Contemplative therapy draws inspiration from contemplative traditions, such as Buddhism and mindfulness meditation, as well as from humanistic, existential, and relational approaches to psychotherapy. It offers clients a path toward greater self-awareness, emotional resilience, and inner peace by integrating ancient wisdom with modern therapeutic techniques.

Mindfulness practices, such as meditation and mindful breathing, are used to help clients become more aware of their thoughts, emotions, and bodily sensations. These practices assist clients in cultivating a compassionate and grounded awareness, allowing them to observe their thoughts, emotions, and experiences with greater clarity and acceptance (Gambrel & Keeling, 2010). Clients learn to relate to themselves and their inner experiences from a place of non-judgmental awareness rather than reacting with habitual patterns of reactivity or self-criticism.

Key concepts of contemplative therapy include:
1. <u>Self-Inquiry</u>: Contemplative therapy invites clients to engage in self-inquiry and introspection. Clients are encouraged to explore their inner experiences, beliefs, and patterns of behavior with curiosity and compassion.
2. <u>Compassionate Acceptance</u>: Contemplative therapy emphasizes the importance of compassionate acceptance toward oneself and others. Clients learn to cultivate self-compassion and kindness, allowing them to approach their struggles and challenges with greater ease and understanding.
3. <u>Integration of Contemplative Practices</u>: Contemplative therapy integrates various contemplative practices, such as mindfulness meditation, loving-kindness meditation, and body scan exercises, into the therapeutic process. These practices are tailored to meet the unique needs and preferences of each client.
4. <u>Holistic Approach</u>: Contemplative therapy takes a holistic approach to healing, addressing the interconnectedness of mind, body, and spirit. Therapists recognize the influence of environmental, cultural, and relational factors on clients' well-being and work to support clients in

cultivating greater harmony and balance in their lives.
5. <u>Cultivation of Presence</u>: Contemplative therapy aims to cultivate presence and authenticity in the therapeutic relationship. Therapists model presence by listening deeply, offering genuine empathy, and creating a safe space for clients to explore their inner experiences without judgment.

Case Study: A College Student's Journey Navigating Family Dynamics, Bridging Cultures, and Contemplative Practice

Introduction

In the journey of a college student, understanding the intricate interplay between family dynamics, cultural identity, and personal development is essential for providing comprehensive support. This case study explores the utilization of a genogram to unravel these complexities, and integrates contemplative practices to empower the student in navigating their challenges with mindful awareness and cultural sensitivity. Additionally, the chaplain utilizes photovoice as a contemplative method to facilitate a reflective dialogue, fostering deeper understanding and connection among family members.

Case Background

Sara, a 20-year-old college student, seeks guidance from a Buddhist chaplain to navigate academic stress and interpersonal conflicts within her family. As a first-generation immigrant from South Asia, Sara grapples with balancing cultural expectations with personal aspirations. She describes feeling torn between familial obligations and the pursuit of her individual goals, yearning to bridge this felt cultural divide within herself and family.

Genogram Creation and Analysis

To begin, the chaplain discussed in advance the intention of creating a genogram with their student and chose a good time to begin the project. In preparation, students are encouraged to come prepared with memories and stories passed down through the generations that feel significant. In the next session, the chaplain collaborated with Sara around a table with a large paper and a variety of colored pens. (Alternatively, a digital genogram can serve the purpose, given the numerous applications available that support its creation. With the aid of digital tools, constructing and sharing genograms becomes more accessible, facilitating collaboration and communication among users).

The chaplain opened up the process by asking Sarah to hold a compassionate and curious presence through the process. As Sara delved into the process, she began by adding details including birthdates, death dates, anniversaries, and significant life events among names and relationships. The chaplain marked milestones with symbols chosen by Sarah – acknowledging the joys and sorrows that have shaped Sarah's family's journey. The chaplain gently shifted the conversation toward relational dynamics by asking contemplative questions as to further elucidated themes like closeness, conflict, substance abuse, and the larger web of familial relationships and cultural influences.

Below are examples of questions:
- How does the family support each other emotionally, financially, and practically?
- What are the roles and responsibilities within the family? How do these roles influence interactions?
- How does the family handle conflict or difficult situations? Are there recurring patterns in conflict resolution?
- Are there any cultural or religious influences that shape family values and traditions?

- How has the family dealt with major life transitions such as births, deaths, marriages, or divorces?
- What are the emotional dynamics between family members? Are there any unresolved issues or tensions?

Tracing the threads of love and tension that weave through the family tapestry helped Sarah have compassion for herself and her extended family. She gained valuable insights on the felt obligations and expectations that influenced her academic goals. And furthermore, she more deeply understood the tension that surrounded her desire for autonomy and her cultural identity. The key insights that emerged from Sarah genogram are as follows.

- Cultural Expectations: Strong emphasis on filial piety and familial duty within Sara's South Asian cultural context. Traditional values shape Sara's familial obligations and expectations, influencing her academic and career choices.
- Interpersonal Dynamics: Tensions arise from the intergenerational gap between Sara, a second-generation immigrant, and her parents, who uphold traditional cultural values. Conflicts emerge regarding Sara's autonomy and cultural identity, contributing to strained familial relationships.
- Acculturation Challenges: Sara navigates the complexities of assimilating into mainstream American culture while preserving her cultural heritage. Conflicting values and societal expectations contribute to Sara's feelings of cultural identity confusion and alienation.
- Intergenerational Communication: Limited communication and understanding hinder the resolution of conflicts within Sara's family. Language barriers and cultural nuances exacerbate misunderstandings and hinder emotional expression.

Intervention Strategies

Drawing upon the genogram analysis, the Buddhist chaplain integrated contemplative practices aimed at fostering well-being, resilience, and familial harmony. Below are specific ways in a contemplative approach was integrated to reduce stress and cultivate a compassionate and insightful frame of mind and presence. These strategies help prepare Sarah to explore more deeply with her family directly in subsequent family sessions.

- Mindfulness-Based Stress Reduction: Exploring mindfulness meditation techniques with Sara to cultivate awareness of her thoughts, emotions, and bodily sensations. Guiding her in practicing mindful breathing and body scans to alleviate academic stress and enhance emotional regulation.
- Cultivating Compassion and Empathy: Facilitating loving-kindness meditation exercises to cultivate compassion towards herself and her family members. Encouraging Sara to reflect on her parents' experiences and challenges, fostering empathy and understanding within familial relationships.
  - Consider your parents' upbringing and life experiences. What do you know about their early life, including any significant events, challenges, or achievements they have shared with you?
  - Reflect on the cultural context in which your parents grew up. How did societal norms, cultural values, and historical events shape their perspectives, beliefs, and behaviors?
  - Reflect on moments when you witnessed your parents' resilience and strength in the face of adversity. What lessons or insights can you draw from their experiences of overcoming challenges and persevering through difficult times?

- Contemplate the emotions and feelings your parents may experience in their daily lives. How do they express joy, sadness, fear, or love? How do their emotional expressions contribute to your understanding of their experiences and challenges?
- Imagine walking in your parents' shoes for a day, experiencing the world from their perspective. What insights or revelations do you gain about their experiences, challenges, and aspirations? How does this exercise deepen your empathy and understanding towards them?

• Self-Exploration and Cultural Affirmation: Encourage cultural immersion experiences, such as participating in cultural events and religious rituals, to deepen Sara's sense of cultural pride and belonging. Guiding Sara in contemplative journaling exercises to explore her cultural identity, values, and aspirations.
- Reflect on your earliest memories associated with your cultural heritage. What customs, traditions, or rituals stand out to you? How have these cultural experiences shaped your identity?
- Contemplate the significance of cultural resilience and cultural pride in your life. How do you draw strength from your cultural heritage during times of adversity or uncertainty?
- Imagine sharing your cultural heritage with others and fostering cross-cultural understanding. What actions or initiatives could you take to promote cultural appreciation and inclusivity within your community or campus environment?
- Explore the values instilled in you by your cultural background. Consider aspects such as family, community, spirituality, education, and work ethic. How do these values influence your decisions, beliefs, and interactions with others?

Contemplative Family Session with Photograph

The chaplain offered a family session to practice deep listening and mindful communication within Sara's family. A contemplative method was integrated with photovoice to facilitate a reflective dialogue, fostering deeper understanding and connection among family members. By doing so, Sara's family could practice deep listening, mindful communication, and contemplative dialogue, leading to greater understanding, connection, and harmony within the family dynamic.

Forms of therapeutic photography have been used to explore and express grief in communion with others and have proven to be a healing ingredient (Thomas, 2024; Weiser, 2004). Similarly, photovoice can be applied therapeutically. Photovoice has been used as a powerful tool in communities and groups to record and reflect on community strengths and concerns while also evoking empathy, compassion, and awareness (Wang, 1997). In this case, the chaplain facilitated photovoice as a family session as a contemplative method to inspire healing and greater awareness. The process might involve:

• Introduction: The session began by introducing the concept of Photovoice to Sara's family members, explaining how it is a participatory method that combines photographs and storytelling to foster dialogue and understanding. The chaplain emphasized that each family member will have the opportunity to express themselves through images and narratives.
• Photo assignment: The chaplain encouraged family members to make photographs of moments, objects, or environments that represent their experiences, emotions, and perspectives within the family dynamic. It was

emphasized that there are no right or wrong photographs, and each image holds significance. Another option is for family members to bring already made photographs that are most significant to them.
- Sharing circle: Gather the family members together in a comfortable setting for a sharing circle. Remind family members that the person who is sharing should not be interrupted, however they are welcome to write down reflections and thoughts on a piece of paper to dialogue about after the sharing process. Start by inviting each family member to share their photographs one by one. As they present their images, encourage them to describe the significance behind each photograph, including thoughts, emotions, and memories associated with it. The chaplain made notes during each family members sharing on significant statements and themes.
- Deep Listening Practice: Encourage active listening and empathy among family members during the sharing circle. Implement deep listening techniques, such as maintaining eye contact, nodding, and paraphrasing to demonstrate understanding and validation. Remind family members to listen without judgment or interruption, creating a supportive and non-threatening atmosphere.
- Contemplative Dialogue: After each family member has shared their photographs, facilitate contemplative dialogues to explore common themes, differences, and insights emerging from the photographs. Encourage family members to reflect on how their perspectives contribute to the family dynamic and interpersonal relationships.
- Reflection and Integration: Conclude the photovoice session with a reflection period where family members can contemplate the insights gained and identify actionable steps for fostering deeper connection and understanding within the family. Encourage ongoing dialogue and reflection outside of the session to promote continued growth and communication.

Conclusion

Through the integration of contemplative practices into intervention strategies, the Buddhist chaplain empowered Sara to navigate the complexities of her college experience with mindfulness, compassion, and cultural sensitivity. By addressing acculturation challenges, improving intergenerational communication, fostering cultural affirmation, and facilitating family sessions, Sara embarks on a transformative journey towards greater resilience, well-being, and cultural integration within her familial and academic spheres. The hope is that Sarah continues to feel less academic stress and interpersonal conflicts as she feels empowered and supported to evolve as she balances her personal aspirations with cultural traditions. Systemically, the hope is that Sarah's family as a whole gained a deeper well of compassion and understanding for one another, including Sarah's desire to grow and choose her own path while also honoring cultural traditions.

References

Bertalanffy, L.V. (1968). *General system theory: Foundations, development, applications*. G. Braziller.

Dahl, C.J., & Davidson, R.J. (2019). Mindfulness and the contemplative life: pathways to connection, insight, and purpose. *Current opinion in psychology*, 28, 60-64.

Feen-Calligan, H., Grasser, L.R., Nasser, S., Sniderman, D., & Javanbakht, A. (2023). Photovoice techniques and art therapy approaches with refugee and immigrant adolescents. *The Arts in psychotherapy*, 83, 102005.

Kerr, M.E. (1981). Family systems theory and therapy. *Handbook of family therapy*, 1, 226-264.

McGoldrick, M., & Gerson, R. Shellenberger (1999). *Genograms. Assessment and Intervention.*

Thomas, J.N. (2016). *Mindful photography and its implications in end-of-life caregiving: An art-based phenomenology.* Sofia University.

Thomas, J.N. (2024) *Choosing Light: Transforming Grief Through Mindful Photography and Self-Reflection.* Rowman & Littlefield.

Titelman, P. (2014). *Clinical applications of Bowen family systems theory.* Routledge.

Wang, C., & Burris, M.A. (1997). Photovoice: Concept, methodology, and use for participatory needs assessment. *Health education & behavior*, 24(3), 369-387.

Weiser, J. (2004). Phototherapy techniques in counselling and therapy – using ordinary snapshots and photo-interactions to help clients heal their lives. *Canadian art therapy association journal*, 17(2), 23-53.

Epilogue

The practices collected in this volume represent simply a few of the Buddhist practical theology strategies pioneered within Buddhist campus chaplaincy. While these adaptations to the Dharma may seem very modern, it can be argued that practical theology has been going on since the time of the historical Buddha, who adapted his teaching to the needs and capacities of his listeners. It is also possible to see the historical records of textual commentary based on the *Prajna Paramita*, the Lojong slogans developed by Atisha, or the Blue Cliff Record as practical theology. Koans can be considered to be a spontaneous and precise response to the present moment: however, the cycles of action and reflection embedded within a koan may continue for a thousand years. And the action-reflection cycle of koans often implicitly critiques a Buddhist practice that has become too reified, inviting the listener to bring a clear mind and direct action to the here-and-now. Within each koan, there is at least one "turning word", a particular word-action that took place, which serves as the basis for reflection.

I will demonstrate this model with the koan, "Zen Master Dongshan is unwell."

The narrative-kernel within this koan is that Zen Master Dongshan has gotten sick, and in the traditional way, is visited by his student. This visiting of the sick dates back to the actions of the historical Buddha, who taught "Whoever tends the sick, tends me." It additionally mirrors the *Vimalakirti Nirdesa Sutra*, which opens with a story in which the teacher Vimalakirti has fallen sick. Buddha enjoins his disciples to visit the layperson. Each one begs off, out of concern that dialogue with Vimalakirti will show the limits of their realization, until they resolve to visit him all together. This story would have been well known to the koan's audience.

> Dongshan's student asks him, is there anyone who doesn't get sick? And he responds, yes, there is.

This question is seeking the True Self, the aspect of consciousness that is beyond birth-and-death. Dongshan affirms its truth.

> The student asks, "Does the person who doesn't get sick take care of you?"
> He says, "I have the opportunity to take care of the person."
> "What happens when you take care of that person?"
> Dongshan replies, "At that time, I don't see the sickness".

Dongshan is offering his student heart-advice: do not spiritually bypass the body. The deeper meaning of this exchange is that our everyday bodymind, with its imperfections, is actually the growing edge. The transient, vulnerable body is the alchemical container. As Zen Master Norm Fischer puts it. "Our strong Zen mind doesn't help us to transcend our illness. It is the other way around. Our human vulnerability humanizes and deepens our Zen mind."

A commentary follows:

> Because of the illness of all sentient beings, Vimalakirti is sick.

So this refers to a traditional story. Vimalakirti in Buddhist tradition was a lay person who was able to practice in whatever situation he found himself. He would go into the taverns to liberate everyone there. He would go to the marketplace and help people to be liberated there. He wasn't confined to practicing in a monastery. When asked the nature of his illness, Vimalakirti responds that he is sick because all beings are sick. Vimalakirti famously shows us to seek enlightenment right where we are, and not to attach to the reified idea of practice.

So the commentary continues,

> Sometimes they composed medicine to heal the sickness.
> At other times, they manifest to heal the medicine.

If we fall into the weeds of delusion, grasping the duality of the world at face value, the medicine of practice will cleanse our perceptions, so that we can break through the self-imposed wall of the isolated, impermanent self.

If we cling to the formality of Buddha's way, that is also a deep ditch.

The commentary continues,

> You should understand that the 10,000 hands and eyes of great compassion are deaf, dumb, and blind.

That's an interesting statement – and the paradox of the Zen koan.

Within the tradition of Mahayana Buddhism, there is an image of the Bodhisattva, the archetype of great compassion, which has 10,000 hands and eyes, to perceive and respond, to reach everywhere. So how could they be deaf, dumb, and blind?

It is like saying that a paper cake will not satisfy our hunger. The wooden Buddha does not have *sharira* (relics). This part of the koan commentary is designed to stop our mind in its tracks. So, if that is the case, then what?

The next part of the commentary poses a response.

> This great earth and all of its multiplicity of forms up to and including you and me are at once medicine. At such a time, where do you find yourself?

So the meaning of this koan is not to hold on to a sense of pure practice, but really to practice right where we are and recognize every moment is the perfect teacher. Keep a practice that's responding directly to the situation rather than depending upon the reified form.

Having reflected upon the practical theology offered by my esteemed colleagues in this volume, I now will offer a skillful means of my own. We need to return to the original affinity and intimacy with nature, which is at the heart of this practice.

The Buddha was born under a tree, got enlightenment under a tree, and died under a tree. In the historical account of the life of the Buddha, we see this radical inclusivity and affinity with nature.

On the occasions in which a student needed clarity, Zen Master Seung Sahn responded, "If you have a question, go ask a tree. The tree will give you a good answer."

So again, let me return us to that koan.

> This great earth and all of its multiplicity of forms up to and including you and me are at once medicine. At such a time, where do you find yourself?

If everything is at once medicine, how can we source from those teachings that we find among the trees, among the natural world?

There is the traditional story about the poet Su Tung Po, who travelled a long way across China to seek the teaching. Upon arriving at the temple, he asked for the Dharma – and was chastised by the teacher,

> How dare you come here seeking the dead words of men? Why don't you open your ears to the living words of nature? Go away.

Su Tung Po was stunned. What could that mean? Totally absorbed, he got on his horse and let the horse find the way home. On their way through the mountains, Su Tung Po heard a waterfall, as if for the first time. He recognized the waterfall was the Buddha's voice, and the mountain as the Earth's body.

Zen Master Dogen said two centuries later,

> Sounds of streams and shapes of mountains
> The sounds never stop and the shapes never cease.
> If you who are valley streams and looming mountains
> can't throw some light on the nature of ridge and rivers, who can?

It's not that we're even evoking nature. It's that we already *are* valley streams and looming mountains. We just have to remember. And, I would say, that deep memory of union with nature is embedded within the structures of ancient languages like Sanskrit, Pali, Tibetan, Hebrew, Arabic, Gaelic, Cherokee, Lakota, Hopi, Quechua.

So then the question really is what are the forms of Buddhism, of this practical Buddhist theology that will help us in this deep re-membering, that will support this reconnection to healthy communities and ecosystems? As I write this, the South has experienced biblical level devastation from Hurricane Helene, and global security is at dramatically heightened risk, with flashpoints in Lebanon, Gaza, Ukraine, Taiwan.

As Peter Senge said in *Necessary Revolution* (2011), we need to live in the present in ways that do not jeopardize our future. The future is awaiting our choices. We need to return to nature, not machines, as our source of inspiration.

> We need to invest seriously and immediately in building a regenerative economy and society that mimics nature as fully as possible (p.38).

So then, what precisely are the practical theologies, the contemporary adaptations of practice that will actively support and help us to remember what it means to have healthy communities and ecosystems. What practices will help us to move from the isolated, lonely "I" to the interconnected "we"?

As I entered service to the college chaplaincies of Tufts and Northeastern Universities just as the pandemic was waning, these were students who had spent their first year of college in isolation, literally "out of touch". There was significant work to rebuild the sanghas. So, this was a very real question.

In traditional Buddhist temple life, there would be a lot of what my Korean teacher called "together action": people cooking together, practicing together, living together. With my college sanghas at Tufts and Northeastern Universities, we have had very powerful experiences by going to a retreat center off the grid (Temenos, in Western Massachusetts). It's difficult to go to the countryside with twenty-five college students and do a retreat off the grid. The conveniences and the support structures that ease the retreat process are not available. But at the same time, when we're able to turn off the phones, the students are able to make a genuine connection. They listen inwardly, and through that deep listening are able to extend generous listening to each other and to nature. We cooked for each other, grounding and nourishing sangha at its roots. Deep in nature, we have then used percussion and Korean *kido* chanting to support what is known in neuropsychology as vertical and horizontal integration. That experience of percussion helps the limbic system and the prefrontal cortex to synchronize together. At that moment, the body and the mind become one, the inside and outside of a person can become one. We have this experience of an inner unity as well as a unity within the community.

That is where transformation happens.

As Chaplain Rebecca Nie and others have discussed in this volume, sparkling moments can be available through celebrating the transitions of the year together with a tea ceremony, or through the ritual of taking refuge, which helps us to remember how connected we are (across time, as well as space) in a way that goes back thousands of years to the time of the historical Buddha.

Roshi John Halifax's GRACE method, described in this volume is a ritual towards embodied intention and presence and giving care is also a lovely and powerful Buddhist practical theology. The practices that Joanna Macy developed in her *Work That Connects*, which adapt the Brahma Viharas to community-building contexts are another skillful means, through which we remember how these qualities of loving kindness and compassion are within us and interconnecting us all the time. The Invisible Chaplains program, brought forth by Associate Dean Matt Weiner, also powerfully shifts the way we conceive of the campus, and the people within it. We have also deeply benefitted from the practical theology of ColorInsight, developed by Rhonda Magee, to engage in challenging conversations about race and cultural difference so as to build a sangha that is also beloved community.

So these are some practical theologies -- ways to help us to re-member, to resource, through awareness of our deep innate connection with each other and the natural world so that we may embody the Dharma in a way that is the most appropriate response to this twenty-first century world.

I will leave us with these words from Zen pioneer and poet Gary Snyder,

> To change the way contemporary human beings live on earth is a kind of Dharma work, a work for dedicated followers of the Way who because of their practice and insight can hope to balance wisdom and compassion and help open the eyes of others.
> *Gary Snyder*,
> Mountains Hidden in Mountains

Gratitude to all dedicated followers of the Way who are pledging themselves to this Dharma work.

Ji Hyang Padma, Ph.D.
September 30, 2024, Year of the Wood Dragon
Boulder, CO

REFERENCES

Fischer, Norm. (2012). Zoketsu Rinsho, Shiho Koan Studies. (Personal Correspondence).

Lozang Trinlae, B . (2014). Prospects for a Buddhist Practical Theology. *International journal of practical theology*, 18(1), 7-22 .

Macy, J. (2006). *The Work That Reconnects*. New Society Publishers.

Magee, R.V., & Kabat-Zinn, J. (2021). *The inner work of racial justice: Healing ourselves and transforming our communities through mindfulness*. Tarcher Perigree.

Sanford, M. (2016). Practical Buddhist Theology: Methods for Putting Wisdom into Practice. In *A Thousand Hands: A Guidebook to Caring for Your Buddhist Community* (pp . 3-15) . essay, Sumeru.

Senge, P.M. (2011). *The necessary revolution: How individuals and organizations are working together to create a sustainable world*. Nicholas Brealey Publishing.

Snyder, G., & Loeffler, J. (2013). *Mountains and rivers without end*. Counterpoint.

Contributor Biographies

Harrison Blum MDiv, MEd, has worked as a Buddhist chaplain in university, medical, psychiatric, and community settings. His publications and presentations focus on the intersections between Buddhism, embodiment, and mindfulness equity. Since 2018 he has served as Director of Religious and Spiritual Life at Amherst College.
Website: movingdharma.org

Julian Bowers-Brown is a Healthcare Chaplain at Nottingham University Hospitals and Sheffield Teaching Hospitals in the UK, with a particular focus on palliative and cancer care. He previously worked as a university academic and compassion-based coach. He is a practicing Soto Zen Buddhist in the lineage of Shunryu Suzuki Roshi.

Eli Ryn Brown (they/she/he) is a QTBIPOC communal healing practitioner who facilitates with Bhumisparsha, Rest for Resistance, and Abolitionist Dreaming Practice. Their practice is grounded in meditation as an act of abolition, and communal healing as part of the radical rest that helps sustain revolutionary action.
Website: elirynbrown.com

Lama Döndrup Drölma is the Resident Lama of Sukhasiddhi Foundation. Her training in the Theravadin and Vajrayana traditions includes a three-year retreat in the Shangpa and Karma Kagyu lineages. In her teaching and writing, she aims to preserve the teachings' authenticity while making them accessible and relevant to 21st Century lives.

Zoketsu Norman Fischer is a poet, author, and Soto Zen priest. A former abbot of the San Francisco Zen Center, he is founder and teacher of the Everyday Zen Foundation.
Website: everydayzen.org

Victor Gabriel is a retired professor from the Department of Buddhist Chaplaincy at the University of the West. He was chair from 2014–2018 and 2022–2024. His research areas include Applied Buddhist "theology," Feminist and Queer theory, Ritual Studies and American Buddhism. He was a psychotherapist and is a Buddhist lay minister.

Rev. Jitsujo T. Gauthier, PhD is an Associate Professor and Chair of Buddhist Chaplaincy at University of the West, teaching courses for Master and Doctorate programs. She is a Zen priest, preceptor, and resident at the Zen Center of Los Angeles, and a Co-Spiritual Director and Seat-Holder for the Zen Peacemaker Order.

Trudy Goodman, PhD is one of the pioneers in Eastern and Western psychology, holding a graduate degree in developmental psychology from Harvard. She has taught Zen and vipassana/mindfulness internationally for 40 years. Trudy is a contributing author of *Clinical Handbook of Mindfulness* (Springer, 2008); *Compassion and Wisdom in Psychotherapy*, (Guilford Press, 2011); and *Mindfulness and Psychotherapy*, (Guilford Press, 2013).
Website: www.trudygoodman.com

Roshi Joan Halifax, PhD is a Buddhist teacher, Founder and Head Teacher of Upaya Zen Center in Santa Fe, New Mexico, a social activist, author, and in her early years was an anthropologist at Columbia University (1964–68) and University of Miami School of Medicine (1970–72). She is a pioneer in the field of end-of-life care. She is Director of the Project on Being with Dying, and Founder of the Upaya Prison Project that develops programs on meditation for prisoners. She is also founder of the Nomads Clinic in Nepal. Website: joanhalifax.org

Rev. Victor Kazanjian, Jr. is a coach and consultant helping individuals and organizations actualize their aspirations through a holistic approach to leadership, life and learning. Victor recently retired as the Executive Director of URI (the United Religions Initiative), a global grassroots intercultural and interfaith peacebuilding network. He previously served as Dean of Intercultural Education, Dean of Religious and Spiritual Life and Co-Director of the Peace and Justice Studies Program at Wellesley College. He is an ordained priest in the Episcopal Church and holds degrees from the Episcopal Divinity School and Harvard University.

Jonathan Makransky is the Multireligious Ministry Initiatives Coordinator at Harvard Divinity School, where he manages the activities of the Buddhist Ministry Initiative. He received his Master of Theological Studies in Buddhism from Harvard and has worked in university spiritual life and ministry settings since then. He is a lifelong Tibetan Buddhist practitioner and has practice leadership and youth mentorship experience in the tradition.

Rev. Ivan (Kusa) Mayerhofer, Ph.D. (he/him) currently serves as the Associate Chaplain for Buddhist Programs, Director of the Meditation Initiative, and Coordinator of Interfaith Programs at Davidson College. He is also an ordained Dharma and Meditation teacher in a Korean Sŏn Buddhist lineage. His ordination master is the Ven. Haju Sunim at the Ann Arbor Zen Temple in Ann Arbor, Michigan.

Nathan Jishin Michon (MA, MDiv, PhD) is ordained as a Shingon Buddhist priest and interfaith minister. Jishin is an instructor with the KYOEN Institute in Kyoto, Japan and director of their "Inward Journeys Japan" initiative. Among other works, they are the editor of *Refuge in the Storm: Buddhist Voices in Crisis Care* and *A Thousand Hands: A Guidebook to Caring for Your Buddhist Community*.

Ernest C.H. Ng, Adjunct Assistant Professor at Hong Kong University and CEO of Tung Lin Kok Yuen Canada Society (TLKYCS), specializes in applying wisdom traditions and spirituality in contemporary society. He serves as a Buddhist Chaplain at the University of British Columbia and Simon Fraser University, and a denominational visitor to healthcare facilities. Website: linktr.ee/ernestngch

Rebecca D. Nie is Stanford University's Buddhist Chaplain-Affiliate. She was ordained as a Dharma Teacher in 2009 and received Zen Master transmission in 2013 through Zen Master Yangil of the Korean Jogye Order. Nie also co-translated *Yin Mountain*, a collection of Daoist women's literature from the 8th to 9th Century.

Ji Hyang Padma, PhD teaches spiritual care at Naropa University, serving as Associate Professor in its Wisdom Traditions Department. She is a Zen teacher with lay entrustment transmission in the Soto Zen lineage of Shunryu Suzuki. Her previous books are *Living the Season: Zen Practices for Transformative Times* and *Field of Blessings: Ritual and consciousness in the work of Buddhist healers*.

Henry C.H. Shiu is the Shi Wu De Professor in Chinese Buddhist Studies at Emmanuel College of Victoria University in the University of Toronto. He has a research interest in Mahayana Buddhist doctrines, contemporary Buddhist movements, the history of Buddhism in Canada, and the development of Buddhist chaplaincy.

Jessica Thomas holds an MS in Marriage and Family Therapy and a PhD in Transpersonal Psychology. She is a therapist, clinical supervisor, grief educator, and organizational consultant. As a professor at Lewis & Clark College and CIIS, she has created coursework and taught on death and grief, psycho-spiritual development and counseling, research methods, and clinical supervision. Her research, Mindful Photography and its Implications in End-of-Life Caregiving, has focused on creative expression and the experience of anticipatory loss.
Website: DrJessicaThomas.com

Mark Unno is Professor of Buddhist Studies and Department Head of Religious Studies at the University of Oregon. He is the 14th-generation minister of Shin Buddhism in his family lineage. He is the author of *Shingon Refractions: Myōe and the Mantra of Light* (2004) and numerous articles. His essays have also appeared in Buddhist journals such as *Tricycle* and *Lion's Roar*.
Website: mtunno5.weebly.com

Matthew Weiner is an Associate Dean in the Office of Religious Life at Princeton University. Before coming to Princeton, he was the Program Director for the Interfaith Center of New York. He holds an MTS from Harvard Divinity School and a PhD from Union Theological Seminary.

Acknowledgments

We owe a debt of gratitude to many people – all those whose insight and help made this book possible.

First, as editor, I would like to thank the authors for their generosity in time, insight and energy. Special gratitude is due to Harrison Blum, Julian Bowers-Brown, Eli Ryn Brown, Lama Döndrup Drölma, Zoketsu Norman Fischer, Victor Gabriel, Rev. Jitsujo T. Gauthier, Roshi Joan Halifax, Rev. Victor Kazanjian, Jr. Jonathan Makransky Rev. Ivan (Kusa) Mayerhofer Nathan Jishin Michon, Leigh Miller, Ernest C.H. Ng Rebecca D. Nie, Henry C.H. Shiu, Ven. Priya Rakkhit Sraman, Jessica Thomas, Mark Unno, and Matthew Weiner for their generous sharing of wisdom.

I thank my colleagues and sanghas at Tufts University, Northeastern University, Omega Institute and Naropa University for supporting my practice and especially providing a home for this writing endeavor.

Thank you to John Kotatsu Bailes, for the immeasurable gifts of your Dharma friendship. Gratitude and praise to Rev. Jitsujo T. Gauthier, Ilduk Kim Kyomunim, Sumi Kim, Ivan (Kusa) Mayerhofer, Jonathan Makransky, Jissan Michelle Nicolle, Rebecca Nie, Doyeon Park, Monica Sanford, Henry C.H. Shiu, Alley Smith, Ven. Priya Rakkhit Sraman and other Buddhist university chaplains who are working together within the Maitreya Association to build chaplaincy community.

Thank you especially to our publisher, Karma Yönten Gyatso (John Negru) for his unfailingly clear judgement and *kshanti* (patient forbearance).

While acknowledging the support I have received from all those mentioned (and many unnamed), I bear sole responsibility for any shortcomings manifested in this work.

www.ingramcontent.com/pod-product-compliance
Lightning Source LLC
Chambersburg PA
CBHW060232240426
43671CB00016B/2923